Critical Essays on
E. M. Forster

Critical Essays on
E. M. Forster

Alan Wilde

G. K. Hall & Co. • Boston, Massachusetts

Library of Congress Cataloging in Publication Data

Main entry under title:

Wilde, Alan.
   Critical essays on E. M. Forster.

   (Critical essays on modern British literature)
   Includes index.
   1. Forster, E. M. (Edward Morgan), 1879–1970–
Criticism and interpretation—Addresses, essays,
lectures. I. Title. II. Series.
PR6011.058Z933   1985   823′.912   85–2763
ISBN 0–8161–8754–1

This publication is printed on permanent/durable acid-free paper
MANUFACTURED IN THE UNITED STATES OF AMERICA

CRITICAL ESSAYS ON MODERN BRITISH LITERATURE

The critical essays series on modern British literature provides a variety of approaches to both the modern classical writers of Britain and Ireland and the best contemporary authors. In general, the series seeks to represent the best in published criticism, augmented, where appropriate, by original essays by recognized authorities. The goal of each volume is to suggest a new perspective on its particular subject.

Alan Wilde's thesis deals with the consistency of E. M. Forster's work. In the plethora of Forster scholarship from all critical quarters (Marxist, psychological, etc.) there is remarkable agreement regarding Forster's beliefs and his "consistent and definable voice." The difficulty arises in assigning Forster a historical niche. The questions of whether he was an Edwardian, a modernist, a postmodernist, even a member of the Bloomsbury group are still the subjects of critical controversy. As disparate as his beliefs and methods seem to be, however, there is a strong unity of effect his work produces and it is this effect that Wilde brilliantly manages to define.

Wilde's is the first major study to place Forster's homosexuality in perspective against his liberal humanism and morality. The importance of the topic, while not paramount, is real in shaping the author's life and his views as they translate into his fiction. Forster's work, especially the major contributions, will continue to be part of the classical canon of modern British Literature, and Wilde's book will play no small role in keeping it there.

Zack Bowen, GENERAL EDITOR

University of Delaware

for Peggy Moan Rowe

CONTENTS

INTRODUCTION

What can one reasonably and usefully say about a body of critical writing that numbered, as of the mid-1970s, some 1,913 items, and that by now easily exceeds the 2,000 mark?[1] It is hardly an exaggeration to assert that the mere bulk of writing devoted to Forster's works and, more recently, to his life threatens to overwhelm not only the beginning student but even those whose interest in Forster spans several decades. And to overwhelm Forster too, sinking his relatively slim production of fiction and nonfiction under the massive weight of interpretation, explication, and evaluation. The problem, however, is in some sense more apparent than real. The amount of commentary lavished on Forster exceeds by far its diversity, and there is to the almost eighty years' worth of accumulated essays, reviews, and books that take him as their subject a quite remarkable uniformity. This is not to say that critics have failed to bring to bear on Forster their own special perspectives—Marxist, Christian, feminist, psychological, psychoanalytic, and so on. But it is to maintain that, whatever their ideological divergencies, those perspectives—whether thematic or technical in emphasis, whether their aim is to praise or to attack—tend to presuppose the same literary criteria, the same value structures, and the same methodological emphases and procedures. In short, a handful of structuralist and poststructuralist essays notwithstanding, almost all commentary on Forster exists within a relatively familiar and traditional realm of critical discourse.

Needless to say, so summary and capacious a generalization derives from a rather distant, bird's-eye view of the field, and it will be necessary later on to modify it in the light of those differences that inevitably present themselves to a more proximate scrutiny. For the moment, however, it may be allowed to stand, since it permits us to ask not only how but why Forster criticism has responded in the way it has—why, that is, it has proved so much less various than the criticism directed at such contemporaries of Forster as D. H. Lawrence, Virginia Woolf, or James Joyce. The most plausible, albeit speculative, answer is that Forster has, in a manner of speaking, called forth and controlled precisely the kind of criticism he has received. Is this possible? Can one imagine the man who, according to his biographer, "was inconspicuous,

1

sometimes to the point of vanishing,"[2] exerting so strong and far-reaching an influence on those drawn to define for themselves the values and meanings of his writing? In fact, yes; but to test the validity of the hypothesis one needs to define what is irreducible in Forster—or, rather, in the Forster who emerges from the fiction and the nonfiction alike by way of a particularly clear set of beliefs and a remarkably consistent and definable voice. Clear, consistent, definable? Immediately and again, questions present themselves. The adjectives may seem at best misguided, at worst perverse, given the quality to which, almost from the beginning, friends and critics have overwhelmingly responded in Forster: his elusiveness. The comparisons of him, for example, to "a vaguely rambling butterfly," "whimsical & vagulous," to "the Cheshire Cat," or to "the elusive colt of a dark horse"[3] (always something animal or fantastic, not quite human or socialized) are only the most imaginative and striking descriptions to be found among the remarks that run from the earliest observations to the most recent.[4] But it is equally important to note that if, as Woolf maintains in the essay reprinted here, "there is something baffling and evasive in the very nature of his gifts"; if, as John Beer suggests, that quality "brings out the difficulty of aligning Forster with any preceding tradition";[5] and if, finally, as Philip Gardner remarks, his elusiveness constitutes "an element which partly accounts for the difficulty experienced by many critics . . . in assigning him his precise 'magnitude,' "[6] still it is no less true that Forster's elusiveness is a stance that describes his strength as much as, or even more than, it does his slipperiness.

No doubt it is difficult to "assign" Forster—to discover not only his magnitude but his filiations. Was he a member of the Bloomsbury Group? Included by S. P. Rosenbaum in *The Bloomsbury Group: A Collection of Memoirs, Commentary and Criticism* (1975), he is excluded from Leon Edel's collective biography, *Bloomsbury: A House of Lions* (1979); and both choices can be seen as plausible. Is his fiction Edwardian and premodernist? Modernist? Both? Again, convincing arguments can be, have been, advanced. At any rate, the questions, while not unimportant, are peripheral: attempts to slot Forster into the categories by which literary history makes sense of literature's always stubborn variousness. What is clear is that, in his life as in his art, the " 'outsider's' view of things" that Beer attributes to Forster,[7] and that for P. N. Furbank makes him "a master of *angle*" determines not only the elusiveness or complexity of his vision but—the word bears repeating—its consistency (consistency but not necessarily coherence, a different and more difficult matter, of which more later).

To speak of complexity is inevitably to summon up Forster's familiar distinction, propounded by Rickie Elliot in *The Longest Journey*, between "the knowledge of good and evil" and "the knowledge of good-and-evil"[8]—to recognize, that is, Forster's temperamental irony and to discover in that irony not merely a collection of satiric techniques but a characteristic way of apprehending the world: a perception of and a response to its fundamental disunity. To speak of consistency, on the other hand, is to gauge the effect of that response on Forster's readers. If the voice of the fiction, and of the nonfiction as well, is continuously busy making us aware of life's disjunctions, unsettling our assurances and certainties, forcing us to make distinctions, it is no less intent on overcoming separation and antinomy. Whether the healing, reconciling countervision succeeds as fully as the originating vision (or irritation)— and whether, incidentally, the source of the latter is to be located in temperament, personality, or, as some more recent commentators hold, sexuality—is not an immediate concern. What matters is the steadying effect of that voice: the assurance it offers, whatever is being said, that we can, not resolve, but come to terms with life's inherent fractures, that we are capable, at the least, of turning the world's muddle into mystery and, at best, of realizing the values that are (so it is implied) within our power to understand and grasp.

All of which is to say that, along with Lawrence, Forster is the preeminent moralist of his age. Speaking of his "passion for moralising," Furbank comments: "He was moralising busily when he was twenty; and he continued, without intermission, for the next seventy years. He plainly regarded it as the business of life; one was on earth to improve oneself and to improve others, and the path to this was moral generalisations." The comparison with Lawrence, however, though valid in some respects, may be misleading. Forster's moral position is less radical, his tone less hectic, his hope more tempered. The last Victorian rather than one of the last Romantics, he seeks not a new order but, as he says in "What I Believe," a reordering of what already exists. Not for Forster Lawrence's injunction to "smash the frame";[9] and it may well be (to return to my original argument) that Forster's critics respond as much to the limits he implicitly imposes on his subversions as to the subversions themselves. Or, alternatively, that Forster elicits, has elicited, a kind of criticism more attentive to the manifest intricacies of his texts than to the less obvious forces that subtend them, the point being that commentary has inclined to take him on his own, ultimately self-limiting and, to a degree, conservative terms, and so to meet him, even when antagonistic, on his own apparently preferred ground.

But these observations, even if true, are too narrowly based, too restrictive in their assessment of Forster as a latter-day sage spooning out dollops of wisdom for the edification of his readers. In fact, just as his "passion for moralising" is absorbed into the aesthetic texture of his fiction, so the aesthetic effect of the novels and stories is moral in a way that transcends the separable generalizations Furbank speaks about— lying instead, as in so much modernist fiction, in its ability to conjure up, by way of hope and desire, alternatives to a world that is, as Forster's fiction envisions it, increasingly out of control. Furthermore, if, like Forster's novels, modernism enacts a dialectic of disorder and order, of thematic irresolution and formal closure, the criticism that it called into being—New Criticism, with its ideal of maximal complexity resolved into unity—offers a way of doing justice to any amount of irony, paradox (*apparent* paradox), and qualification while preserving a belief in the integrity of the work as a whole. It follows, finally, since Forster's critics (when they are not simply impressionistic) fall overwhelmingly into the New Critical camp, that his fictions tend to be valued or devalued to the degree that, in the face of their complexities, they achieve or fail to achieve at the last a demonstrable unity of effect.

Still, to point up the congruence between Forster and his critics is very likely to say no more than can be alleged of Forster's contemporaries and their critics. The question remains: What is it that, despite his elusiveness, constrains his critics to see him as he would be seen? The answer, it appears, is to be found in Lionel Trilling's shrewd observation that Forster "is not merely a writer, he is a figure"—one, he explains, who "acts out in public the role of the private man."[10] In other words, Forster, from the beginning to the end of his career, and in a way different from Joyce or Woolf, imposed on his readers, consciously or not, a particular way of perceiving him which has persisted into the present and which accounts for the fact that at the moment he seems to many rather old-fashioned. "I used to admire Forster's work much more than I do now," Angus Wilson said in a recent interview, adding with an eerie echo of Trilling's words: "Forster has receded from me as a figure."[11] And in a still more recent comment, Lillian D. Bloom describes the writers discussed in the book she is reviewing as "all of them (with the arguable exception of E. M. Forster) 'great' and presumably secure in a literary galaxy."[12]

Has Forster in fact, despite the continued outpouring of books and essays devoted to him, receded from readers in general? And is his reputation less secure than it once was? According to Frederick P. W. McDowell, the leading scholar of Forster criticism, "Forster will undoubtedly occupy a place somewhat less august in the annals of contemporary literature than he did in the years 1945 to 1970, but it is safe to say that he will never sink into the obscurity that overtook him, in the period 1930 to 1943, as an important novelist."[13] But even this tempered estimate may seem too sanguine in the light of Wilson's and Bloom's remarks. (And they are not alone in their disparagements: several years ago, in response to a *Times Literary Supplement* questionnaire, a number of writers described Forster as the most overrated novelist of the century.) Nevertheless, McDowell is surely right. The virtues of at least the major novels have been established, and if Forster as a presence seems for now less lustrous and exciting than many of his contemporaries, it may well be because of the way in which he has been viewed. This is, to repeat, a matter not of the quality of Forster criticism but of its scope or, better, of its grid. The best of that writing does perhaps constitute, as McDowell says, "a lump of pure gold,"[14] but something more, it seems, is required to rescue Forster from the trough into which his self-created myth has plunged him. In sum, it may be said that Forster has been as much the victim as the beneficiary of the criticism dedicated to him; and it may be said with equal justice that his critics have in turn been the victims, the willing victims perhaps, of Forster as "figure": the elusive moralist with, as Trilling once remarked, a whim of iron.

Such an overview, however, risks, even courts, simplification; and as it is possible to exaggerate the singleness or singlemindedness of Forster, who, Furbank argues, "had a variety of literary personalities,"[15] so it is possible to overstate the unanimity of his critics and to underplay the interest and importance of their family quarrels. For the fact is that if criticism of Forster rests on a base of common procedures and assumptions, it is by no means of a piece; and the problem is how best to represent its variety. One might, of course, seek out large configurations, dividing the criticism, as McDowell plausibly and persuasively does, into three periods: 1905–38, the time in which "review comment prevails"; 1938–57, the years of "the Forster revival" (initiated by Trilling's study) and of "a more authoritative and systematic appraisal of Forster's work"; and 1958–the present, years that account for over sixty per cent of the items listed in McDowell's bibliography, among them almost all of the full-length books.[16] Or, alternatively, one might single out (as McDowell also does) major and representative statements on Forster, a short, chronological, and necessarily personal list which would include Woolf's "The Novels of E. M. Forster" (1927) and F. R. Leavis's "E. M. Forster" (1938), both seminal in arguing for a division in Forster between realistic and symbolic impulses; Trilling's *E. M. Forster* (1943) and Frederick C. Crews's *E. M. Forster: The Perils of Humanism* (1962), two studies centering on the nature and limitations of Forster's liberal humanism; James McConkey's *The Novels of E. M. Forster* (1957), an examination of Forster's fictional strategies in terms of the categories set forth in *Aspects of the Novel*; Wilfred Stone's *The Cave and the Mountain: A Study of E. M. Forster* (1966), in which Forster undergoes a full-scale, controversial psychological analysis and in which *A Passage to India* is elaborately and impressively examined as a novel whose theme "is that, for all our differences, we are in fact *one*"[17] (a reading to be contrasted with Crews's and with Alan Wilde's in *Art and Order: A Study of E. M. Forster* [1964]); George H. Thomson's *The Fiction of E. M. Forster* (1967), a provocative attempt to answer, in ways that will become apparent shortly, the criticisms of writers like Leavis and Woolf; and, finally, John Colmer's *E. M. Forster: The Personal Voice* (1975) and Claude Summers's *E. M. Forster* (1983), which in their admirably lucid examinations of the whole of Forster's career suggestively bring into play the evidence of the posthumous works.

The list is skimpy and inadequate: it does not, for example, mention notable essays or books by, among others, John Beer, Malcolm Bradbury, E. K. Brown, G. K. Das, K. W. Gransden, Michael Ragussis, Stephen Spender, or Austin Warren (for all of which, see McDowell's bibliography and bibliographical essays). Nor does it allude to most of the works printed below or to such invaluable resource books for students of Forster as McDowell's *Annotated Bibliography* (1976), Philip Gardner's *E. M. Forster: The Critical Heritage* (1973), S. P. Rosenbaum's *The Bloomsbury Group* (1975), P. N. Furbank's *E. M. Forster: A Life* (1977–78), or the splendid Abinger Edition, edited by the late Oliver Stallybrass, which has given us at last authoritative texts to work with. Still, it is long enough to suggest some of the major steps in the history of Forster criticism and to acknowledge the changes that have taken place in it over the course of the last several decades.

In any case, the meagerness of the sampling is intended as a comment not on the vitality of Forster criticism but on the inadequacy, for the purposes of this introduction, of an exclusively diachronic approach. Partly because that approach has been so well pursued by others already mentioned, partly because of reasons already set forth above, and partly because, as Gardner claims, "the understanding of Forster by his earlier contemporaries was no worse, if no better, than that demonstrated by his later,"[18] it seems wiser and more fruitful to grasp that sprawling body of criticism topically. In other words, one must, as far as possible, imagine his critics—despite the historical and ideological constraints that necessarily condition their attitudes—as Forster imagines writers of different ages in *Aspects of the Novel*: all of them "at work together in a circular room."[19] What is it they are discussing? Forster's liberal humanism, certainly; his homosexuality, very likely; no doubt, in the light of Furbank's biography, the relations between the man and the work; and of course, and as always, the proper interpretation of the fiction. Other topics too, naturally, but these will serve to suggest the characteristic and recurring issues that define a general topography and its boundaries.

To begin with Forster's humanism is not to put ideas before art but to acknowledge again the persuasiveness and influence of Trilling's notion of Forster as a figure: one of those, to quote further from his definition, "who live their visions as well as write them, who *are* what they write, whom we think of as standing for something as men because of what they have written in their books. They preside, as it were, over certain ideas and attitudes."[20] The description suits best, perhaps, the Forster who emerged in the 1930s and 1940s, "the antiheroic hero," as Christopher Isherwood fondly called him, whose voice spoke at once quietly and powerfully in the shadow of economic and political crises and, finally, of war. But it is no less true to assert that the ideas given their most memorable expression in "What I Believe" (1939) shape Forster's public thinking and attitudes throughout his long career, as they shape the attitudes of his critics to him and his work. What is at issue is, first of all, a particular set of beliefs: in the irreducible centrality of the individual; in the importance, whatever their actual limits and failures, of personal relations; in the virtues of "tolerance, good temper and sympathy";[21] in the value of diversity and differences; and, more generally, in the capacity of human beings for taking pleasure in their world. But Forster's humanism is also a *way* of perceiving and coming to terms with the world, one that involves, as we've already seen, a sense of its intrinsic complexity: that inextricable mixture of good-and-evil that calls forth in those able to recognize it a spirit of restlessness and inquiry, an openness to experience, and, above all, an unrelenting tentativeness in the face of the competing absolutes and faiths that always and everywhere loudly assert their exclusive possession of Truth.

It is easy enough to understand, even to anticipate, the objections of non- or antihumanists to Forster's beliefs,[22] objections, primarily, to the unprogrammatic nature of his political ideas and to his thoroughly undoctrinaire sense of the world's mystery. More to the point are the reactions by liberals themselves to what Trilling (in the essay reprinted here) speaks of as Forster's "refusal to be great" and his concommitant espousal of "the relaxed will," which put him "for all his long commitment to the doctrines of liberalism . . . at war with the liberal imagination." Praising his "moral realism," Trilling admits to an occasional irritation with Forster; and other critics, even sympathetic ones, have gone further, some, like Crews, detecting in Forster or his work "a certain shallowness that is inherent in his liberalism."[23] In any case, many of the critics in the pages that follow (see, especially, Widdowson and Parry) have felt the need to weigh the strengths of Forster's liberal humanism against its putative inadequacies when faced with the social, political, and metaphysical realities revealed in the major novels especially. Very likely, the last word has been said in the essay by Wilfred Stone, an eminently subtle and sinuous examination of "Forster's personal witness for softness," which urges all that can be said in opposition to his beliefs but sees them as finally constituting "a position toughly held and not weakly acted out."

Explicitly or implicitly, Stone's essay takes account of and answers a whole range of familiar objections: those of F. R. Leavis, and, still more, of his followers, which fault Forster for associating himself with and for "accepting, it seems, uncritically, the very inferior social-intellectual milieu [of Bloomsbury]";[24] those of critics like Samuel Hynes, for whom Forster's "liberalism was never much more than sentimental humanism";[25] and, finally and most effectively, those of commentators like Cynthia Ozick, who, in answer to her rhetorical question, "Does it devalue the large humanistic statement to know that its sources are narrowly personal?," resoundingly (and a bit smugly) replies "Yes."[26] The

narrowly personal sources are for Ozick, as for Hynes, to be located in
Forster's homosexuality; and there is little question but that, along with
his humanism, Forster's sexual preferences are the aspect of his life
that has generated the most heat (more rarely, light) among his critics.
Ought one to be surprised? Obviously not, given the persistence of
exactly those societal attitudes that kept Forster from publishing his
homosexual novel during his lifetime—attitudes that, as he sadly and
acutely noted in 1960, had undergone no more than a "change from
ignorance and terror to familiarity and contempt."[27] And yet there is
something odd about the reactions that followed the publication of
Maurice, The Life to Come, and Furbank's biographical studies. For the
fact is that Forster's homosexuality was an open secret in American
academic circles at least as long ago as the 1950s, perhaps earlier; and
if critics refrained from referring to it—or referred to it gingerly—their
reasons had less to do with ignorance than with discretion. What
emerged, then, after Forster's death was less the fact of his homosexuality (though no doubt some critics, along with the public, were
taken by surprise) than its special configuration. In particular, that Forster, as Furbank says in the essay reprinted below, "found [sex] easier
with people outside his own social class" and that "he valued sex for
its power to release his own capacities for tenderness and devotion,
but ... never expected an *equal* sexual relation" helps enormously to
explain the nature and urgency of the subsexual attractions in several
of the novels, even as these facts and the additional one that "he
achieved physical sex very late" (these and *not* the homosexuality itself) enable us better to comprehend the failure his books frequently
display to connect passion imaginatively and convincingly with love.

The importance of Forster's homosexuality (and of its special patterns) to an understanding of his life and work is generally agreed upon.
What that understanding is or should be is another matter. Critics like
Hynes and Ozick, both of them reviewing *Maurice* unfavorably, con-
clude that "Forster may have disliked and resented his condition" and
that he "thought homosexuality wrong: naturally wrong, with the sort
of naturalness that he did not expect to date."[28] In the light of such
beliefs, Ozick's revaluation and deconsideration of Forster's humanism
as a function of his sexuality is hardly unexpected, however wrong-
headed and offensive her views inevitably appear to better-informed
minds. Other critics, Judith Scherer Herz and Claude Summers among
them, begin with the more plausible contention that, in Herz's words,
"the heterosexual/homosexual distinction is quite artificial" and that
"sexual energy has been a component of Forster's fiction from the start."
Both critics, in short, find in Forster's homosexuality areas of literary
strength and in his work a heretofore insufficiently explored dimension;
and it seems undeniable that henceforth no criticism can afford to overlook, indeed to explore fully, the impact of Forster's sexual behavior and
fantasies on his fiction.

And yet, Furbank maintains firmly that "We must not expect, then, when reading Forster's letters, any more than from reading his biography, to trace the creator to his lair, or to find 'explanations' of his novels."[29] One understands the warning implicit in these words: the caution against a kind of biographical reductiveness. Most critics, however, like Stone "consult[ing] Forster's fiction and biography as different aspects of one record—as I believe in essentials they are," are reluctant to forego whatever illumination the life may be seen to shed on the work, particularly in a work so filled, as we are beginning to see and as Herz so persuasively argues, with double plots and energizing subtexts. It is possible, though, to agree that what critics are likely to look for in the future is not an explicit correlation between the life and the fiction (the psychological method) but, as the phenomenologist Maurice Merleau-Ponty suggests, a style, "the system of equivalences that [the artist] makes for himself for the work which manifests the world he sees."[30]

In another sense, then, Furbank is right; and although critics are unlikely to ignore the biographical record, it is in the writings that one must finally seek the inscription and manifestation of the life—as many have, of course, from the start. It has already been noted that several of the best early critics focus their remarks in terms of what Forster's friend Goldsworthy Lowes Dickinson called his "double vision."[31] "Here, then," Virginia Woolf remarks in the essay reprinted below, "is a difficult family of gifts to persuade to live in harmony together: satire and sympathy; fantasy and fact; poetry and a prim moral sense"; and she comments later in the same essay on "an ambiguity at the heart of Mr. Forster's novels." (Like Dickinson, Woolf felt that in A Passage to India "the double vision . . . was in process of becoming single.") Reviewing Forster criticism in 1966, Malcolm Bradbury commented: "The sense that Forster proceeds simultaneously in two areas of the novel not normally brought together—the areas of social observation and comedy, and the area of symbolic romance—has . . . been common enough among critics of Forster; and in most post-war criticism one or the other side of Forster has been stressed."[32] What needs to be emphasized, however, is not the fact of Forster's foot-in-both-worlds stance but its consequences for the interpretation and evaluation of his achievement.

These consequences became fully apparent with the publication of George H. Thomson's The Fiction of E. M. Forster. Arguing against what he describes as the realist assumptions of critics such as Woolf, Leavis, Trilling, Crews, and Wilde, Thomson opens his book with the following credo: "Four things may be said about the fiction of E. M. Forster: first, that his works are romance rather than novel; second, that symbolism is central to his achievement in the romance form; third, that the principal source of his symbols is ecstatic experience; and fourth, that through the power of ecstatic perception his symbols achieve archetypal significance and mythic wholeness."[33] Clearly, to accept these propositions is to view Forster's fiction in one way, while to reject them is to see it very differently indeed. Whether, for example, one chooses to regard such symbolic characters as Stephen Wonham in *The Longest Journey* or *Howards End*'s Mrs. Wilcox as successful archetypal creations or as poorly soldered amalgams of conflicting intentions; whether one detects in much of Forster's symbolism integrity or strain; whether one finds in various of the plots the internal warfare of contradictory impulses or their successful resolution; and, finally, whether Forster's fiction in general does or does not appear to embody a vision of unity and wholeness—in all these cases the answer depends on the degree to which one is willing to credit Thomson's reading of Forster "as a visionary whose aim was to transmute his realistic material."[34]

If Thomson was not the first to approach Forster as a writer of romance (see the essays by John Edward Hardy and Louise Dauner), it is also the case that his interpretation has not brought realist critics to their knees (see Peter Widdowson's persuasive oppositional reading, also included in this collection). And if, as has been repeatedly argued in this introduction, the assumptions of *both* realist and romance critics are in some fundamental sense the same—that is, if one group deplores the absence of a coherence, in characterization, in the manipulation of symbols, in structure, and in vision, the presence of which the other group applauds—nevertheless Thomson's argument has probably done more than any other to draw the lines that have so far defined the map of Forster criticism. For this reason, Thomson's distinction hovers over much of what follows in this collection, particularly in the second section, where his own study of the early stories as "romance moralities" confronts Woolf's overview of Forster's career and Trilling's alignment of him with the liberal imagination, and in the fourth, where a half-dozen critics examine the major novels. (It should be said here that despite the occasional eccentric judgment—most notably W. H. Auden's [in his foreword to the Abinger Edition of *Goldsworthy Lowes Dickinson*] that Forster's somewhat limping and pedestrian biography of his friend was his best book—*Howards End* and *A Passage to India* are understood to represent the highpoint of Forster's achievement.)

Although almost all critics—Trilling is a notable exception—regard *A Passage to India* as the greatest of Forster's works, his major and rightful claim to a place in the history of twentieth-century fiction, it could plausibly be argued that for most readers *Howards End* presents itself as Forster's most immediately accessible and rewarding novel. Morally impassioned, tonally various, rich in its elaboration of characters and of the contexts that add dimension to their separate quests, the book best represents the individuality and range of Forster's voice and the fictional incarnation of Trilling's figure. At the same time, *Howards End* is, as McDowell rightly notes, "the most controversial of Forster's novels."[35] Critics have argued endlessly and passionately over the plausibility of Margaret Schlegel's marriage to Henry Wilcox, Henry's liaison with Jacky Bast, and Helen Schlegel's brief affair with Leonard Bast; over Leonard's credibility as a character; over the integrity or obtrusiveness of the novel's "rhythms" (or, as Forster says, its internal stitching); and, most of all, over the novel's ending and the evidence it offers of either a "structural unity," which for John Edward Hardy is ratified in the "fertility ritual" of the final chapter, or of an "unresolved tension between situation and values," which for Peter Widdowson reveals the crisis both "of liberalism and liberal-humanism in the twentieth century" and "of the realistic novel itself."[36] In short, Hardy anticipates Thomson's romance reading of the novel, while Widdowson, urging "realist" criteria, rejects it; and between them the two interpretations demonstrate the principal and antithetic responses that critics have had to *Howards End* from the start. But not necessarily, even in these cases, the only possible ones. It is worth noting Widdowson's suggestive assertion that "it is precisely in the tensions, irresolutions and ambiguities of the novel that its strength resides"[37]—an observation that shows not only that one can criticize *and* value the book but, more important, that the integrity of Forster's undertaking is not simply to be equated with the coherence of this or that individual book.

If *A Passage to India* has prompted a smaller number of discrete interpretative clashes among critics, that is only to say that the clashes have been more focused, not that they have been less passionate and intense, even, at times, acrimonious. In her discussion of the criticism devoted to the novel, June Perry Levine contends that "two main areas of opinion—that the novel represents either a positive vision of love, order, and unity or a negative vision of despair, chaos, and separation—account for the great majority of critical responses."[38] The formulation is a bit too neat, but it will serve nevertheless to identify the extremes within which commentary on the novel generally operates. Some studies, notably Benita Parry's *Delusions and Discoveries: Studies on India in the British Imagination 1880–1930* (1972) and Jeffrey Meyer's *Fiction and the Colonial Experience* (1973), have set the book firmly in its Indian context; the majority have chosen to concentrate on its personal and metaphysical implications, seeing it as the culmination, transcendence, or collapse of Forster's religious and humanist beliefs. The interpretations that approximate most closely Levine's divisions ("whether *A Passage to India* reveals a pessimistic or optimistic view of the universe"[39]) are probably, in reverse order, those of Thomson, who ends his chapter on the novel by asserting that "through its concrete, sensuous, and visionary unity, Forster's mythic India gives immediate and incarnate assurance that the universe is one"[40] and of Crews, for whom "the strands of the novel are unified by the thematic principle that unity is not to be obtained."[41]

Thomson and Crews thus enact once again the assumptions of romance and realist criticism. Most critics, however, tend to less extreme positions; and the critical division—based almost always on varying readings of the meaning of the caves in the second part of the novel and on the significance of the temple ceremonies and their consequences in the third—may perhaps be better phrased as follows: that whereas for one group (see Wilde's *Art and Order* and Reuben Brower's essay in *The Fields of Light* [1951]) the caves represent an awareness of negation that is never or never fully overcome and the symbolic events of "Temple" express only the *desire* for unity, for the other (including McDowell and Dauner in the essays reprinted below) the caves "comprise," in McDowell's words, "the sum total of all experience" and "Temple," to quote him again, promises that "temporal discordances will in time yield to a merging of hitherto abrasively active dichotomies." The concentration in the first set of readings on a desired unity and, in the other, on its achievement "in time" makes for divisions that are perhaps more matters of emphasis than of absolute opposition and helps to suggest again the metaphor of family quarrels. Further, what seems to be implied is that the most fruitful interpretations, like those of Parry (which closes this collection), begin *and* end with the awareness that *A Passage to India* is itself less a work of thematic resolution or irresolution than the site of conflicting urgencies contained within (or by) a formal perfection that does not so much overcome as distance and suspend the problematics it initiates and explores.

Not all of the essays and comments gathered here are to be seen in terms of Thomson's realist-romance paradigm. Those in the first section, for example, respond to Forster the man, addressing by way of anticipation or hindsight the conventional wisdom about Trilling's "figure." So, not only Furbank's discussion of (among other things) Forster's homosexuality and Stone's powerful reconsideration of his humanism but Lawrence's perceptive, if partial, insight into Forster's temperamental and sexual crisis in the early years of World War I (and before his first fully consummated relationship with another man), all play off against Isherwood's more familiar portrait of Forster as the very embodiment of the relaxed will. Evidently, it is no longer possible to avoid the awareness that Forster has in some sense splintered before our eyes, and if the sentimental view finds more to regret than to applaud in the fracturing of the once traditional image, one may legitimately doubt that Forster, who after all anticipated and allowed the publication of the posthumous works, would have concurred.

In the same spirit, and more directly, the essays that make up the third section of this collection engage the impact of Forster's sexuality on his writing, and although they argue from different moral positions and with a different sense of what meaning and value is to be attributed to the overtly homosexual works, they are at one in accepting the need to come to terms with the literary and biographical revelations of the 1970s. These essays have, however, been chosen for other reasons as well. Called upon to do double, even triple, duty, they serve both to establish other critical positions in the body of Forster criticism and to offer readings of novels and stories not dealt with elsewhere in the book. Of these, the first published (apart from a handful of stories) is *Where Angels Fear to Trend*; and it remains something of a mystery why, except in full-length studies, the book has been, though praised, generally neglected. Considered by Woolf and Leavis to be Forster's most successful prewar novel, a better novel indeed than *Howards End*, *Where Angels Fear to Tread* perhaps offers too little by way of resistance to critical exegetes. At once restricted in scope and masterly in execution, the book challenges, or appears to challenge, less than its successors. And yet it can be argued (see the essay by Alan Wilde below) that the novel announces in a variety of ways Forster's divided aims and "the uneasy balance between them" that the book finally achieves.

The next two novels are the subject of Judith Scherer Herz's stimulating essay, which, while taking issue with Wilde's attempt to establish various stages in Forster's career and with his evaluation of the stories in *The Life to Come*, carries still further the idea of doubleness. "A good deal of [Forster's] strength as a novelist," she writes, "thus depends upon the tension generated by the collision of two story lines, the surface heterosexual romance and the interior homosexual romance." The remark applies as much to *Where Angels Fear to Tread* as to the two books she considers; and not the least value of her analysis is that it allows readers to approach all three of the early novels (though this, it should be said, is not precisely what she intends) as at once self-contradictory and filled with barely suppressed energy and desire— to avoid, that is, the choice between the mutually exclusive arguments of realism and romance, and the need to overpraise works that are at once minor and flawed. Few critics would accept McDowell's estimate of *A Room with a View* as a "masterpiece,"[42] given its generally recognized failure to confront the kinds of problems raised by the depiction of George Emerson or to make of his father more than a sentimental deus ex machina; and there is no need to. One can, instead, both respond to the novel's geniality and high spirits and recognize in Forster's evasions and sublimations the workings of a mind radically, if surreptitiously, at war with society and with itself.

Larger claims can be—and are—made for *The Longest Journey* by such critics as Thomson or John Magnus ("Ritual Aspects of E. M. Forster's *The Longest Journey*" [1967]), who read the novel "as romance or as symbolic parable."[43] For those who cannot, *The Longest Journey* at worst betrays "disabling immaturities in valuation"[44] on Forster's part and at best reveals, as Herz says, "the thinnest skin stretched over the most turbulent inner action." Few critics, on the other hand, are inclined to deny the novel its many and compelling merits—above all, its subtle and modulated portrayal of Rickie Elliot, its philosophical breadth and poetic reach, and its conceptual largeness—and fewer still will challenge its value as a quasi-autobiographical document indispensible to the understanding of Forster's troubled imagination. As for *Maurice*, the other novel that meant so much to Forster himself, it is probably too soon to say what its final place in his canon will be. If critics like Ozick and Hynes and even Herz have stressed its imaginative thinness, its lack of tension, its "poverty of feeling,"[45] still the book has not lacked intelligent defenders, most notably Claude Summers, whose reading of *Maurice* in this collection fascinatingly situates the novel in the context of two contemporary and opposing views of homosexuality (John Addington Symonds's and Edward Carpenter's),[46] responds to the charges that have been brought against it, and argues persuasively for a revaluation of "Forster's most undervalued work."

Finally, there are the homosexual stories of *The Life to Come*, criticism of which, despite a number of studies (see, for example, Norman Page's *E. M. Forster's Posthumous Fiction* [1977], chapter eight of Summers's *E. M. Forster* [1983], and Wilfred Stone's " 'Overleaping Class': Forster's Problem in Connection" [1978], in addition to the essays by Wilde and Herz below), must be regarded, even more than in the case of *Maurice*, as still in its preliminary stages, so wide are the disagreements about their value both individually and collectively. What can be asserted is that, however they come finally to be regarded, their importance in challenging, along with *Maurice* and Furbank's biographical studies, the standard view of Forster is beyond question. If much of Forster criticism has till now seen him steadily, it must now carry forward the undertaking begun in the nineteen-seventies of seeing him differently and whole—or, at any rate, as the sum of interrelated but dispersed and not always easily reconcilable parts.

The essays that follow have been chosen both for their own rewarding insights and for what they reveal about the perspectives, quarrels, and attitudes that inform the body of Forster criticism.[47] But precisely because they repeatedly argue with one another, they cannot be said to represent, except in the ways indicated earlier, *a* viewpoint, *a* way of seizing Forster and his fiction. Nor, indeed, does the achievement of a definitive reading (assuming the unlikely case that such an interpretation were possible) matter nearly so much as defining the terms under which all readings of Forster are likely to be conducted in the near future—if, at any rate, their aim is to ratify the interest, importance, and availability of his fiction to contemporary readers. Most criticism of Forster carries an invisible banner on which is inscribed a motto from *A Room with a View*: "The sadness of the incomplete—the sadness that is often Life, but should never be Art . . ."[48] Certainly, Forster contrasted throughout his career the coherence of art—"the one orderly product which our muddling race has produced"[49]—with "the chaotic nature of our daily life,"[50] and did so all the more after he himself virtually ceased writing fiction. At the same time, Forster's novels, the early ones especially, demonstrate an abiding distrust of any tendency to view life in aesthetic categories, to constrain its messiness and vitality to the willed fixities of the detached and spectatorial mind. Which is to say that Forster is by no means, or in any case not always, at one with those of his critics who find in art's elegance and control an *answer* to life's recalcitrant complexities.

As we've seen, Forster's ironic and increasingly hectic sense of life's inherently fragmented nature generates in all his work, and by way of compensation, a desire for, a reaching after, unity of one kind or another. Writing to Robert Trevelyan in connection with his first novel, he says: "What I want, I think, is the sentimental, but the sentimental reached by no easy beaten track"; and following the consummation of his relationship with Mohammed el Adl, he expresses to Florence Barger the happiness he feels "not for the actual pleasure but because the last barrier has fallen."[51] To cross or down barriers is in some sense the motive of all Forster's fiction (the key words of *A Room with a View*'s central fourth chapter are "cross" and "across"), a motive that is sentimental to the degree that it seeks to dissolve differences, as in *Maurice*'s greenwood, into a oneness free of complexity and contingency alike. But Forster is also, and more famously, the spokesman for "eternal differences,"[52] for a connection that takes as its end not the eradication but the recognition and integration of life's antinomies. The incompatibility between these ideals (although everywhere in the prewar fiction and especially in *Maurice* Forster seeks, with relative degrees of success or failure, to reconcile them) only alerts us to the further divisions that make up the very texture of the novels. Love and truth, comradeship and sexuality, the ideal and the actual, above all consciousness and desire, in each case one urgency wars with another, manifesting irreconcilability in a clash of surface and subsurface aims, or of rhetorical strategies, or even (as in the balancing of Margaret Schlegel's pursuit of "sustained relations" against her sister's experience of "passing emotion")[53] of moral imperatives.[54]

Given this pervasive uneasiness and strain, what, then, does the promise or, at times, notably in *A Passage to India*, the fulfillment of art's "vital harmony"[55] signify to the reader of Forster's novels? The *idea* of reconciliation or transcendence, certainly. For the modernists generally, as for the New Critics, art *is* order: the proof of the imagination's power and achievement; a source of consolation; and, if less overtly, a moral desideratum as well. But in the wake of an expiring modernism, we have come to realize that formal unity, the hallmark of Forster's belief in art as a "self-contained entity,"[56] is precisely an idea and an ideal—not in itself the resolution of conflict but its *containment*, the implicit expression of a desire that half recognizes its own futility. Does this mean that Forster's fiction, along with much of what we value in modernism, is to be written off as failure? Not at all. The issue, again, is one of the enabling preconceptions all of us bring to literature. And it is just possible that if, in this postmodernist, post-structuralist age—one that finds more to celebrate in the incomplete than in the complete, that detects meaning in gaps and impasses, in blindness and paradox—if under these new circumstances critics can be brought to forego some of their traditional assumptions about the primacy of aesthetic coherence, they may discover, as in different ways Stone, Herz, Summers, Widdowson, and Parry do, heretofore unsuspected levels of complexity in Forster's works.

To see the novels and stories in this manner is to regard them as no doubt less perfectly unified and autonomous creations, but also to cease berating them for their failures to achieve the smooth assurance of the settled and integrated vision. At stake is a figure more diverse, complex, and riven than Trilling's, enacting not only in but through the fiction an emblematic relationship to self and world, which expresses neither the abstract serenity of achieved wisdom nor the fervent, unitary search for it that critics have variously identified, but the frictional, tensive interplay between them—and, still more, between competing energies and impulses that are at once rationally contradictory and experientially interwoven. As Herz says in words that apply to more than the clash of the heterosexual and homosexual plot lines she is discussing, "it is from this conflict . . . that the novels take their energy." To be sure, energy, Blake's devil notwithstanding, is not enough, but that is not all Forster has to offer to the newer, more sinuously questioning, less complacent criticisms of the present, for which the unified self or work is always insidiously fractured: a scene of random desires and languages problematically attached to being. The Forster who has emerged in the last fifteen years—not only and not primarily the historical man but the man mediated by the whole range of his work—encompasses the more familiar liberal humanist but only as one part, if still an important part, of a more intricate, less stable amalgam. Ozick and Hynes to the contrary, Forster's values gain rather than lose by virtue of the struggles from which they grow. Thus Glen Cavaliero writes: "The transformation of a private and personal estrangement into an engaged concern with the very society which implicity rejected him is one of Forster's triumphs as humanist and artist."[57] There is, in short, no need to choose among competing Forsters, since the competition is precisely the point. The task is, instead, to surround the official voice with other, till now less audible ones, thereby complicating and dispersing its singular authority. At which point, ironically enough, even the traditional Forster—the Forster, most notably, of *Howards End* and of the essays in *Two Cheers for Democracy*—begins to take on new and unexpected life. After all, the complexities of the relaxed will speak (or should speak) with special force to a generation intent on finding alternatives to a rigid "symmetry of choices,"[58] just as Forster's determination to establish small enclaves of value in the face of the self's and the universe's ultimate incomprehensibility sounds (or should sound) a note congenial to contemporary writers and readers skeptical of all-inclusive solutions and all-encompassing forms.

If, for many, this is not in fact the case, it may be because Forster has come to seem, along with a number of other modernist writers, one of "the great dead men with their injunctions. Make it new. Only connect."[59] But to see these injunctions or Furbank's "moral generalisations" not as complacencies and certainties but as tentative, provisional gestures of ongoing exploration and accommodation is to restore to the novels especially the presence of an energizing density of contradiction, conflict, and vacillation that is rightly theirs. Criticism's job consists, of course, not in wrenching works out of their historical contexts but in bringing to light for successive groups of readers elements heretofore undetected or misconstrued, a process helped along in Forster's case by the publication of *Maurice* and *The Life to Come* and of Furbank's *Life*; and if for the moment what those books have told us has served rather to sink than to raise Forster's reputation, there is every reason to think of the situation as temporary. Attuned to a more elastic notion of literary order and development and to a more problematical conception of the authorial self, contemporary criticism is now in a position, even while recognizing Forster's writings as the inevitable products of their time, to recuperate them for our own.

. . . .

I would like to thank this volume's contributors, and particularly those who have allowed me to cut, abridge, or otherwise modify their work in the interests of achieving a reasonably sized book.

Zack Bowen has been a model editor: patient, supportive, and encouraging.

As always, I have benefited from the advice, help, and patience of my friends Timothy Corrigan, Jayne Kribbs, Frederick P. W. McDowell, and Robert Storey; and still more from the unstinting generosity and support of Daniel O'Hara and Jack Undank.

I could not possibly have carried through this project without the imaginative, intelligent, and thoughtful cooperation of Mary Tiryak, who has helped me in every possible way in the completion of this book. I am especially grateful to her.

ALAN WILDE

Temple University

Notes

1. One thousand nine hundred and thirteen is the number of items listed in Frederick P. W. McDowell's *E. M. Forster: An Annotated Bibliography of Writings About Him* (De Kalb, Ill.: Northern Illinois Univ. Press, 1976). The bibliography, as McDowell notes, is incomplete for the years 1974 and 1975.

2. Quotations from essays that appear in this collection—in this case, P. N. Furbank's "The Personality of E. M. Forster"—will not be documented in the notes.

3. See, respectively, Anne Olivier Bell, ed., *The Diary of Virginia Woolf*, I (London: Hogarth Press, 1977), 295, 291; David Garnett, "Forster and Bloomsbury," in *Aspects of E. M. Forster*, ed. Oliver Stallybrass (London: Edward Arnold, 1969), p. 32; and John Maynard Keynes, "My Early Beliefs," in *Two Memoirs* (New York: Augustus M. Kelley, 1949), p. 81.

4. See Philip Gardner's "Introduction" to *E. M. Forster: The Critical Heritage* (London and Boston: Routledge and Kegan Paul, 1973), p. 27, where he notes "the fairly frequent occurrences of the word 'elusive' in earlier reviews" and also John Beer's "Introduction: The Elusive Forster," in *E. M. Forster: A Human Exploration, Centenary Essays*, ed. G. K. Das and John Beer (London and Basingstoke: Macmillan Press, 1979).

5. Beer, p. 3.

6. Gardner, p. 12.

7. Beer, p. 3.

8. E. M. Forster, *The Longest Journey* (New York: Random House-Vintage Books, n.d.), p. 186. Although the Abinger Edition provides definitive texts of Forster's works, I have quoted, because of their accessibility, from popular American editions.

9. The phrase appears in a part of Lawrence's letter to Forster (12 Feb. 1915) not quoted below. See Harry T. Moore, ed., *The Collected Letters of D. H. Lawrence*, I (New York: Viking Press, 1962), 320.

10. Lionel Trilling, "George Orwell and the Politics of Truth," in *The Opposing Self: Nine Essays in Criticism* (London: Secker and Warburg, 1955), p. 156.

11. Betsy Draine, "An Interview with Angus Wilson," *Contemporary Literature*, 21 (Winter 1980), 13.

12. Lillian D. Bloom, "Moral and Creative Insights," *Novel*, 17 (Winter 1984), 183.

13. Frederick P. W. McDowell, " 'Fresh Woods, and Pastures New': Forster Criticism and Scholarship since 1975," in *E. M. Forster: Centenary Revaluations*, ed. Judith Scherer Herz and Robert K. Martin (Toronto and Buffalo: Univ. of Toronto Press, 1982), p. 311.

14. Frederick P. W. McDowell, "Forster Scholarship and Criticism for the Desert Islander," in *E. M. Forster: A Human Exploration*, p. 282.

15. Mary Lago and P. N. Furbank, eds., *Selected Letters of E. M. Forster*, I (Cambridge, Mass.: Harvard Univ. Press, 1983), xi. The quotation is from Furbank's section of the introduction.

16. McDowell, *Annotated Bibliography*, pp. 9, 10. Forster criticism has been so exhaustively and intelligently explored and documented by McDowell that it has seemed redundant to append a bibliography to this collection. Readers who wish to pursue further the history of that criticism and to discover reasoned, reliable assessments of particular works and critics are advised to read, in the following order, the three essays by McDowell already referred to: "Forster Scholarship and

Criticism for the Desert Islander"; the "Introduction" to the *Annotated Bibliography*; and " 'Fresh Woods, and Pastures New.' " Also very much worth consulting are Gardner's "Introduction" (see n. 4), which concentrates on criticism of the years 1905–28 (but takes note of later criticism as well) and Malcolm Bradbury's model "Introduction" to *Forster: A Collection of Critical Essays* (Englewood Cliffs, N. J.: Prentice Hall-Spectrum Books, 1966).

17. Wilfred Stone, *The Cave and the Mountain: A Study of E. M. Forster* (Stanford: Stanford Univ. Press; London: Oxford Univ. Press, 1966), p. 339.

18. Gardner, p. 3.

19 E. M. Forster, *Aspects of the Novel* (New York: Harcourt, Brace-Harvest Books, 1954), p. 14.

20. Trilling, *The Opposing Self*, p. 155.

21. E. M. Forster, "What I Believe," in *Two Cheers for Democracy* (New York: Harcourt, Brace, 1951), p. 67. On the same subject, see Forster's less well-known piece, "A Letter," *Twentieth Century*, 157 (Feb. 1955), 99–101.

22. See, for example, D. S. Savage, *The Withered Branch: Six Studies in the Modern Novel* (London: Eyre & Spottiswoode, 1950) and Ernest Beaumont, "Mr. E. M. Forster's Strange Mystics," *Dublin Review*, 453 (3d Quarter 1951), 41–51.

23. Frederick C. Crews, *E. M. Forster: The Perils of Humanism* (Princeton: Princeton Univ. Press, 1962), p. 172.

24. F. R. Leavis, "E. M. Forster," in *The Common Pursuit* (London: Chatto and Windus, 1952), p. 276.

25. Samuel Hynes, "Forster's Cramp," in *Edwardian Occasions: Essays on English Writing in the Early Twentieth Century* (New York: Oxford Univ. Press, 1972), p. 121.

26. Cynthia Ozick, "Forster as Homosexual," *Commentary*, 52 (Dec. 1971), 85.

27. E. M. Forster, "Terminal Note" to *Maurice* (New York: W. W. Norton, 1971), p. 255.

28. See Hynes, p. 115 and Ozick, p. 84.

29. Furbank, *Selected Letters*, p. vii.

30. Maurice Merleau-Ponty, *Signs*, trans. Richard C. McCleary (Evanston, Ill.: Northwestern Univ. Press, 1964), p. 54.

31. The phrase comes from a letter quoted in E. M. Forster's *Goldsworthy Lowes Dickinson* (London: Edward Arnold, 1947), p. 216.

32. Bradbury, p. 10.

33. George H. Thomson, *The Fiction of E. M. Forster* (Detroit: Wayne State Univ. Press, 1967), p. 13.

34. Thomson, p. 17.

35. McDowell, *Annotated Bibliography*, p. 23.

36. Hardy's essay is reprinted below (in abridged form), as is part of Widdowson's book on the novel. The remarks quoted here, however, come from an earlier part of Widdowson's monograph. See *E. M. Forster's "Howards End": Fiction as History* (London: Chatto and Windus, for Sussex Univ. Press, 1977), pp. 12–14.

37. Widdowson, p. 12.

38. June Perry Levine, *Creation and Criticism: "A Passage to India"* (Lincoln: Univ. of Nebraska Press, 1971), pp. 127–28.

39. Levine, p. 119.

40. Thomson, p. 250.

41. Crews, p. 142.

42. Frederick P. W. McDowell, *E. M. Forster*, rev. ed. (Boston: Twayne Publishers, 1982). The remark occurs in the preface, which is unpaginated.

43. McDowell, "Forster Scholarship and Criticism for the Desert Islander," p. 280.

44. Leavis, p. 268.

45. Hynes, p. 121.

46. This argument, as Summers indicates in his notes, has been made by Robert K. Martin in his essay "Edward Carpenter and the Double Structure of *Maurice,*" *Journal of Homosexuality*, 8 (Spring/Summer 1983), 25–46.

47. Restrictions of space have made necessary the exclusion not only of much valuable criticism but of essays devoted exclusively or primarily to the nonfiction. It should be said, however, that the definitive essay on Forster's criticism has still to be written.

48. E. M. Forster, *A Room with a View* (New York: Random House-Vintage Books, n.d.), p. 140.

49. E. M. Forster, "Art for Art's Sake," in *Two Cheers*, p. 92.

50. E. M. Forster, *Howards End* (New York: Vintage Books, 1956), p. 106.

51. See Lago's and Furbank's *Selected Letters*, pp. 83, 274.

52. Forster, *Howards End*, p. 338.

53. Forster, *Howards End*, p. 25.

54. For a more detailed presentation of this problem, see Alan Wilde, *Horizons of Assent: Modernism, Postmodernism, and the Ironic Imagination* (Baltimore and London: Johns Hopkins Univ. Press, 1981), pp. 71–80.

55. Forster, "Art for Art's Sake," p. 90.

56. Forster, "Art for Art's Sake," p. 89.

57. Glen Cavaliero, *A Reading of E. M. Forster* (Totowa, N.J.:Rowman and Littlefield, 1979), p. 130.

58. Thomas Pynchon, *The Crying of Lot 49* (New York: Bantam Books, 1972), p. 136.

59. Renata Adler, *Speedboat* (New York: Random House, 1976), p. 73. The allusion is to the epigraph of *Howards End*.

Perspectives on Forster:
The Man and the Figure

The Personality of E. M. Forster

P. N. Furbank*

I am not sure it is the time to talk about E. M. Forster. It is too late to speak of the living man and too soon to summon up his ghost. For the moment he lies out of reach and won't give up his secret. And he had a secret—it's not just sentimental to say it; nothing so spectacular as "voices," but he knew how to live in daily touch with his own depths. This set him apart, so that it was no mistake for people to have reverenced him—as they did and do. He was a rare creature, contrived of the strangest materials.

A rare creature, but a problem to his biographer. Reverence is a luxury a biographer cannot afford. And then, how to make a narrative of the life of a man for whom time stood still? Also, a smaller matter, there's the difficulty that no one ever described Forster as a young man. People record their impressions of a contemporary because he is famous or because he impinged on them personally; and Forster did not impinge—he was inconspicuous, sometimes to the point of vanishing. Moreover, for most of his life, no one could remember a word he said in conversation. So—till he becomes famous—we have to depend largely on his own account of himself. Still, his contemporaries seem to have agreed he was exactly the same at twenty as he was at ninety, so perhaps the problem is not so grave. One can work backwards from what one knows, and I shall do so here. Where shall I begin? As good a place as any would be his attitude to friends, for it was central to him, and in some ways very odd and original, and it leads naturally on to all the other questions.

Forster gave endless time and attention to his friends. He also gave them total loyalty; he never casually dropped people, as most of us do, out of mere forgetfulness or through change of circumstances. Though he sometimes dropped them, with perfect deliberateness, if they offended him in some vital way; and then he was implacable. It was another principle of his never to listen to apologies or explanations; and

*Reprinted from *Encounter* 35 (Nov. 1970), 61–68, by permission of the author and Encounter Limited.

when he had made up his mind against anyone, fairly or unfairly, he was most unlikely to change it.[1]

Otherwise, if someone became a friend of his, that was that; he continued to be so for life; it was merely a matter of which grade or circle in his system of friendships he should be assigned to (and over the years he might from time to time gravitate or be shifted from one to another). The habit of keeping his friends steadily in mind was basic to Forster. For one thing, he always looked for permanencies in life. He never placed his hopes in the future or wanted to leave bits of his past behind, as people with his degree of ambition mostly do; though since he lived fully in the moment, making a definite event of the most casual meal or conversation or journey, he did not grow stale. More importantly, he regarded people and affections as the sole reality, and keeping them in mind was tantamount to living itself. That this reality was perishable too, in the perspective of eternity, he regarded as the ultimate principle of existence, beyond which there was no looking.

On the other hand, he never "gave" himself fully to friends. To begin with, he never liked being laughed at. It would be wrong to say he couldn't bear it; he swallowed it for friendship's sake, if he had to, but it was no part at all of his idea of the pleasures of friendship, and he winced or bristled so visibly under teasing that people usually didn't try it twice. Equally, he was no good at quarrels. That is to say, they always assumed giant proportions for him; he nerved himself up to a quarrel with immense effort, and he remembered it for months or years afterwards, writing thousands of words about it in letters or keeping a *dossier* on it. He had curious ways of describing a quarrel. If he were not involved personally, he spoke as though he were—"So *we* were in trouble . . ."; and if he were involved, he would put the whole thing between inverted commas—"I have been *insulted!*," he might say, as if he only just thought of the name for what had taken place. He could not conceive of enjoying quarrels or of their being a natural part of a relationship, and when his married friends quarrelled he was quite sure their marriage must be breaking up.

Again, though he took his friends' troubles to heart more than the average person (and sometimes more than they deserved) and was forever listening to confessions, with a beautiful attentiveness and sympathy, he set definite limits to the bearing of others' burdens. "My aim in life," he once wrote to a friend, "is to be as sensitive as I can up to a point. When that point is passed one bursts or dies, so a secondary aim is introduced: not to pass it, and every now and then to repaint and mend the sorry fabric of one's armour." He was very much against the Christian doctrine of vicarious suffering and had a whole repertoire of self-protective devices. One of them, in times of stress, was to cultivate erotic thoughts.

For all the duties and responsibilities he imposed on himself, there was something self-pleasing in his approach to people. It came out particularly plainly in his sex life. He achieved physical sex very late and found it easier with people outside his own social class, and it remained a kind of private magic for him—an almost unattainable blessing, for which another person was mainly a pretext. He valued sex for its power to release his own capacities for tenderness and devotion, but he never expected an *equal* sexual relationship. His chief feeling towards anyone who let him make love to them was gratitude. Intense gratitude led him to romanticise them, at least with one part of his mind, and by romanticising them he managed to keep them at a distance. He was infinitely attentive and thoughtful and exacting, always determined to keep his lover "up to the mark"—not be slack or idle, write proper letters and so on—but he never showed any wish to set up house with him. One can't picture him doing it. He could imagine two lovers living together in the "greenwood" but hardly in a flat in Kensington or a house in Potter's Bar. Of course he knew many homosexual ménages and found them perfectly congenial, but it never crossed his mind to be part of one. But then, it would be wrong to put this down just to temperament. He quite seriously, and on fully thought-out grounds, distrusted marriage as an institution and fretted at having to write "marriage-fiction." He suspected marriage might produce more harm than good; he was sure, at least, that there were finer possibilities outside it.

I was puzzled by the list of virtues Joe Ackerley attributed to him in his posthumous obituary in the *Observer* (14 June 1970). The article is one of the best evocations of Forster there has been; but the list itself doesn't seem right. "I would say" says Ackerley,

> that in so far as it is possible for any human being to be both wise and worldly wise, to be selfless in any material sense, to have no envy, jealousy, vanity, conceit, to contain no malice, no hatred (though he had anger), to be always reliable, considerate, generous, never cheap, Morgan came as close to that as can be got.

It says a lot that he could evoke such wholesale and loving admiration from a close friend. Still, I don't think Forster was without vanity; he had a considerable share of it, as almost all authors have. He thought highly of his own work, though he saw its limitations clearly enough, and had a strong sense of his position. He thought respect was due to it and was very quick to resent slights, and not at all inclined to pass them over, though he didn't make scenes, and showed annoyance in quiet and barbed ways. Certainly he often acted "humbly" from a social point of view. He was inclined to search out the shyest or most commonplace person at a party (just as he would attend politely, as if hearing it for the first time, when total strangers explained what was wrong with the plot of *The Longest Journey*). This was genuinely kind and delicate behaviour (though he was quite capable, too, of doing it to shame his host or hostess); also he *liked* "boring" people and frequently made lifelong friendships with them. Still he was perfectly conscious of the effect he was making and the part his fame was playing in it. Humility hardly comes in.

Nor do I feel that lack of vanity was quite the key to his dowdy appearance—his way of moving through life, as William Plomer puts it, looking like the man who comes to wind the clocks. After all, he was dandy enough in his prose-style; as well as being a flexible artistic instrument, it was a very smart costume, the prose of a man who took great pains with his appearance. It is true he was always defeatist about his looks. In his boyhood he played up, in a precocious, only-son manner, to family jokes about his "beauty" and the injury it suffered from sores and sticking-plaster; and he went on making the same kind of joke to himself. He was sure he was physically unattractive, just as he knew, or found out, that in the way of friendship he could attract anyone he really wanted to. Thus he came to terms with his situation very satisfactorily; it was part of a larger decision to be content with a dowdy and suburban way of existence. Still, I imagine that somewhere self-punishment entered in. Men of homosexual temperament often have a strong urge for personal display, they would like to be peacocks and attract all eyes; and if their upbringing forbids it (such a puritan middle-class upbringing as Forster's or Samuel Butler's) they react by making the worst of themselves.

Again, to return to Joe Ackerley's list, Forster was perfectly capable of jealousy. His life being arranged as it was, occasions for jealousy did not often arise; but when they did, he suffered and fought in a very normal, and not especially saint-like, way.

Which makes it all the more striking that he was, as Ackerley says, completely without envy. So far as I can tell, he never once experienced the emotion. The nearest he came to it was after the success of *Howards End*. By a characteristic trick of psychology, as soon as he had experienced success he began to be sure there must be failure in store for him, and started asking himself what would happen when his reputation sank and others overtook him. Would he begin to envy his rivals? In a way, the test actually presented itself; by the end of the war he was relatively a forgotten figure—certainly not a household name like Galsworthy or even Lawrence. And although he was depressed at his sterility and worried about how he was going to live, envy never once entered his thoughts. If one were urging his claims to sainthood (my own ideas about saints are too vague), this would be a weighty argument.

Another would be his generosity, as Ackerley rightly mentioned. Throughout his life he had one clear idea about money, that it was an opportunity to perform acts of loving-kindness. His mother also had a very strong sense of duty about money. Forster took over her attitude, raising it from the level of duty to a more imaginative benevolence. Even in early youth he was perpetually giving money to his family and to friends; half his quite small earnings from his early writings went on sending friends on foreign holidays or getting cousins out of scrapes. I suppose hardly anyone in his intimacy did not receive, at some time or other, the well-timed gift of a large sum of money. And one must remember that, until the 1940s, he was by no means a rich man, hardly even comfortably off. During World War I, while he was in Alexandria, he urged his mother to sell his typewriter to help her pay for a cure; and even in the 1930s he was quite worried by the cost of the train-fare to Wiltshire. He thought a great deal about money and worked out his own theory of giving. One should give large sums; large gifts did not create embarrassment as small ones did—people regarded them as an act of God. Loans were a different matter; they could be very small—and if he lent someone ten shillings and it was not returned by Thursday, as stipulated, he was very quick to ask the reason why.

So much for his virtues. As for his other traits, I think the most characteristic was his passion for moralising. He was moralising busily when he was twenty; and he continued, without intermission, for the next seventy years. He plainly regarded it as the business of life; one was on earth to improve oneself and to improve others, and the path to this was moral generalisations. A landscape, personal crises or the sorrows of others, books, paintings, incidents at the tea-table or international disasters, were, for him, all occasions for drawing a moral. Had he been born a contemporary of George Eliot, this might have passed without notice; but in his own age it sets him apart as an English writer—more so than any oddity of upbringing, like being a miner's son or a Polish sea-captain. It was a dominating influence on his writing. The technical originality of his novels lies in his being more Victorian than ever George Eliot or Thackeray were, more godlike in manipulating his characters and telling us what to think of them; or rather it lies in his working his godlike intrusions more inextricably into his fictional fabric. In a recent BBC radio discussion K. W. Gransden complained, and rightly, that Forster sometimes didn't trust the reader enough and commented where comment was unnecessary. But the point seems incidental. For one unnecessary intrusion, there are ten which are necessary and intrinsic. So much does his method depend on them, one forgets to notice them and is only reminded by the queer and spectral thinness of stage-versions of his novels. Moreover the habit grew on him; his commenting presence is more dominating in *A Passage to India* than ever before. He found moralising a device of endless potentiality; there was room for his whole genius in it.

I think he may have taken over this moralising habit from his mother. Carlylean denunciation, moral heroics, earnest evangelical exhortation are perhaps more of a male *forte*; but a habit of putting people right, in season and out, and of giving them the benefit of a general stock of moral knowledge, came to no one more naturally than a Victorian matron. Forster remade his inheritance, if that is what it was; he did not lay down the law like a trumpeting dowager or bossy governess. He was much more various and elusive, by turns gruff and scout-masterly, grave and prophetic and feline and flickering in a mercurial and "camp" manner. The combination was disconcerting but all of a piece. Unlike so many homosexuals, he suffered very little from internal conflicts, and such female characteristics as he adopted were pure strength to him.

His moralising made him formidable, though. One felt his eye on one, like any unwary child or servant. Joe Ackerley has described his unnerving manner of listening, with an attention which seemed to go far beyond the words that were said. His sureness attracted people who were unsure of themselves; but they did not find him an easy companion. They got a great deal out of him, as he did of them; for many, he touched a personal chord no one else had ever sounded, and they were proportionately devoted to him. Still, if you *were* unsure of yourself, there were plenty of snubs to swallow. Though not at all a copious conversationalist, no one ever *managed* conversations more inexorably, and people in his company were always finding words freeze on their lips. And in fact, though he had endless and fruitful experience of shy people, he did not particularly value shyness. Actually, what he liked best, if given the choice, was robust, unfidgety people, at ease in their bodies, people who could cut through his own cobwebs and express affection—as he could not—in a free and demonstrative way. If he trusted people, they could not display affection too lavishly for him.

A good way of visualising Forster, I find, is to imagine him when introduced to a dog or cat. I never witnessed this, but can picture him putting himself on a level with the animal, approaching it tolerantly but non-committally. It *might* be a nice animal, but then again it might not; it was a mistake to have preconceptions about such matters; and at all events it didn't matter *much* what character an animal had—but it mattered a little. That would be his tone, I think; and he would shoot glances at the animal, in the intervals of conversation, examining it from queer angles, till he had made up his mind about it.

This was rather the way he behaved as a critic. From many points of view he was a superb literary critic. He felt this himself, and had a pert way of exclaiming how acute he was, and what an easy business criticism turned out to be. His letters of literary advice to friends are admirable. No one was better, as they acknowledged, at sensing their intentions or putting his finger on the spot where things went wrong. As a critic he *looked*, he scrutinised the object as if nothing else like it had ever existed, and he emerged with a brand new, freshly-minted formula, fitting not only the work in question but, potentially, a whole new class of works. His published criticism has the same virtues; many of his judgments in *Aspects of the Novel* seem dated now, but his formulae are as lively as ever.

However, there was a price to pay for this *ad hoc* approach to criticism. He was so distrustful of system in all matters of art, as in matters of the heart and conduct, that he could not enter into the frame of mind of artists to whom system mattered. He could never get his mind round Henry James, for instance, though he thought about him, off and on, all his life. He would write James off as a futile cobweb-spinner; then he would pick up a new novel of his and be astonished at its marvellous power and solidity. The thing seemed a great mystery to him; it never occurred to him that James might have wanted to do one thing in one novel and another in another—that there was a system and larger artistic plan in his literary career. During the Second World War he took it into his head to make an analysis of Beethoven's piano sonatas. As literature it is very attractive and full of fresh inspirations and *aperçus*; but as music criticism, so far as I can judge, it is a semi-failure (a musical friend of mine thought the same). He feels his way too empirically from incident to incident in the music, acclaiming this and puzzling over that; he pushes, picking and choosing beyond its natural scope.

I mention his limitations as a critic because they help to define his virtues, which were also his virtues as a thinker and writer in general. His mind was a vast breeding-ground for discriminations. He endlessly picked and chose and could distinguish between two blades of grass. No one ever made such restrictive remarks. I can hear them so vividly: "So-and-so, with an intelligent face, fairly"; or, "I am devoted to so-and-so's son, slightly." I remember him once chatting with Lord Beveridge in his club. "What a charmer!" he said afterwards—then, considering his words more carefully, "What an ill-informed distinguished old man." Again, both as a critic and a creator, he was a master of *angle*. As all his friends remarked, nobody came at things from queerer angles. It was not whimsicality; it arose from his seeing things more concretely than other people. (It shows his respect for the concreteness of the world that he always realised his metaphors. Describing himself as having, like a rat, deserted the ship of fiction, he continues "and *swam* towards biography.") He planted himself firmly in the world and took sighting from where he stood; there was this that one could see and that which was concealed by the lie of the land. Of course, one could change one's viewpoint. . . . His great strength as a novelist was his sense for the angles at which people stood to one another and to the universe surrounding them and the constant dance of changing angles from which he makes us view them. For him, the art of fiction, like the art of life, lay in finding one's bearings. "One must face facts," a friend once said to him. "How can I," he replied, "when they're all around me?"

This leads me to what you might call his "secret" and his deepest originality; I mean his feeling for life. His knowledge of society was not particularly remarkable; what was superior to him was his knowledge of the possibilities of life. It seemed he could see through to life; it was not a vague generality to him but a palpable presence, and he could hear its wingbeat. I remember him once describing some friends of his and their fondness, when they were children, for an older companion who was not quite right in the head. He spoke of it in a delighted tone, which I find hard to interpret; but it seemed to convey that this was what life was made up of. Everything was there, if one took the trouble to look for it. There was no need, and it would be wrong, to ask oneself if this was a small incident or a large one, or to place it in any category or system at all. The whole of life was present in it, and there was nothing beyond. I remember another even tinier incident. We were sharing a hotel bedroom, and as he undressed the coins dropped out of his pocket. He said, in a tone of mock-superstitious resignation, "When they begin to sing, it's all up with them." There was the same joyful note in his voice. It was oddly ghostly and impressive, as if he truly had some private insight into the workings of providence.

Notes

1. Politically, too, he was never much interested in justice; though perhaps in this case he thought there were enough people already looking after it.

[Letter to Bertrand Russell]   D. H. Lawrence*

We have had E. M. Forster here for three days. There is more in him than ever comes out. But he is not dead yet. I hope to see him pregnant with his own soul. We were on the edge of a fierce quarrel all the time. He went to bed muttering that he was not sure we—my wife & I—weren't just playing round his knees: he seized a candle & went to bed, neither would he say good night. Which I think is rather nice. He sucks his dummy—you know, those child's comforters—long after his age. But there is something very real in him, if he will not cause it to die. He is *much* more than his dummy-sucking, clever little habits allow him to be. . . .

*Excerpted from a letter to Bertrand Russell, 12 Feb. 1915, and reprinted from George Zytaruk and James T. Boulton, eds., *The Letters of D. H. Lawrence*, II (Cambridge, London, New York: Cambridge Univ. Press, 1981), 282–85, by permission of Laurence Pollinger Ltd., Cambridge University Press, Viking Penguin, Inc., and the estate of Mrs. Frieda Lawrence Ravagli. Copyrght 1932 by the estate of D. H. Lawrence. © renewed 1960 by Angelo Ravagli and C. M. Weekley, executors of the estate of Frieda Lawrence Ravagli.

Forster is not poor, but he is bound hand & foot bodily. Why? *Because he does not believe that any beauty or any divine utterance is any good any more.* Why? Because the world is suffering from bonds, and birds of foul desire which gnaw its liver. Forster knows, as every thinking man now knows, that all his thinking and his passion for humanity amounts to no more than trying to soothe with poetry a man raging with pain which can be cured. Cure the pain, don't give the poetry. Will all the poetry in the world satisfy the manhood of Forster, when Forster knows that his implicit manhood is to be satisfied by nothing but immediate physical action. He tries to dodge himself—the sight is pitiful.

But why can't he act? Why can't he take a woman and fight clear to his own basic, primal being? Because he knows that self-realisation is not his ultimate desire. His ultimate desire is for the continued action which has been called the social passion—the love for humanity—the desire to work for humanity. That is every man's ultimate desire & need. Now you see the vicious circle. Shall I go to my Prometheus and tell him beautiful tales of the free, whilst the vulture gnaws his liver? I am ashamed. I turn my face aside from my Prometheus, ashamed of my vain, irrelevant, impudent words. I cannot help Prometheus. And this knowledge rots the love of activity. . . .

The repeating of a known reaction upon myself is sensationalism. This is what nearly *all* English people now do. When a man takes a woman, he is *merely* repeating a known reaction upon himself, not seeking a new reaction, a discovery. And this is like self-abuse or masterbation [sic]. The ordinary Englishman of the educated class goes to a woman now to masterbate himself. Because he is not going for discovery or new connection or progression, but only to repeat upon himself a known reaction.

When this condition arrives, there is always Sodomy. The man goes to the man to repeat this reaction upon himself. It is a nearer form of masterbation. But still it has some *object*—there are still two bodies instead of one. A man of strong soul has too much honour for the other body—man or woman—to use it as a means of masterbation. So he remains neutral, inactive. That is Forster. . . .

[From *Down There on a Visit*]   Christopher Isherwood*

Well, *my* "England" is E. M.; the antiheroic hero, with his straggly straw mustache, his light, gay, blue baby eyes and his elderly stoop.

*Excerpted from *Down There on a Visit* (New York: Simon and Schuster, 1962), pp. 162, 175–76. Reprinted by permission of Candida Donadio & Associates, Inc. © 1962 by Christopher Isherwood.

Instead of a folded umbrella or a brown uniform, his emblems are his tweed cap (which is too small for him) and the odd-shaped brown paper parcels in which he carries his belongings from country to town and back again. While the others tell their followers to be ready to die, he advises us to live as if we were immortal. And he really does this himself, although he is as anxious and afraid as any of us, and never for an instant pretends not to be. He and his books and what they stand for are all that is truly worth saving from Hitler; and the vast majority of people on this island aren't even aware that he exists. . . .

What a tonic for me it was, having lunch with E.M. today! He says he's afraid of going mad, of suddenly turning and running away from people in the street. But, actually, he's the last person who'd ever go mad; he's far saner than anyone else I know. And immensely, super-humanly strong. He's strong because he doesn't try to be a stiff-lipped stoic like the rest of us, and so he'll never crack. He's absolutely flexible. He lives by love, not by will.

That last statement smells unpleasantly of the Christian jargon. But E.M., of course, has no religion. If he did, he wouldn't be E.M. I must admit, he doesn't seem to loathe it as I do; in fact, when he talks about it, he's very moderate and open-minded. But, all the same, he's one more living proof that nobody who is really great can have any truck with that filth.

While we were eating, the manager of the restaurant came over to tell us he'd just heard on the wireless that Hitler has allowed six days for the evacuation of the Sudeten areas. "*Six days!*" I exclaimed. "Why, that's marvelous!" At once I felt idiotically gay. It was as if we had all had an almost indefinite reprieve from the crisis. Time has slowed down nowadays to such an extent that six days are about equal to six ordinary months. . . .

To celebrate our reprieve I ordered champagne, just for the pleasure of being extravagant, and we both got rather drunk. E.M. became very gay and made silly jokes. His silliness is beautiful because it expresses love and is the reverse side of his passionate minding about things. The other kind of silliness—ugly, unfunny bar stories, joyless swishing and clowning—expresses aggression and malice and is the reverse side of insensitive not-caring. We need E.M.'s silliness more than ever now. It gives courage. The other kind depresses and weakens me more than the worst prophecies of disaster. . . .

E. M. Forster's
Subversive Individualism

Wilfred Stone*

I

It is appropriate on this centenary of Forster's birth to take a look at some aspects of his social philosophy—his liberalism, his well-known creed of "personal relations," his lifelong contention with the vexed problem of *power*. It is appropriate because Forster made his mark not just as a novelist, but also as a humanist; not just as an artist, but as a moral influence; not just as the author of *A Passage to India*, but also as the author of "What I Believe." It is appropriate as well because Forster's social attitudes are deeply personal, and now that P. N. Furbank's biography is out, and Forster is out of the closet in other ways, the materials are available for a reassessment. His position as a novelist is, I believe, forever secure, whereas his position as a humanist, as the liberal moral philosopher, is, I think, more problematical. But his influence in this role has been immense, and this centenary year will doubtless be the occasion for many people to reevaluate the impact of Forster's influence upon them.

Let me begin with that striking statement Forster made in his postwar broadcast talk "The Challenge of Our Time" (1946):

> I belong to the fag-end of Victorian liberalism, and can look back to an age whose challenges were moderate in their tone, and the cloud on whose horizon was no bigger than a man's hand. In many ways it was an admirable age. It practised benevolence and philanthropy, was humane and intellectually curious, upheld free speech, and had little colour-prejudice, believed that individuals are and should be different, and entertained a sincere faith in the progress of society. The world was to become better and better, chiefly through the spread of parliamentary institutions. The education I received in those far-off and fantastic days made me soft and I am very glad it did, for I have seen plenty of hardness since, and I know it does not even pay. Think of the end of Mussolini—the hard man, hanging upside-down like a turkey, with his dead mistress swinging beside him.[1]

I disinctly remember my shocked reaction when I first read that statement—shortly after I had spent four years in an unwanted military uniform. How, I wanted to cry out, did Forster suppose that that hard man Mussolini got his comeuppance, except at the hands of other hard men, or men who had been trained to be hard? Did he suppose that some abstract force of history, operating automatically and inevitably,

*Excerpted from Judith Scherer Herz and Robert K. Martin, eds., *E. M. Forster: Centenary Revaluations* (Toronto and Buffalo: Univ. of Toronto Press; London and Basingstoke: Macmillan Press, 1982), pp. 15–16, 23–34, by permission of the author, University of Toronto Press, and Macmillan Press, London and Basingstoke.

took care of these threats to civilization without human intervention? What kind of bloodless dream of history was this? And by what right did Forster the non-combatant stand on the sidelines of conflict and assure us that the hard ones always lost, just a few years after they had come so desperately close to winning? To citizens of the twentieth century who have known trenches and breadlines and concentration camps for their inheritance, Forster's defence of "softness" can seem at best unrealistic and at worst infuriating. Yet the idea of softness is at the heart of Forster's liberal philosophy; it is literally soft at the centre.

So our question is: How valuable is a creed so centred? Is it a responsible code or is it a cop-out—a denial of complexity and a turning away from history? How seriously can we take Forster's personal witness for softness in a world increasingly dominated by the hard impersonality of gigantic armaments, gigantic corporations, gigantic machines, gigantic populations, gigantic cities? In engaging with that question, I shall consult Forster's fiction and biography as different aspects of one record—as I believe in essentials they are. And I shall approach the question via Forster's personal experience, for it is that personal experience more than any theoretical belief that is written into "What I Believe" and those other credal pronouncements of Forster's sixth decade. To ask what meaning that creed has for our day, we must first ask what meaning it had for Forster himself. . . .

II

The event that perhaps tested Forster's liberal humanism most acutely and painfully was the First World War. All Bloomsbury felt, says Furbank, that "it was not *their* war,"[2] and Forster aligned himself with this attitude. The war filled him with nothing less than "panic and emptiness," and his first response was to find refuge in friends, exercising the old pattern of dissolving the "gang" into individuals. "He was doubly disturbed," Furbank tells us, "—by the war itself, and by the inadequacy of his own response to it."[3] That response *was* inadequate. Essentially he just ran away—to the safety of a cushy job with the Red Cross in Alexandria—and when in 1916 he was threatened with conscription (technically, the duty to "attest"), he simply went to pieces. Here is Furbank's account:

> He was now in a serious dilemma. He was determined not to attest, yet could not easily explain his reasons—for he knew that, in a strict sense, he was not a conscientious objector. For a few days he was badly thrown by the contretemps, and—as once or twice later in life in times of stress—he developed a kind of falling sickness and had bouts of hurling himself against the furniture.[4]

He finally managed to stay out of the army through some wirepulling with high-ranking friends—a conspicuous instance of using his social rank as a "protector." "I am quite shameless over this wirepulling," Forster wrote to his mother in 1916; "If I can't keep out of the army by fair means then hey for foul! Let alone that there conscience. I know I should be no good, and haven't the least desire to pacify the parrots who cry 'All must go.' "[5] One cannot, of course, fail to share Forster's horror of the war and his desire to escape it, but neither can one refrain from asking the obvious, embarrassing question: What about those hundreds of thousands who had no high-ranking friends and no wires to pull? This is but one of the many times in his life that Forster invoked special privilege in order to save himself—and is but an extended pattern of that tearful escape home from school.

During these war years in Alexandria Forster experienced an intense retreat inward. There was, of course, a movement outward as well—to an interest in the history and politics of Egypt that led to *Alexandria: A History and A Guide* (1922), *Pharos and Pharillon* (1923), and his long essay "The Government of Egypt" for the Labour Research Department (1920). It was this period, as Lionel Trilling has said, that gave Forster "a firm position on the Imperial question."[6] But I think these outgoing efforts were, in part at least, a kind of moral compensation for having so narcissistically sought sanctuary during the war years.[7] Part of that inward retreat expressed itself as an embrace of "decadence." After having read Huysmans' *A Rebours* and Eliot's *Prufrock* in 1917, he wrote: "Oh, the relief of a world which lived for its sensations and ignored the will ... Was it decadent? Yes, and thank God."[8] And speaking specifically of Prufrock he wrote: "Here was a protest, and a feeble one, and the more congenial for being feeble. For what, in that world of gigantic horror, was tolerable except the slighter gestures of dissent?" (*AH*, 107). Eliot would have been surprised, I think, to know that anyone read *Prufrock* as a "protest." Forster's reasons are interesting:

> He who measured himself against the war, who drew himself to his full height, as it were, and said to Armadillo-Armageddon "Avaunt!" collapsed at once into a pinch of dust. But he who could turn aside to complain of ladies and drawing-rooms preserved a tiny drop of our self-respect, he carried on the human heritage. (*AH*, 107)

This is salvation via nostalgia. What Forster is saying is that he felt safe in such rooms with such ladies—perhaps even saved—and there is little question that his embrace of "decadence" as a value in this period is a kind of fantasy return to the womb. He loved Eliot's poems because they "were innocent of public-spiritedness: they sang of private disgust and diffidence, and of people who seemed genuine because they were unattractive or weak" (*AH*, 106). Can there be any doubt that this is Forster looking into his own mirror? He is building a defence for the "unattractive or weak," for softness, and I think that it is during these years that Forster crystallized that defence into something like a principle—and into a political position that touched more than the Imperial question. He was confronted with the clear choice of either being ashamed of himself or being proud of himself, and he elected to be proud of himself. Unless the world is made safe for the soft individual it cannot, for Forster, be a tolerable world: he wanted a literal translation of the hope that the meek should inherit the earth. Decadence? Forster refuses to hear it as a bad word. Years later, in 1939, when these conflicts had been reduced to a creed, Forster declared that decadence is what some people call those intervals in history when "force and violence" do not "get to the front." Forster calls those absences "civilization" and finds in such interludes "the chief justification for the human experiment."[9]

But Forster did not arrive at such views easily. His letters to friends out of Alexandria are full of trouble and sadness, and he by no means managed to "let alone that there conscience." Alexandria was a time of sexual awakening for Forster and he was excited by the streams of soldiers pouring into the Montazah Convalescent Hospital where he worked; but he was conscious as well that they came from a hell he had no part of. "It makes me very happy yet very sad," he writes to Lowes Dickinson in July 1916; "they come from the unspeakable all these young gods, and in a fortnight at the latest they will return to it . . ." But what comes next? Does Forster consider joining them? Partaking of their suffering like a brother? On the contrary, he clings to his privileged position, and his conscience erodes into a daydream of what might be: "Why not a world like this?" (referring to the comforts the soldiers knew at the hospital). Why not a world "that should not torture itself by organized and artificial horrors?"[10] This is no way to "face facts," and friends who were not pacifists (as Dickinson was) criticized Forster for his evasions; but during this period that dream of a world without violence became, in some strange way, confused in Forster's mind with moral action. He looked out on the "real" world as if from a kind of hibernation, a drugged quarantine; and though he sensed that there was something "unreal" about his position, he clung to it. Thus he writes to Bertrand Russell in 1917:

> Here I have been for nearly two years. Harmless and unharmed. Here in Egyptian hospitals. I live in their wards, questioning survivors. It has been a comfortable life. How unreal I shan't know till I compare it with the lives others have been leading in the period. I don't write, but feel I think and think I feel. Sometimes I make notes on human nature under war conditions . . . I love people and want to understand them and help them more than I did, but this is oddly accompanied by a growth of contempt. Be like them? God, no.[11]

There is class snobbery here and maybe something worse, but this passage gives us a glimpse at the workings of Forster's "conscience." Love warring with contempt measures the degree of Forster's self-contempt—

and the guilt (evaded rather than suppressed) arising from his position
of special privilege. But such exclusiveness is inseparable from Forster's
liberal humanism, for the softness it defends is his own softness, and
in that defence Forster again and again implicitly declares himself to
be a special case and deserving of special treatment. In spite of having
"magical feelings about his own life" and feeling in some way exempted
from the common human fate, he at the same time felt that his situation
was somehow "unreal." But Forster is never openly apologetic over a
position that some people saw as plain cowardice; and Alexandria, I
believe, was the testing place where he gained the confidence to accept
himself as he was, and to be his own kind of liberal.

During the war, Forster felt that history was sweeping him away,
that he could not get anywhere by the exercise of will, that in all the
big things he was helpless. Like Cavafy (and perhaps with Cavafy's
help), he reduced history to personal relations, to relations—in his case—
based on homosexual love. And he elevated "decadence" to something
like an ideal.

But the germ of an opposing attitude was alive in him. And after
the war, as if to make up for his wartime retreat, he came out of his
cocoon and engaged in a wide variety of political actions. Throughout
the 'twenties he was an active critic of England's imperialistic crimes in
India and Egypt; as first president of the National Council for Civil
Liberties, he did what he could to defend free speech on the BBC and
elsewhere; he led a wide-ranging assault with his pen on bureaucracy,
in the military and in government offices (hitting a high point with that
fine satire, "Our Deputation"); he was active in fighting literary cen-
sorship and the prudery behind it, defending Radclyffe Hall's *Well of
Loneliness* (1928) and, much later, Lawrence's *Lady Chatterley's Lover*
(1960); he was active in the PEN Club and in 1928 became the first
president of the "Young PEN," a club for young and unknown writers;
he continually spoke out against homosexual and racial prejudice. As
another war loomed, Forster became somewhat disillusioned with ac-
tivism, and on the eve of the Munich crisis he was asked by Goronwy
Rees, assistant editor of the *Spectator*, "Why have you given up politics?"
He replied, "Because I want just a *little* result."[12]

To be sure, Forster was an activist only in liberal causes, which is
to say only causes for which words are weapons. But he had emerged
from hiding and become a fighter with words, and he no longer acquiesced in the belief that history operated by its own forces and could
not be affected by the will. If Forster became less organizationally engaged in the late 'thirties and early 'forties, he assuredly did not become less articulate. In these years Forster uttered a flood of speeches,
broadcasts and essays defining his liberal humanist position—the greatest
of which is "What I Believe" in 1939. In them all, Forster stood his
ground in defence of softness, but it was a position toughly held and
not weakly acted out. Julian Bell, before he was killed in the Spanish

Civil War in 1937, had challenged Forster's pacifism as an archaic posture in a world threatened by Hitlers and Mussolinis. But in reply Forster refused to "chuck gentleness" and went on to say. "If one has been gentle, semi-idealistic, and semi-cynical, kind, tolerant, demure, and generally speaking a liberal for nearly sixty years, it is wiser to stick to one's outfit."[13] And it was about this time that Christopher Isherwood in *Lions and Shadows* (1938) had talked about the need for the "Truly Weak Man" to submit himself to what he called the "Test." Forster would have none of this, and wrote to Isherwood in February 1938:

> *Bother the Test*—am so certain I shall fail mine that I can't think about it. Now and then I get toward facing facts, but get too tired to keep on at it. I only hope I shan't let any one down badly: *that* thought does present itself rather alarmingly.[14]

If this is still somewhat self-indulgent, it is at least honest; Forster is sure of who he is and unabashed about acting the part.

During the second war, Forster's stance became one of "keeping calm and cheerful." He did not succumb to despair—though he had a tragic sense that the old order had forever "vanished from the earth"[15] and he turned out, during the war years, a steady stream of propaganda broadcasts, one of them beginning memorably with the words, "This pamphlet is propaganda!"[16] But throughout the war he concerned himself less with winning battles than with reminding his countrymen and women that it was "civilisation" they were fighting for, not victory. What would be gained if in defeating the Nazis we allowed our culture to become "governmental" like theirs? All would be lost. And his PEN speech in the autumn of 1941—to a hall full of anti-Hitler writers and refugees, all highly committed—began, "I believe in art for art's sake."[17]

III

But all these utterances can be glossed by references to the one classic statement of 1939, "What I Believe." It is all there. Forster in his level speaking voice and colloquial vocabulary, without pomposity or prophetic intonation, made a statement that has become a classic in the modern liberal/humanist tradition. Since most readers probably know this essay almost by heart, I shall dip into it only briefly. He comes out as the defender of weakness ("the strong are so stupid"); of a saving élite ("an aristocracy of the sensitive, the considerate and the plucky"); of free speech ("I believe in [Parliament] *because* it is a Talking Shop"); of something like deconstruction ("The more highly public life is organized, the lower does its morality sink"); and, of course, of personal relations, the key to the whole creed:

> . . . there is even a terror and a hardness in this creed of personal relationships, urbane and mild though it sounds. Love and loyalty to an

individual can run counter to the claims of the State. When they
do—down with the State, say I, which means that the State would
down me.

(TCD, 68, 70, 67, 71, 66)

These are tough statements. If this author is not much good with his
fists or the sword, he has learned to be very good with words. And if
this is a creed born of weakness and dependency, it no longer sounds
like a cry from the beleaguered schoolboy. Forster lived in a free
country and would not be jailed—not yet—for sounding treasonous.
Nevertheless, these are radical things to say on the eve of a war and it
took courage to say them. No one could accuse Forster of playing it
safe or of currying favour with the powerful.

But—to return to the question with which we began—how viable
is such a creed as a programme of action, as creed to be *followed*? In
attempting to answer that, I should like to invoke the name of a writer
behind the Iron Curtain, the Hungarian novelist George Konrád. In
Konrád's career and words, superficially so different from Forster's, I
find Forster's creed validated in some critical ways. Konrád as a writer
assumes an oppositional stance against the state that, in interesting ways,
parallels Forster's—and dramatizes how Forster's creed could be put to
work in a "real" confrontation. Konrád is an Eastern European and a
Jew who has known repression first hand. Only four of the one hundred
students who attended his small-town Jewish elementary school are
alive today. "I have known ever since," he writes, "that you cannot trust
the state, only a few friends at best."[18] Those who ran the death camps
were loyal citizens of the state and that, writes Konrád, is the greater
part of their evil. On the dangers of bureaucracy and the power of the
non-violent individual in opposing it, Konrád agrees with Forster down
the line. Forster we remember, in "What I Believe," addresses not an
age of anarchy but an age of "faith," not a world unorganized, but a
world too highly organized and growing more so—in which the top dog
is the bureaucrat, civil or military. Both Forster and Konrád would
agree with Max Weber in seeing the threat to the future as coming not
from the left or the right but from the bureaucracy; and Konrád extols
friendship as a value in the face of a cruelly oppressive state in words
that virtually paraphrase Forster's. Forster says, "If I had to choose
between betraying my country and betraying my friend, I hope I should
have the guts to betray my country" (*TCD*, 66). Konrád says, "The
true symbol of the totalitarian state is not the executioner, but the
exemplary bureaucrat who proves to be more loyal to the state than to
his friend."[19] . . .

Here is a freedom fighter who believes in personal relations, who
loathes violence, and who is convinced that the "guerrillas of the typewriter"[20] can, if persistent, win every time in the face of superior armed
might. "This quiet revolution begins," writes Konrád, "with people who

do not subordinate their conscience to the needs of the state."[21] Konrád's prediction is that "during the fourth quarter of this century citizens in their slow and cunning ways, will 'humanize' the state."[22] They will do this not through violence, but through being a yeast, a kind of Arnoldian "saving remnant," that will spread its virtue like an ink blot or a beneficent disease. It is the same faith that Forster places in his "aristocracy of the sensitive, the considerate and the plucky"—an aristocracy not of power but of those elect souls found in all ages, classes, and nations who represent "the true human condition, the one permanent victory of our queer race over cruelty and chaos" (TCD, 70).

Is this faith naïve? Well, obviously, it would only work under certain conditions. In opposing an Idi Amin or a Shah of Iran—two overthrown despots who depended on torture rather than words as the instruments of their power—such a faith would have no more effect than, as Forster might say, love or a flower. It is a creed potent only in societies that have some respect for law and tradition, some sensitivity for human rights, some reluctance simply to wipe out or jail their dissidents. Apparently modern-day Hungary, however precariously, qualifies as this kind of society, for Konrád—though he was briefly arrested in 1973 for collaborating on a book about the rise of intellectuals to class power—has managed to stay out of prison while continuing to turn out novels and essays severely critical of the state. To be sure, Konrád walks a tightrope that Forster, in his much freer society, never had to. Nevertheless, the fact that Konrád puts his beliefs to risk in an active political arena—and against a formidable state power—for me authenticates Forster's position in important ways. They both hold creeds admirably designed to wear away the establishment, to keep it off balance, to remind it that governments exist to serve human beings and not for their own sakes. It may not always be true that "the strong are . . . stupid" or that "the more a society is organized, the lower does its morality sink" (Forster, TCD, 71), or that "An ideal is deformed as soon as it is adopted by a system"[23] (Konrád), but it is true much of the time, and these are useful precepts in the unending war for decency in human society. So, though Forster's creed of liberal humanism in large part grew out of his own sense of dependency and weakness, it need not be soft at the centre. Though Forster was never tested as Konrád was tested—and both are essentially men of words and not of action—it is clear to me that in the Second World War Forster was quite ready to stand and die for what he believed if called upon to do so. That hope that he should "have the guts" to betray his country before he betrayed his friend would have been, I believe, a fulfilled hope. Forster's dream of "civilisation" repudiates the fighting attitude, but Forster could fight—with words—when he had to; his dream was of a womb, a quiet place, but over the years Forster had learned that huddling there was not the way to solve problems or find self-respect. He became a fierce non-combatant—most impressively in "What I Believe."

The great social need of the modern world is to keep bureaucracy human, to bring bigness down to size, to keep power from becoming abstract. Both Forster and Konrád are evidence that the weak can be strong in this task—especially if they hold on to their faith as artists—the faith, in Konrád's words, that "The act of creation is always a radical act"[24] and in Forster's that "Creation lies at the heart of civilisation like fire in the heart of the earth."[25]

After making that claim for "creation," Forster went on to say, "In this difficult day [1939] ... it is a comfort to remember that violence has so far never worked" (*TCD*, 41–42). It is virtually the same statement he made in 1946 when he said that "hardness ... does not even pay." What Forster means is that violence and hardness do not, in his mind, work in *the long run*, and those words, appropriately enough, make up the title of an essay Forster wrote in 1938 that I would like to close with. He is talking back to the Communists:

> Talking with Communists makes me realise the weakness of my own position and the badness of the twentieth-century society in which I live. I contribute to the badness without wanting to. My investments increase the general misery, and so may my charities. And I realise, too, that many Communists are finer people than myself—they are braver and less selfish, and some of them have gone into danger although they were cowards, which seems to me finest of all ... [But] their argument for revolution—the argument that we must do evil now so that good may come in the long run—it seems to me to have nothing in it. Not because I am too nice to do evil, but because I don't believe the Communists know what leads to what. They say they know because they are becoming conscious of "the causality of society." I say they don't know, and my counsel for 1938–39 conduct is rather: Do good, and possibly good may come from it. Be soft, even if you stand to get squashed.[26]

If one is really ready to be squashed rather than fight—as both Forster and Konrád in different ways claim they are—one has, in a sufficiently liberal society, some heroic potentialities. It is the role of the hero as nuisance, as gadfly—and perhaps as martyr. If, more formally speaking, ours is the age of the anti-hero, then the hero might well be the victim who carefully picks the cause he suffers or dies for. Both Forster and Konrád fall in that role—or potentially fall in it. The advice to "Be soft, even if you stand to get squashed" is Forster's way of defending his personal inheritance and experience, but it is also his way of saying to a violent world that he will not "do evil now so that good may come in the long run." He has no faith in such futures; he has faith only in the individual and in personal relationships—and in the love and loyalty that make them vital.

Once again we ask; Is this a viable faith? The answer, I think, is yes, but it is not a creed for everyone—especially not for those sentimentalists who can embrace the "aesthetic" Forster, the believer in art for art's sake, but who deny or forget Forster the serious humanist and moralist. To stand up and say that goodness equals softness, as Forster does, carries conviction only when we are persuaded that the speaker has the "guts" to live his creed to the uttermost, to pay the ultimate price for being soft in a hard world. I believe that Forster, by 1939, stood ready to pay that price if need be—to betray his country before his friend, to be squashed rather than resort to violence. The creed stands or falls on whether Forster's personal witness to this belief is convincing. To me it is. Forster did not always pay the price that hardness demands of softness, but I believe that by 1939 he had matured to a point where he was ready to pay it. One cannot prove this, for Forster was never tested *in extremis*, but the whole bent of his experience points in this direction. Forster *is* a special case. More than most men he lived his life in terms of ends rather than means, in terms of final values rather than of movements or causes—and this aspect of his fortune makes him seem, at times, not one of us. But Forster did not exempt himself. He went into spiritual danger although he was a coward, and "What I Believe" is the distilled testimony of how he made himself brave for others. It is one of the best reminders I know that human beings may, after all, possess the power of redeeming themselves.

Notes

1. "The Challenge of Our Time," *Two Cheers for Democracy*, ed. Oliver Stallybrass, Abinger edn. (London: Edward Arnold, 1972), p. 54.

2. P. N. Furbank, *E. M. Forster: A Life* (New York: Harcourt Brace Jovanovich, 1977), II, p. 1.

3. Furbank, II, p. 1.

4. Furbank, II, p. 26.

5. Furbank, II, p. 27.

6. Lionel Trilling, *E. M. Forster* (Norfolk, Conn.: New Directions, 1943), p. 138.

7. In 1917 Forster wrote to G. Lowes Dickinson: "I have never had the energy or intelligence to understand contemporary civilization, have never done more than loaf through it and jump out of its way when it seemed likely to hurt me" (Furbank, II, p. 26). In 1939, in "What I Believe," Forster wrote, "I look the other way until fate strikes me. Whether this is due to courage or to cowardice in my own case I cannot be sure" (*Two Cheers for Democracy*, p. 68). These are not simple avoiding reactions, but part of a struggle in Forster, a life-long struggle, between courage and cowardice.

8. E. M. Forster, "T. S. Eliot," *Abinger Harvest* (London: Edward Arnold, 1961), p. 106.

9. Forster, "What I Believe," *Two Cheers for Democracy*, p. 68.

10. Furbank, II, p. 34.

11. Quoted in Jane Lagoudis Pinchin, *Alexandria Still: Forster, Durrell and Cavafy* (Princeton: Princeton University Press, 1977), p. 99.

12. Furbank, II, pp. 222.

13. Furbank, II, p. 224.

14. Furbank, II, p. 223.

15. E. M. Forster, "They Hold Their Tongues," *Two Cheers for Democracy*, p. 29.

16. E. M. Forster, *Nordic Twilight* (London: Macmillan, 1940), p. 3.

17. E. M. Forster, "The New Disorder," *Horizon*, IV (1941), 379.

18. George Konrád, "The Long Work of Liberty," *The New York Review of Books*, XXIV (26 January 1978), 38.

19. Konrád, p. 38.

20. Konrád, p. 39.

21. Konrád, p. 39.

22. Konrád, p. 38.

23. Konrád, p. 39.

24. Konrád, p. 38.

25. E. M. Forster, "What Would Germany do to Us?" *Two Cheers for Democracy*, p. 41.

26. E. M. Forster, "The Long Run," *New Statesman and Nation* (n.s.), XVI (1938), 971–2.

Realism and Romance

The Novels of E. M. Forster

I

There are many reasons which should prevent one from criticizing the work of contemporaries. Besides the obvious uneasiness—the fear of hurting feelings—there is too the difficulty of being just. Coming out one by one, their books seem like parts of a design which is slowly uncovered. Our appreciation may be intense, but our curiosity is even greater. Does the new fragment add anything to what went before? Does it carry out our theory of the author's talent, or must we alter our forecast? Such questions ruffle what should be the smooth surface of our criticism and make it full of argument and interrogation. With a novelist like Mr. Forster this is specially true, for he is any case an author about whom there is considerable disagreement. There is something baffling and evasive in the very nature of his gifts. So, remembering that we are at best only building up a theory which may be knocked down in a year or two by Mr. Forster himself, let us take Mr. Forster's novels in the order in which they were written, and tentatively and cautiously try to make them yield us an answer.

The order in which they were written is indeed of some importance, for at the outset we see that Mr. Forster is extremely susceptible to the influence of time. He sees his people much at the mercy of those conditions which change with the years. He is acutely conscious of the bicycle and of the motor-car; of the public school and of the university; of the suburb and of the city. The social historian will find his books full of illuminating information. In 1905 Lilia learned to bicycle, coasted down the High Street on Sunday evening, and fell off at the turn by the church.

*Reprinted from the *Collected Essays*, I (London: Hogarth Press, 1966), 342–51, by permission of the author's Literary Estate and The Hogarth Press. Originally published in *The Death of the Moth and Other Essays* by Virginia Woolf, copyright 1942 by Harcourt Brace Jovanovich, Inc.; © renewed 1970 by Margaret T. Parsons, executrix. Reprinted by permission of the publisher.

For this she was given a talking to by her brother-in-law which she remembered to her dying day. It is on Tuesday that the house-maid cleans
out the drawing-room at Sawston. Old maids blow into their gloves
when they take them off. Mr. Forster is a novelist, that is to say, who
sees his people in close contact with their surroundings. And therefore
the colour and constitution of the year 1905 affect him far more than any
year in the calendar could affect the romantic Meredith or the poetic
Hardy. But we discover as we turn the page that observation is not an
end in itself; it is rather the goad, the gadfly driving Mr. Forster to provide a refuge from this misery, an escape from this meanness. Hence we
arrive at that balance of forces which plays so large a part in the structure of Mr. Forster's novels. Sawston implies Italy; timidity, wildness;
convention, freedom; unreality, reality. These are the villains and heroes
of much of his writing. In *Where Angels Fear to Tread* the disease, convention, and the remedy, nature, are provided if anything with too eager
a simplicity, too simple an assurance, but with what a freshness, what
a charm! Indeed it would not be excessive if we discovered in this slight
first novel evidence of powers which only needed, one might hazard, a
more generous diet to ripen into wealth and beauty. Twenty-two years
might well have taken the sting from the satire and shifted the proportions of the whole. But, if that is to some extent true, the years have
had no power to obliterate the fact that, though Mr. Forster may be sensitive to the bicycle and the duster, he is also the most persistent devotee of the soul. Beneath bicycles and dusters, Sawston and Italy, Philip,
Harriet, and Miss Abbott, there always lies for him—it is this which
makes him so tolerant a satirist—a burning core. It is the soul; it is reality; it is truth; it is poetry; it is love; it decks itself in many shapes,
dresses itself in many disguises. But get at it he must; keep from it he
cannot. Over brakes and byres, over drawing-room carpets and mahog-
any sideboards, he flies in pursuit. Naturally the spectacle is sometimes
comic, often fatiguing; but there are moments—and his first novel provides several instances—when he lays his hands on the prize.

Yet, if we ask ourselves upon which occasions this happens and
how, it will seem that those passages which are least didactic, least
conscious of the pursuit of beauty, succeed best in achieving it. When
he allows himself a holiday—some phrase like that comes to our lips;
when he forgets the vision and frolics and sports with the fact; when,
having planted the apostles of culture in their hotel, he creates airily, joy-
fully, spontaneously, Gino the dentist's son sitting in the café with his
friends, or describes—it is a masterpiece of comedy—the performance of
Lucia di Lammermoor, it is then that we feel that his aim is achieved.
Judging, therefore, on the evidence of his first book, with its fantasy, its
penetration, its remarkable sense of design, we should have said that
once Mr. Forster had acquired freedom, had passed beyond the boundaries of Sawston, he would stand firmly on his feet among the descendants

of Jane Austen and Peacock. But the second novel, *The Longest Journey*, leaves us baffled and puzzled. The opposition is still the same: truth and untruth; Cambridge and Sawston; sincerity and sophistication. But everything is accentuated. He builds his Sawston of thicker bricks and destroys it with stronger blasts. The contrast between poetry and realism is much more precipitous. And now we see much more clearly to what a task his gifts commit him. We see that what might have been a passing mood is in truth a conviction. He believes that a novel must take sides in the human conflict. He sees beauty—none more keenly; but beauty imprisoned in a fortress of brick and mortar whence he must extricate her. Hence he is always constrained to build the cage—society in all its intricacy and triviality—before he can free the prisoner. The omnibus, the villa, the suburban residence, are an essential part of his design. They are required to imprison and impede the flying flame which is so remorselessly caged behind them. At the same time, as we read *The Longest Journey* we are aware of a mocking spirit of fantasy which flouts his seriousness. No one seizes more deftly the shades and shadows of the social comedy; no one more amusingly hits off the comedy of luncheon and tea party and a game of tennis at the rectory. His old maids, his clergy, are the most lifelike we have had since Jane Austen laid down the pen. But he has into the bargain what Jane Austen had not—the impulses of a poet. The neat surface is always being thrown into disarray by an outburst of lyric poetry. Again and again in *The Longest Journey* we are delighted by some exquisite description of the country; or some lovely sight—like that when Rickie and Stephen send the paper boats burning through the arch—is made visible to us forever. Here, then, is a difficult family of gifts to persuade to live in harmony together: satire and sympathy; fantasy and fact; poetry and a prim moral sense. No wonder that we are often aware of contrary currents that run counter to each other and prevent the book from bearing down upon us and overwhelming us with the authority of a masterpiece. Yet if there is one gift more essential to a novelist than another it is the power of combination—the single vision. The success of the masterpieces seems to lie not so much in their freedom from faults—indeed we tolerate the grossest errors in them all—but in the immense persuasiveness of a mind which has completely mastered its perspective.

II

We look then, as time goes on, for signs that Mr. Forster is committing himself; that he is allying himself to one of the two great camps to which most novelists belong. Speaking roughly, we may divide them into the preachers and the teachers, headed by Tolstoy and Dickens, on the one hand, and the pure artists, headed by Jane Austen and Turgenev, on the other. Mr. Forster, it seems, has a strong impulse to belong

to both camps at once. He has many of the instincts and aptitudes of the
pure artist (to adopt the old classification)—an exquisite prose style, an
acute sense of comedy, a power of creating characters in a few strokes
which live in an atmosphere of their own; but he is at the same time
highly conscious of a message. Behind the rainbow of wit and sensibility there is a vision which he is determined that we shall see. But his
vision is of a peculiar kind and his message of an elusive nature. He has
not great interest in institutions. He has none of that wide social curiosity which marks the work of Mr. Wells. The divorce law and the poor
law come in for little of his attention. His concern is with the private
life; his message is addressed to the soul. "It is the private life that holds
out the mirror to infinity; personal intercourse, and that alone, that ever
hints at a personality beyond our daily vision." Our business is not to
build in brick and mortar, but to draw together the seen and the unseen. We must learn to build the "rainbow bridge that should connect
the prose in us with the passion. Without it we are meaningless frag-
ments, half monks, half beasts." This belief that it is the private life that
matters, that it is the soul that is eternal, runs through all his writing.
It is the conflict between Sawston and Italy in *Where Angels Fear to
Tread*; between Rickie and Agnes in *The Longest Journey*: between Lucy
and Cecil in *A Room with a View*. It deepens, it becomes more insistent
as time passes. It forces him on from the lighter and more whimsical
short novels past that curious interlude, *The Celestial Omnibus*, to the
two large books, *Howards End* and *A Passage to India*, which mark his
prime.

But before we consider those two books let us look for a moment at
the nature of the problem he sets himself. It is the soul that matters;
and the soul, as we have seen, is caged in a solid villa of red brick somewhere in the suburbs of London. It seems, then, that if his books are to
succeed in their mission his reality must at certain points become ir-
radiated; his brick must be lit up; we must see the whole building satur-
ated with light. We have at once to believe in the complete reality of
the suburb and in the complete reality of the soul. In this combination
of realism and mysticism his closest affinity is, perhaps, with Ibsen. Ibsen has the same realistic power. A room is to him a room, a writing
table a writing table, and a waste-paper basket a waste-paper basket.
At the same time, the paraphernalia of reality have at certain moments
to become the veil through which we see infinity. When Ibsen achieves
this, as he certainly does, it is not by performing some miraculous con-
juring trick at the critical moment. He achieves it by putting us into
the right mood from the very start and by giving us the right materials
for his purpose. He gives us the effect of ordinary life, as Mr. Forster
does, but he gives it us by choosing a very few facts and those of a highly
relevant kind. Thus when the moment of illumination comes we accept
it implicitly. We are neither roused nor puzzled; we do not have to ask

ourselves, What does this mean? We feel simply that the thing we are looking at is lit up, and its depths revealed. It has not ceased to be itself by becoming something else.

Something of the same problem lies before Mr. Forster—how to connect the actual thing with the meaning of the thing and to carry the reader's mind across the chasm which divides the two without spilling a single drop of its belief. At certain moments on the Arno, in Hertfordshire, in Surrey, beauty leaps from the scabbard, the fire of truth flames through the crusted earth; we must see the red-brick villa in the suburbs of London lit up. But it is in these great scenes which are the justification of the huge elaboration of the realistic novel that we are most aware of failure. For it is here that Mr. Forster makes the change from realism to symbolism; here that the object which has been so uncompromisingly solid becomes, or should become, luminously transparent. He fails, one is tempted to think, chiefly because that admirable gift of his for observation has served him too well. He has recorded too much and too literally. He has given us an almost photographic picture on one side of the page; on the other he asks us to see the same view transformed and radiant with eternal fires. The bookcase which falls upon Leonard Bast in *Howards End* should perhaps come down upon him with all the dead weight of smoke-dried culture; the Marabar caves should appear to us not real caves but, it may be, the soul of India. Miss Quested should be transformed from an English girl on a picnic to arrogant Europe straying into the heart of the East and getting lost there. We qualify these statements, for indeed we are not quite sure whether we have guessed aright. Instead of getting that sense of instant certainty which we get in *The Wild Duck* or in *The Master Builder*, we are puzzled, worried. What does this mean? we ask ourselves. What ought we to understand by this? And the hesitation is fatal. For we doubt both things—the real and the symbolical: Mrs. Moore, the nice old lady, and Mrs. Moore, the sibyl. The conjunction of these two different realities seems to cast doubt upon them both. Hence it is that there is so often an ambiguity at the heart of Mr. Forster's novels. We feel that something has failed us at the critical moment; and instead of seeing, as we do in *The Master Builder*, one single whole we see two separate parts.

The stories collected under the title of *The Celestial Omnibus* represent, it may be, an attempt on Mr. Forster's part to simplify the problem which so often troubles him of connecting the prose and poetry of life. Here he admits definitely if discreetly the possibility of magic. Omnibuses drive to Heaven; Pan is heard in the brushwood; girls turn into trees. The stories are extremely charming. They release the fantasticality which is laid under such heavy burdens in the novels. But the vein of fantasy is not deep enough or strong enough to fight single-handed against those other impulses which are part of his endowment. We feel that he is an uneasy truant in fairyland. Behind the hedge he always hears the motor horn and the shuffling feet of tired wayfarers, and soon he must return. One slim volume indeed contains all that he has allowed himself of pure fantasy. We pass from the freakish land where boys leap into the arms of Pan and girls become trees to the two Miss Schlegels, who have an income of six hundred pounds apiece and live in Wickham Place.

III

Much though we may regret the change, we cannot doubt that it was right. For none of the books before *Howards End* and *A Passage to India* altogether drew upon the full range of Mr. Forster's powers. With his queer and in some ways contradictory assortment of gifts, he needed, it seemed, some subject which would stimulate his highly sensitive and active intelligence, but would not demand the extremes of romance or passion; a subject which gave him material for criticism, and invited investigation; a subject which asked to be built up of an enormous number of slight yet precise observations, capable of being tested by an extremely honest yet sympathetic mind; yet, with all this, a subject which when finally constructed would show up against the torrents of the sunset and the eternities of night with a symbolical significance. In *Howards End* the lower middle, the middle, the upper middle classes of English society are so built up into a complete fabric. It is an attempt on a larger scale than hitherto, and, if it fails, the size of the attempt is largely responsible. Indeed, as we think back over the many pages of this elaborate and highly skillful book, with its immense technical accomplishment, and also its penetration, its wisdom, and its beauty, we may wonder in what mood of the moment we can have been prompted to call it a failure. By all the rules, still more by the keen interest with which we have read it from start to finish, we should have said success. The reason is suggested perhaps by the manner of one's praise. Elaboration, skill, wisdom, penetration, beauty—they are all there, but they lack fusion; they lack cohesion; the book as a whole lacks force. Schlegels, Wilcoxes, and Basts, with all that they stand for of class and environment, emerge with extraordinary verisimilitude, but the whole effect is less satisfying than that of the much slighter but beautifully harmonious *Where Angels Fear to Tread*. Again we have the sense that there is some perversity in Mr. Forster's endowment so that his gifts in their variety and number tend to trip each other up. If he were less scrupulous, less just, less sensitively aware of the different aspects of every case, he could, we feel, come down with greater force on one precise point. As it is, the strength of his blow is dissipated. He is like a light sleeper who is always being woken by something in the room. The poet is twitched away by the satirist; the comedian is tapped on the shoulder by the moralist; he never loses himself or forgets himself for long in sheer delight in the beauty or the interest of things as they are. For this reason the lyrical passages in his books, often of great beauty in themselves, fail of their due effect in the context. Instead of flowering naturally—as in Proust, for instance—from an overflow of interest and beauty in the object itself, we feel that they have been called into existence by some irritation, are the effort of a mind outraged by ugliness to supplement it with a beauty which, because it originates in protest, has something a little febrile about it.

Yet in *Howards End* there are, one feels, in solution all the qualities that are needed to make a masterpiece. The characters are extremely real to us. The ordering of the story is masterly. That indefinable but highly important thing, the atmosphere of the book, is alight with intelligence; not a speck of humbug, not an atom of falsity is allowed to settle. And again, but on a larger battlefield, the struggle goes forward which takes place in all Mr. Forster's novels—the struggle between the things that matter and the things that do not matter, between reality and sham, between the truth and the lie. Again the comedy is exquisite and the observation faultless. But again, just as we are yielding ourselves to the pleasures of the imagination, a little jerk rouses us. We are tapped on the shoulder. We are to notice this, to take heed of that. Margaret or Helen, we are made to understand, is not speaking simply as herself; her words have another and a larger intention. So, exerting ourselves to find out the meaning, we step from the enchanted world of imagination, where our faculties work freely, to the twilight world of theory, where only our intellect functions dutifully. Such moments of disillusionment have the habit of coming when Mr. Forster is most in earnest, at the crisis of the book, where the sword falls or the bookcase drops. They bring, as we have noted already, a curious insubstantiality into the "great scenes" and the important figures. But they absent themselves entirely from the comedy. They make us wish, foolishly enough, to dispose Mr. Forster's gifts differently and to restrict him to write comedy only. For directly he ceases to feel responsible for his characters' behaviour, and forgets that he should solve the problem of the universe, he is the most diverting of novelists. The admirable Tibby and the exquisite Mrs. Munt in *Howards End*, though thrown in largely to amuse us, bring a breath of fresh air in with them. They inspire us with the intoxicating belief that they are free to wander as far from their creator as they choose. Margaret, Helen, Leonard Bast, are closely tethered and vigilantly overlooked lest they may take matters into their own hands and upset the theory. But Tibby and Mrs. Munt go where they like, say what they like, do what they like. The lesser characters and the unimportant scenes in Mr. Forster's novels thus often remain more vivid than those with which, apparently, most pain has been taken. But it would be unjust to part from this big, serious, and highly interesting book without recognizing that it is an important if unsatisfactory piece of work which may well be the prelude to something as large but less anxious.

IV

Many years passed before *A Passage to India* appeared. Those who hoped that in the interval Mr. Forster might have developed his technique so that it yielded rather more easily to the impress of his whimsical mind and gave freer outlet to the poetry and fantasy which play about him were disappointed. The attitude is precisely the same foursquare attitude which walks up to life as if it were a house with a front door, puts its hat on the table in the hall, and proceeds to visit all the rooms in an orderly manner. The house is still the house of the British middle classes. But there is a change from *Howards End*. Hitherto Mr. Forster has been apt to pervade his books like a careful hostess who is anxious to introduce, to explain, to warn her guests of a step here, of a draught there. But here, perhaps in some disillusionment both with his guests and with his house, he seems to have relaxed these cares. We are allowed to ramble over this extraordinary continent almost alone. We notice things, about the country especially, spontaneously, accidentally almost, as if we were actually there; and now it was the sparrows flying about the pictures that caught our eyes, now the elephant with the painted forehead, now the enormous but badly designed ranges of hills. The people too, particularly the Indians, have something of the same casual, inevitable quality. They are not perhaps quite so important as the land, but they are alive; they are sensitive. No longer do we feel, as we used to feel in England, that they will be allowed to go only so far and no further lest they may upset some theory of the author's. Aziz is a free agent. He is the most imaginative character that Mr. Forster has yet created, and recalls Gino the dentist in his first book, *Where Angels Fear to Tread*. We may guess indeed that it has helped Mr. Forster to have put the ocean between him and Sawston. It is a relief, for a time, to be beyond the influence of Cambridge. Though it is still a necessity for him to build a model world which he can submit to delicate and precise criticism, the model is on a larger scale. The English society, with all its pettiness and its vulgarity and its streak of heroism, is set against a bigger and more sinister background. And though it is still true that there are ambiguities in important places, moments of imperfect symbolism, a greater accumulation of facts than the imagination is able to deal with, it seems as if the double vision which troubled us in the earlier books was in process of becoming single. The saturation is much more thorough. Mr. Forster has almost achieved the great feat of animating this dense, compact body of observation with a spiritual light. The book shows signs of fatigue and disillusionment; but it has chapters of clear and triumphant beauty, and above all it makes us wonder, What will he write next?

Forster and the Liberal Imagination   Lionel Trilling*

E. M. Forster is for me the only living novelist who can be read again and again and who, after each reading, gives me what few writers can give us after our first days of novel-reading, the sensation of having learned something. I have wanted for a long time to write about him and it gives me a special satisfaction to write about him now, for a consideration of Forster's work is, I think, useful in time of war.

In America Forster has never established a great reputation. Perhaps his readers are more numerous than I suppose, but at best they make a quiet band, and his novels—excepting *A Passage to India,* and that for possibly fortuitous reasons—are still esoteric with us. In England, although scarcely a popular writer, he is widely known and highly regarded; still, it is not at all certain whether even in England he is properly regarded and truly known. Some of the younger writers—among them Christopher Isherwood and Cyril Connolly—hold him in great esteem and have written well about him; I. A. Richards' remarks about Forster are sometimes perceptive, Elizabeth Bowen has spoken of him briefly but well, and the late Peter Burra's essay (now the introduction to the Everyman edition of *A Passage To India*) is a sound appreciation. But both Rose Macaulay and Virginia Woolf, who write of Forster with admiration, perceive the delicacy but not the cogency of his mind. As for the judgment canonized in *The Concise Cambridge History Of English Literature,* it is wholly mistaken; the "shy, unworldly quality" of work "almost diffidently presented" by a man who is "at heart a scholar" simply does not exist. The author of this comment has taken an irony literally and has misinterpreted a manner.

It is Forster's manner, no doubt, that prevents a greater response to his work. That manner is comic; Forster owes much to Fielding, Dickens, Meredith and James. And nowadays even the literate reader is likely to be unschooled in the comic tradition and unaware of the comic seriousness. The distinction between the serious and the solemn is an old one, but it must be made here again to explain one of the few truly serious novelists of our time. Stendhal believed that gaiety was

*Reprinted from the introductory chapter of *E. M. Forster* (Norfolk, Conn.: New Directions Publishing, 1943), pp. 7–24, copyright 1943 by New Directions Publishing Corporation, and reprinted by permission of New Directions, Laurence Pollinger Limited, and The Hogarth Press.

one of the marks of the healthy intelligence, and we are mistakenly sure that Stendhal was wrong. We suppose that there is necessarily an intellectual "depth" in the deep tones of the organ; it is possibly the sign of deprivation—our suspicion of gaiety in art perhaps signifies an inadequate seriousness in ourselves. A generation charmed by the lugubrious—once in O'Neill, Dreiser and Anderson, now in Steinbeck and Van Wyck Brooks—is perhaps fleeing from the trivial shape of its own thoughts.

Forster is not only comic, he is often playful. He is sometimes irritating in his refusal to be great. Greatness in literature, even in comedy, seems to have some affinity with greatness in government and war, suggesting power, a certain sternness, a touch of the imperial and imperious. But Forster, who in certain moods might say with Swift, "I have hated all nations, professions and communities, and all my love is for individuals," fears power and suspects formality as the sign of power. "Distrust every enterprise that requires new clothes" is the motto one of his characters inscribes over his wardrobe. It is a maxim of only limited wisdom; new thoughts sometimes need new clothes and the seriousness of Forster's intellectual enterprise is too often reduced by the unbuttoned manner he affects. The quaint, the facetious and the chatty sink his literary criticism below its proper level; they diminish the stature of his short fiction and they even touch, though they never actually harm, the five novels; the true comic note sometimes drops to mere chaff and we now and then wish that the style were less comfortable and more arrogant.

But while these lapses have to be reckoned with, they do not negate the validity of the manner of which they are the deficiency or excess. Forster's manner is the agent of a moral intention which can only be carried out by the mind *ondoyant et divers* of which Montaigne spoke. What Forster wants to know about the human heart must be caught by surprise, by what he calls the "relaxed will," and if not everything can be caught in this way, what is so caught cannot be caught in any other way. Rigor will not do, and Forster uses the novel as a form amenable to the most arbitrary manipulation. He teases his medium and plays with his genre. He scorns the fetish of "adequate motivation," delights in surprise and melodrama and has a kind of addiction to sudden death. Guiding his stories according to his serious whim—like the anonymous lady, he has a whim of iron—Forster takes full and conscious responsibility for his novels, refusing to share in the increasingly dull assumption of the contemporary novelist, that the writer has nothing to do with the story he tells and that, *mirabile dictu*, through no intention of his own, the story has chosen to tell itself through him. Like Fielding, he shapes his prose for comment and explanation, and like Fielding he is not above an explanatory footnote. He summarizes what he is going to show, introduces new themes when and as it suits him to do so, is not awed by the sacred doctrine of "point of view" and, understanding that verisimilitude, which more than one critic has defended from his indifference, can guarantee neither pleasure nor truth, he uses exaggeration and improbability. As a result, the four novels up to *A Passage To India* all suggest that they have been written after a close application to the dramatic principles of *The Winter's Tale*.

In all this Forster is not bizarre. He simply has the certainty of the great novelists that any novel is a made-up thing and that a story, in order to stand firmly on reality, needs to keep no more than one foot on probability. Against this belief is opposed our increasingly grim realistic prejudice: we have learned to believe that *The Winter's Tale* is great poetry but bad dramaturgy. Our literal and liberal intelligence jibs at an interruption of sixteen years, at what we are convinced is an improbability not only of event but of emotion—we think it wrong that Mamillius and Antigonus should die so casually, or that anyone should "exit, pursued by a bear," or that Polixenes should fly into his brutal rage after having so charmingly taken part in Perdita's great flower scene, for it confuses us that good and evil should co-exist and alternate. To accept Forster we have to know that *The Winter's Tale* is dramatically and morally sound and that improbability is the guide to life.

This means an affirmation of faith in the masters of the novel, in James, Meredith, Dickens—and in Hawthorne, whose notion of the "romance" (for he was forced to distinguish his own kind of novel from the more literal kind) is here so suggestive.

> When a writer calls his work a Romance, it need hardly be observed that he wishes to claim a certain latitude, both as to its fashion and material, which he would not have felt himself entitled to assume had he professed to be writing a Novel. The latter form of composition is presumed to aim at a very minute fidelity, not merely to the possible, but to the probable and ordinary course of man's experience. The former—while, as a work of art, it must rigidly subject itself to laws, and while it sins unpardonably so far as it may swerve aside from the truth of the human heart—has fairly a right to present that truth under circumstances, to a great extent, of the writer's own choosing or creation.

Hawthorne is no doubt the greater artist and perhaps the greater moralist, yet Forster stands with him in his unremitting concern with moral realism. All novelists deal with morality, but not all novelists, or even all good novelists, are concerned with moral realism, which is not the awareness of morality itself but of the contradictions, paradoxes and dangers of living the moral life. To the understanding of the inextricable tangle of good and evil and of how perilous moral action can be, Hawthorne was entirely devoted. Henry James followed him in this devotion and after James, though in a smaller way, comes Forster, who can say of one of his characters that he was "cursed with the Primal Curse, which is not the knowledge of good and evil, but the knowledge of good-and-evil."

It is here that the precise point of Forster's manner appears. Forster's plots are always sharp and definite, for he expresses difference by means of struggle, and struggle by means of open conflict so intense as to flare into melodrama and even into physical violence. Across each of his novels runs a barricade; the opposed forces on each side are Good and Evil in the forms of Life and Death, Light and Darkness, Fertility and Sterility, Courage and Respectability, Intelligence and Stupidity—all the great absolutes that are so dull when discussed in themselves. The comic manner, however, will not tolerate absolutes. It stands on the barricade and casts doubt on both sides. The fierce plots move forward to grand simplicities but the comic manner confuses the issues, forcing upon us the difficulties and complications of the moral fact. The plot suggests eternal division, the manner reconciliation; the plot speaks of clear certainties, the manner resolutely insists that nothing can be quite so simple. "Wash ye, make yourselves clean," says the plot, and the manner murmurs, "If you can find the soap."

Now, to the simple mind the mention of complication looks like a kind of malice, and to the mind under great stress the suggestion of something "behind" the apparent fact looks like a call to quietism, like mere shilly-shallying. And this is the judgment, I think, that a great many readers of the most enlightened sort are likely to pass on Forster. For he stands in a peculiar relation to what, for want of a better word, we may call the liberal tradition, that loose body of middle class opinion which includes such ideas as progress, collectivism and humanitarianism.

To this tradition Forster has long been committed—all his novels are politically and morally tendentious and always in the liberal direction. Yet he is deeply at odds with the liberal mind, and while liberal readers can go a long way with Forster, they can seldom go all the way. They can understand him when he attacks the manners and morals of the British middle class, when he speaks out for spontaneity of feeling, for the virtues of sexual fulfillment, for the values of intelligence; they go along with him when he speaks against the class system, satirizes soldiers and officials, questions the British Empire and attacks business ethics and the public schools. But sooner or later they begin to make reservations and draw back. They suspect Forster is not quite playing their game; they feel that he is challenging *them* as well as what they dislike. And they are right. For all his long commitment to the doctrines of liberalism, Forster is at war with the liberal imagination.

Surely if liberalism has a single desperate weakness, it is an inadequacy of imagination: liberalism is always being surprised. There is always the liberal work to do over again because disillusionment and fatigue follow hard upon surprise, and reaction is always ready for that moment of liberal disillusionment and fatigue—reaction never hopes, despairs or suffers amazement. Liberalism likes to suggest its affinity with science, pragmatism and the method of hypothesis, but in actual conduct it requires "ideals" and absolutes; it prefers to make its alliances only when it thinks it catches the scent of Utopia in parties and governments, the odor of sanctity in men; and if neither is actually present, liberalism makes sure to supply it. When liberalism must act with some degree of anomaly—and much necessary action is anomalous—it insists that it is acting on perfect theory and is astonished when anomaly then appears.

The liberal mind is sure that the order of human affairs owes it a simple logic: good is good and bad is bad. It can understand, for it invented and named, the moods of optimism and pessimism, but the mood that is the response to good-and-evil it has not named and cannot understand. Before the idea of good-and-evil its imagination fails; it cannot accept this improbable paradox. This is ironic, for one of the charter-documents of liberalism urges the liberal mind to cultivate imagination enough to accept just this improbability.

> Good and evil we know in the field of this world grow up together almost inseparably; and the knowledge of good is so involved and interwoven with the knowledge of evil, and in so many cunning resemblances hardly to be discerned, that those confused seeds which were imposed upon Psyche as an incessant labor to cull out, and sort asunder, were not more intermixed. It was from out the rind of one apple tasted, that the knowledge of good and evil, as two twins cleaving together, leaped forth into the world. And perhaps this is that doom which Adam fell into of knowing good and evil, that is to say of knowing good by evil.

And the irony is doubled when we think how well the great conservative minds have understood what Milton meant. Dr. Johnson and Burke and, in a lesser way at a later time, Fitzjames Stephen, understood the mystery of the twins; and Matthew Arnold has always been thought the less a liberal for his understanding of them. But we of the liberal connection have always liked to play the old intellectual game of antagonistic principles. It is an attractive game because it gives us the sensation of thinking, and its first rule is that if one of two opposed principles is wrong, the other is necessarily right. Forster will not play this game; or, rather, he plays it only to mock it.

This indifference to the commonplaces of liberal thought makes the very texture of Forster's novels and appeared in the first of them. The theme of *Where Angels Fear To Tread* is the violent opposition between British respectability and a kind of pagan and masculine integration. D. H. Lawrence, who played the old game of antagonistic principles for all it was worth—and it was worth something in his hands—gave us many characters like Forster's Gino Carella, characters who, like Gino, were cruel (the scene of Gino's cruelty is, incidentally, one of the most remarkable in modern fiction) or, like Gino, indifferent to the "higher" and romantic emotions. But here Lawrence always stopped; from this point on all his effort went to intensifying his picture, and by this he no doubt gained, as against Forster, in sheer coercive power. For the poor, lost, respectable British people, Gino may serve as the embodiment of the masculine and pagan principle, but Forster knows that he is also coarse, dull, vain, pretentious, facilely polite and very much taken with the charms of respectability.

And it is irritating to be promised a principle and then to be given only an hypothesis. The hypothesis, having led us to criticize respectability, is useful, but we had wanted it to be conclusive. And Forster refuses to be conclusive. No sooner does he come to a conclusion than he must unravel it again. In *A Room With A View*, to take another example, he leads us to make the typical liberal discovery that Miss Bartlett, the poor relation who thinks she is acting from duty, is really acting from a kind of malice—she has been trying to recruit the unawakened heroine into "the armies of the benighted, who follow neither the heart nor the brain." But Forster does not stop at this conventionality, even though in 1908 it was not quite so conventional. For when the heroine at last fulfills her destiny, deserts Miss Bartlett and marries the man she had unconsciously loved (this is, to all appearance, a very modest little novel), she comes to perceive that in some yet more hidden way Miss Bartlett had really desired the union. And we have been prepared for this demonstration of the something still further "behind" the apparent by the action of the tolerant and enlightened clergyman, Mr. Beebe, who has ceased to be the angel of light and has set himself against the betrothal.

Forster's insistence on the double turn, on the something else that lies behind, is sometimes taken for "tolerance," but although it often suggests forgiveness (a different thing), it almost as often makes the severest judgments. And even when it suggests forgiveness it does not spring so much from gentleness of heart as from respect for two facts co-existing, from the moral realism that understands the one apple tasted. Forster can despise Gerald of *The Longest Journey* because Gerald is a prig and a bully, but he can invest Gerald's death with a kind of primitive dignity, telling us of the maid-servants who weep, "They had not liked Gerald, but he was a man, they were women, he had died." And after Gerald's death he can give Agnes Pembroke her moment of tragic nobility, only to pursue her implacably for her genteel brutality.

So much moral realism is rare enough to be a kind of surprise, and Forster, as I have said, likes to work with surprises mild or great. "Gerald died that afternoon," is the beginning of a chapter which follows immediately upon a description of Gerald full of superabundant life. We have to stand unusually far back from Forster's characters not to be startled when they turn about, and the peculiar pleasure to be had from his books is that of a judicious imperturbability. He is always shocking us by removing the heroism of his heroes and heroines; in *A Passage To India*, Mrs. Moore, of whom we had expected high actions, lets herself be sent away from the trial at which her testimony would have been crucial; Cyril Fielding, who as a solitary man had heroically opposed official ideas, himself becomes official when he is successful and married; and Dr. Aziz cannot keep to his role of the sensitive and enlightened native. It is a tampering with the heroic in the manner not of Lytton Strachey but of Tolstoy, a kind of mithridate against our being surprised by life. Let us not deceive ourselves, Forster seems to say, it is with just such frailties as Mrs. Moore and Mr. Fielding, and with and for such unregeneracies as Dr. Aziz that the problem of, let us say, India must be solved. The moments of any man's apparent grace are few, any man may have them and their effects are not easily to be calculated. It is on a helter-skelter distribution of grace that Forster pins what hopes he has; but for years after *A Passage To India*—it is still his latest novel—he has had the increasing sense of possible doom.

Perhaps it is because he has nothing of the taste for the unconditioned—Nietzsche calls it the worst of all tastes, the taste that is always being fooled by the world—that Forster has been able to deal so well with the idea of class. The liberal mind has in our time spoken much of this idea but has failed to believe in it. The modern liberal believes in categories and wage-scales and calls these class. Forster knows better, and in *Howards End* shows the conflicting truths of the idea—that on the one hand class is character, soul and destiny, and that on the other hand class is not finally determining. He knows that class may be truly represented only by struggle and contradiction, not by description, and preferably by moral struggle in the heart of a single person. When D. H. Lawrence wrote to Forster that he had made "a nearly deadly mistake glorifying those *business* people in *Howards End*. Business is no good," he was indulging his own taste for the unconditioned. It led him to read Forster inaccurately and it led him to make that significant shift from "business people" to "business." But Forster, who is too worldly to suppose that we can judge people without reference to their class, is also too worldly to suppose that we can judge class-conditioned action until we make a hypothetical deduction of the subject's essential humanity. It is exactly because Forster can judge the "business people" as he does, and because he can judge the lower classes so without sentimentality, that he can deal firmly and intelligently with his own class, and if there is muddle in *Howards End*—and the nearly allegorical reconciliation is rather forced—then, in speaking of class, clear ideas are perhaps a sign of ignorance, muddle the sign of true knowledge; surely *Howards End* stands with *Our Mutual Friend* and *The Princess Casamassima* as one of the great comments on the class struggle.

To an American, one of the most notable things about Forster's work is the directness and consciousness of its connection with tradition. We know of Foster that he is a Hellenist but not a "classicist," that he loves Greece in its mythical and naturalistic aspects, that Plato has never meant much to him, perhaps because he mistrusts the Platonic drive to the absolute and the Platonic judgment of the body and the senses. He dislikes the Middle Ages and all in Dante that is medieval. He speaks of himself as a humanist and traces his descent to Erasmus and Montaigne. He is clearly in the romantic line, yet his admiration for Goethe and Shelley is qualified; Beethoven is a passion with him but he distrusts Schumann. He has no faith in the regenerative power of Christianity and he is frequently hostile to the clergy, yet he has a tenderness for religion because it expresses, though it does not solve, the human mystery; in this connection it is worth recalling that he once projected a book on Samuel Butler. I list these preferences of Forster's not because I wish to bound his intellectual life—so brief a list could not do that—but because enumerating them will help to suggest how hard it would be to name an American novelist whose connection with intellectual tradition is equally clear. In America the opinion still prevails, though not so strongly as it once did, that a conscious relation with the past can only debilitate a novelist's powers, dull his perceptions and prevent his experience of life.

Yet if we test the matter we must come to a contrary conclusion. Sherwood Anderson, for example, though at first it may seem strange to say so, had much in common with Forster. The original gifts of the two men, so far as we can measure such things, might for purposes of argument be judged nearly equal. Each set himself in opposition to the respectable middle class of his own country and each found a symbolic contrast in an alien and, as it seemed, a freer race. Each celebrated the salvation of the loving heart, the passionate body and the liberated personality. Yet as Anderson went on, he grew more and more out of touch with the life he represented and criticized, and it was as if, however much he might experience beyond a certain point, he had not the means to receive and order what he felt, and so ceased really to feel. In his later years he became, as gifted men of a certain temperament tend to become, symbolic and visionary, but, never understanding how to handle his ultimate hopes and his obscurer insights, he began to repeat himself and became increasingly vague. The vision itself began to fail when Anderson could not properly judge its importance and could not find for it the right symbols and the right language; and in his later years he made the impression, terribly touching, of being lost and alone.

He was indeed lost and alone, though he need not have been. But the men with whom he might have made community were not to be found where he thought they were, in the stable and the craftsman's shop. The men of Anderson's true community were the members of

the European tradition of thought. But Anderson was either indifferent
to the past or professionally contemptuous of it; he subscribed to the
belief that American art must throw off the shackles of tradition and
work only with intuition and observation. Anderson saw "culture" as gen-
tility; and he saw it too, one feels, as a kind of homogeneous mass to
be accepted or rejected only in totality; he did not know that it was a
collection of individuals much like himself with whom he might claim
kinship and equality, nor did he know that what he was demanding for
life had been demanded by other men time out of mind. Anderson's
books, like so many other American books, had at first a great and taking power; then, like so many other American books that have astonished and delighted us, they fell out of the texture of our lives, they
became curiosities.

Let us say the worst we can of Forster—that beside a man like Anderson with his tumble of emotions and child-like questions, Forster
might seem to have something donnish about him. But then we must
at once say that Forster has a sense of the way things go which Anderson, for all his great explicit impulse toward actuality, never had—the
sense of what houses, classes, institutions, politics, manners and people
are like. Forster knows, as Anderson never knew, that things are really
there. All his training has helped bring his impulses to consciousness,
and the play of consciousness over intuition and desire gives him his
curious tough insight.

The great thing Forster has been able to learn from his attachment to tradition and from his sense of the past is his belief in the
present. He has learned not to be what most of us are—eschatological.
Most of us, consciously or unconsciously, are discontented with the nature rather than with the use of the human faculty; deep in our assumption lies the hope and the belief that humanity will end its career by
developing virtues which will be admirable exactly because we cannot
now conceive them. The past has been a weary failure, the present cannot matter, for it is but a step forward to the final judgment; we look to
the future when the best of the works of man will seem but the futile and
slightly disgusting twitchings of primeval creatures: thus, in the name
of a superior and contemptuous posterity, we express our self-hatred—
and our desire for power.

This is a moral and historical error into which Forster never falls;
his whole work, indeed, is an implied protest against it. The very relaxa-
tion of his style, its colloquial unpretentiousness, is a mark of his acceptance of the human fact as we know it now. He is content with the
human possibility and content with its limitations. The way of human
action of course does not satisfy him, but he does not believe there are
any new virtues to be discovered; not by becoming better, he says, but
by ordering and distributing his native goodness can man live as befits
him.

This, it seems to me, might well be called worldliness, this acceptance of man in the world without the sentimentality of cynicism and
without the sentimentality of rationalism. Forster is that remarkably
rare being, a naturalist whose naturalism is positive and passionate, not
negative, passive and apologetic for man's nature. He accepts the many
things the liberal imagination likes to put out of sight. He can accept,
for example, not only the reality but the power of death—"Death destroys a man, but the idea of death saves him," he says, and the fine
scene in *The Longest Journey* in which Rickie forces Agnes to "mind"
the death of Gerald is a criticism not only of the British fear of emotion
but also of liberalism's incompetence before tragedy. To Forster, as to
Blake, naturalism suggests not the invalidity or the irrelevance of human emotions but, rather, their validity and strength: "Far more mysterious than the call of sex to sex is the tenderness that we throw into that
call; far wider is the gulf between us and the farmyard than between
the farmyard and the garbage that nourishes it."

He is so worldly, indeed, that he believes that ideas are for his
service and not for his worship. In 1939 when war was certain and the
talk ran so high and loose about Democracy that it was hard to know
what was being talked about, Forster remarked with the easy simplicity
of a man in his own house, "So two cheers for Democracy; one because
it admits variety and two because it permits criticism. Two cheers are
quite enough: there is no occasion to give three. Only Love the Beloved
Republic deserves that." He is so worldly that he has always felt that
his nation belonged to him. He has always known that we cannot love
anything bigger until we first love what Burke called "the little platoon"
and so it has been easy for him to speak of his love for his country with
whose faults he has never ceased to quarrel; and now he has no void
to fill up with that acrid nationalism that literary men too often feel
called upon to express in a time of crisis. He is one of the thinking people who were never led by thought to suppose they could be more than
human and who, in bad times, will not become less.

Romance Moralities   George H. Thomson*

"The novel . . . is a perpetual quest for reality, the field of its research
being always the social world, the material of its analysis being always
manners as the indication of the direction of man's soul."[1] Forster would
agree with this definition. The traditional novel, he says (speaking of
Virginia Woolf's *Night and Day*), "is an exercise in classical realism,

*Reprinted from *The Fiction of E. M. Forster* (Detroit: Wayne State Univ. Press,
1967), pp. 45–52, by permission of the author and Wayne State University Press.

and contains all that has characterised English fiction, for good and evil, during the last two hundred years: faith in personal relations, recourse to humorous side-shows, geographical exactitude, insistence on petty social differences."[2]

What then is the nature of the reality so persistently sought by the novelist?

> If we examine more closely our ordinary notions of reality, perhaps we should find that we do not consider real what actually happens but a certain manner of happening that is familiar to us. In this vague sense, then, the real is not so much what is seen as foreseen; not so much what we see as what we know. When a series of events takes an unforeseen turn, we say that it seems incredible. That is why our ancestors called the adventure story a fiction. Adventure shatters the oppressive, insistent reality as if it were a piece of glass. It is the unforeseen, the unthought-of, the new. Each adventure is a new birth of the world, a unique process.[3]

No better words could be found than these by Ortega y Gasset to take us from the novel to the romance, and so to the writings of E. M. Forster which, though they incorporate elements of the novel, are pre-eminently romance.

Romance arises when man ceases to believe in the cosmology and history of his myths and epics, when the heroic figures of the past no longer grip his imagination. Then he turns to idealized figures of a more subjective mould. The libido, anima, and shadow (Jung) find expression in the hero, heroine, and villain. The story, no longer thought of as literally true, may expand and stretch itself through any number of fabulous adventures. The subject matter, no longer thought of as religiously based, may be handled with a freedom and lightness of touch unthinkable in myth and epic.

With the decline of poetic romance at the end of the Renaissance, we observe romance elements making strong incursions into the prose fiction of Rabelais and Cervantes. But the rise of the novel, by definition realistic and socially oriented, drove romance into a corner from which it has never escaped. For two centuries readers and critics have inclined to the view that romance is acceptable and admirable only so long as it is subordinated to the requirements of realism. Hawthorne, Melville, and the Brontës broke with this predilection and paid for it by being widely misunderstood. The same misunderstanding, which insists on judging romance by standards appropriate only to the novel, has infected most commentary on Forster's fiction and distorted critical evaluation of it.[4]

An appreciation of Forster's work is further complicated by the fact that it combines romance with important elements from the realistic novel. Central to all romance is the archetype of an unfallen world, a golden age in which an idealized hero and heroine experience marvelous adventures in a strange and beautiful landscape. It is a world of innocence and energy. Evil enters this world in the form of wasteland settings, monsters, ogres, and unqualified villains. The remarkable thing about Forster's stories is this: the romance vision of innocence is portrayed with extraordinary purity and directness; but the romance vision of evil or experience is largely excluded from his work. Instead the vision of evil is taken over directly from the Fielding-Austen tradition of the novel where it is exclusively social.

I have put the facts boldly for the sake of clarity; now I must qualify them. There are two kinds of evil in Forster's fiction. The one kind is social and adheres to the characters. The other kind is transcendent and, though it is sometimes expressed through a character, has an existence apart from the characters. It is ominous and inexplicable. The perverted cruelty of Harcourt Worters ("Other Kingdom"), the ultimate horror behind the sham respectability of Michael ("The Point of It"), the terrifying mindlessness of the tentacles of the Mending Apparatus ("The Machine Stops"), and the priest pushing the bride-mother over the cliff ("The Story of the Siren") are like the goblins that walk inexorably over the universe and the Marabar echoes that infect all life: they allow us to glimpse a dark and appalling universe. Elizabeth Bowen has hit upon an image to convey this sense we have of evil, "the sense of conscious life's being built up over a somehow august vault of horror, that rings under the foot, that exhales coldly through cracks."[5] The images associated with this transcendent evil—the monster-like tentacles of the machine, the black figure of the evil priest, the goblins—have parallels with the evil figures of romance. But they do not as in romance have a prominent role to play. They appear only for a moment, just long enough to give us a glimpse of some underlying horror.

Forster's bad characters cannot convey this sense of horror. The point about them is that they are too obtuse even to know it exists. In so portraying them, Forster attempted what he believed to be a true portrait of the average Englishman who is incapable of deliberate wrong, incapable of worshipping the Devil. "His character, which prevents his rising to certain heights, also prevents him from sinking to these depths. Because he doesn't produce mystics he doesn't produce villains either. . . ." His badness is the result of muddle and negation, a kind of moral consumption such as overtakes Jane Austen's Mr. and Mrs. Dashwood during their prolonged deliberations about the appropriate sum to be settled on Mr. Dashwood's sisters.[6]

In exploiting the Fielding-Austen tradition of the novel, however, Forster reinterprets the forces of corruption and gives his socially evil characters a new twist. They became appalling because their destructive power creates an illusion of naturalness; their ignorance, obtuseness, self-righteousness, and egotistical altruism appear as a kind of perverted innocence. In Fielding, Austen and, to take a later example, James, the carriers of social evil are felt to be responsible for their own destinies and for the devastation they bring on others. In Forster, though they are the cause of devastation and are damned on that account, they are not distinguished by the albatross of guilt or responsibility. They are spiritually negative and neither deserve nor justify any further judgment.

We have reached a point now where we can ask how the horror which underlies and overarches Forster's world is related to the bad characters who move on its surface. The answer is that, though they cannot express it, we glimpse the horror through them. In moments of crisis their smooth-functioning worldly surfaces crack and we catch sight of the abyss: "Though they do not generate evil they do, like blocked gutters, receive, store and exhale it."[7] Mr. Bons confronts Achilles in abject suicidal terror ("The Celestial Omnibus"); Henry Wilcox reveals the panic and emptiness adumbrated by the goblins as they walk over the universe from end to end.

Experience-and-evil, with its two levels, is all of a piece and stands as the complete negation of innocence-and-goodness. This brings it into conformity with the romance tradition. The assertion that Forster's people are either saved or damned, are either capable or not capable of vision, is true. The implication that this attitude points to hardness of heart and a kind of arrogance is false. Were Forster a social philosopher his attitude might seem arrogant. Likewise, were Homer a theologian, his treatment of the gods might seem frivolous, or were Tolstoy an historian, his treatment of the past might seem fabricated. We may note that when Forster comes forward as social philosopher or commentator in his nonfictional writing his vision of a sheep-or-goat humanity is severely modified; he is well aware of the dangers of arrogance. But in his fiction the drastic separation of good and evil is essential to the romance tradition in which he works. He does not allow his vision to be narrowed (as Hawthorne did) by "that tiresome little receptacle, a conscience."[8] To complain that he is unjust to the Anglo-Indians, unfair to the Wilcoxes (in fact he tries too hard to give them their due), and overly obvious in the short stories is to condemn an essential characteristic of the romance tradition and to ignore the fact that the conventions taken over from realistic fiction are being used for other than realistic ends.

To the support of this bold confrontation of innocence and experience, good and evil, the saved and the damned, Forster brings a firm moral vision. This is not to deny, of course, that he has always deplored righteousness and dogmatism. Yet his favorite novelist is Jane Austen, who misses being dogmatic only because her truths seem too apparent to need underlining and who misses being righteous only because it does not occur to her that she can be anything but right. At his deepest and most creative level Forster has a cluster of moral convictions almost as assured as Jane Austen's. These convictions admirably support his romance vision and at the same time underpin his satirical thrusts at the wicked. For romance has traditionally depended on the boldness of black and white and "the mountains of Right and Wrong,"[9] and satire has always depended on morality for its bite.

Obviously, Forster chose the romance form because it suited his didactic propensities. But if we ask the *why* of his didactic propensities we are driven to a deeper level at which we observe that the romance form suited the nature of his experience and interests. His experience was visionary. As such it could not be directly described without destroying its quality of transcendence. It had to be symbolized; and for this purpose the greatest possible freedom was needed in selecting images to convey its extraordinary quality. Romance, which has at its disposal a universe of subjectively mediated images, gave him this freedom of selection and allowed him to express the inexpressible.

Forster's psychological interests were equally well-suited to the romance form. He had little interest in exploring the psychological drama of inner conflict; he had a deep interest in externalizing psychological conflict, in rendering it wholly dramatic by expressing the contending forces in separate characters and symbols. This kind of outwardly expressed conflict worked like magic to stimulate his creative powers. Under its spell, evil emerged with sharpness, bite, and remarkable solidity while good emerged with resonant and soaring conviction.

The romance form also suited Forster's satirical bent. An important theme in the more bourgeois novel is the parody of the romance and its ideals: "The tradition established by *Don Quixote* continues in a type of novel which looks at a romantic situation from its own point of view, so that the conventions of the two forms make up an ironic compound instead of a sentimental mixture."[10] Forster reverses this tradition. His type of fiction looks at a novelistic situation from a romance point of view and exposes the situation to ridicule and satirical judgment. Much of his humor and irony stems from this juxtaposing of situation and perspective at odds with each other. Such a procedure fits beautifully into the romance tradition of clearly distinguished worlds of good and evil. At the same time it explains why Forster's evil world is taken over from the tradition of the realistic novel. It is the situations of this evil world which are exposed by being seen through the eyes of romance.

Forster's interest in looking at novelistic situations from the romance point of view also explains why he did not portray his bad people as morally responsible beings. To have done so would have given them too great a stature and spoiled the satire. But a deeper reason is to be found in the nature of his good people. At their most profound they resemble the bad people in this one respect only, that they are not morally responsible beings. And they are not morally responsible because their moments of vision are *given*. Though they are worthy of the revelation that comes to them, they cannot be said quite to have earned it. In so presenting the situation, Forster is true to the essentially

subjective world of romance. We do not feel responsible for the goodness of our deepest insights. The goodness is simply given; likewise, the
evil is simply present. Romance dramatizes this truth about our subjective experience.

It is not too much to say that Forster's success as a writer depends
on this recognition of the limits of moral responsibility. His is not a dark
or ominous vision like that of Melville, Conrad, or Faulkner. It allows
us only to glimpse the darkness. And though it encroaches on the un-
imaginable, it creates a sense of luminousness and lucidity. It is a vision
which must be taken seriously and at the same time must be handled
with lightness of touch. Had Forster taken his bad people overseriously
he would almost certainly have lost his urbanity and have succumbed
to indignation and righteousness. Had he taken his good people overseriously he would have lost his lightness of touch and succumbed to
high-mindedness and sentimentality. His conception of the individual as
not morally responsible for either the best or worst in human existence
saved him from these dangers.

On the other hand, the sense of a somehow transcendent good and
evil, permeating the imagination of the author and his reader, gives rise
to a final moral vision as decisive as it is prophetic. The implication is a
little surprising, for the reader learns from this vision that man is, after
all, a fully responsible moral being. The limitations of responsibility
within the fiction were simply devices of the storyteller who found them
valuable in constructing his complete image. Because romance is subjective and allegorical in the sense that it pulls apart and externalizes in
separate images the elements that make up our inner life, only this complete image can give us a whole vision of man's nature. And only the
complete man can in all respects be regarded as a morally responsible
being.

I have been generalizing about all of Forster's fiction. The time has
now come to distinguish between the novels and short stories. With each
novel that Forster wrote he resisted more strenuously the temptation to
become a moral legislator of the fallen world or a prophet of the unfallen world. He became more tentative in his moral valuations with the
result that his style showed an increase in tension and irony. And these
qualities make up one side of his integrity and his personal style. But
they are not the dominant note. In the novels, Forster remains prophet
and judge despite himself.

Ansell in *The Longest Journey* fails to acknowledge the physical
presence of Agnes Pembroke because in the spiritual sense she is not
real. Much the same point is made in *Howards End*. The truth is that
the people who cannot say "I" for lack of a center within themselves and
so go round and round in the social circle of Forster's fallen world are
never, in the eyes of their creator, quite alive or real. On the other hand,
those characters and scenes which express the vitality and innocence of

the unfallen world glow with a beauty and serene passion that lends to them an unforgettable reality. It is within this context that we encounter the eternal moment, the instant of revelation in which tension and irony are resolved and we, with the creator, become one with a world of pristine joy. With each novel that Forster wrote the eternal moment appears with less frequency. This is not because it is absent but because it has been transmuted and is experienced as a subdued and diffused effect rather than as a single moment. Even at its most subdued, however, the sense it gives of revelation is so absolute and is in such decisive contrast to society's sterile habitude that Forster, for all his diffidence and modesty, becomes both judge and prophet.[11]

Now the distinction to be made is this: in the short stories Forster is neither diffident nor modest. In the sharpest possible terms he contrasts the two worlds of innocence and experience. None of the tension or irony comes from tentative valuation. All of it comes from an awareness that the unseeing and unfeeling machinations of society threaten to ensnare the spirit of man. The short stories break with "the demons of Realism and Literal Illusion";[12] they reveal with uncomplicated directness the essential romance pattern of Forster's created world.

Notes

1. Lionel Trilling, *The Liberal Imagination: Essays on Literature and Society* (New York, 1950), p. 212.

2. E. M. Forster, *Two Cheers for Democracy* (New York: Harcourt, Brace, 1951), p. 246. He said the same thing in 1925—*Abinger Harvest* (London: Edward Arnold, 1953), p. 127. Editions of other works by E. M. Forster referred to in the text are *Aspects of the Novel* (London: Edward Arnold, 1949); *The Collected Tales of E. M. Forster* (New York: Alfred A. Knopf, 1947); *Howards End* (London: Edward Arnold, 1947); *The Longest Journey* (London: Edward Arnold, 1947); and *A Passage to India* (London: Edward Arnold, 1947). Ed. note.

3. José Ortega y Gasset, *Meditations on Quixote*, trans. E. Rugg and D. Marin (New York, 1961), p. 132.

4. See Northrop Frye's "Four Forms of Prose Fiction," now incorporated in his *Anatomy of Criticism* (Princeton, 1957), pp. 302–14, in which he discusses the four forms: novel, romance, confession, and anatomy. On epic, romance, and novel see also Ortega, esp. pp. 118–34.

5. Elizabeth Bowen, *Collected Impressions* (New York, 1950), p. 121. This sense of evil distinguishes Forster from Bloomsbury. Maynard Keynes notes that the devotees of G. E. Moore, among whom he numbers himself, were the victims of a rationality which led to superficiality. They repudiated the notion of there being "insane and irrational springs of wickedness in most men." They "were not aware that civilization was a thin and precarious crust erected by the personality and the will of a very few, and only maintained by rules and conventions skillfully put across and guilefully preserved." See *Two Memoirs* (London, 1949), pp. 99–100.

6. *Abinger Harvest*, pp. 21–22.

7. Bowen, p. 125.

8. *Aspects of the Novel*, p. 132. Forster's freedom from a niggling conscience is well expressed in this 1959 statement: "I never had much sense of sin and when

I realized that the main aim of the Incarnation was not to stop war or pain or poverty, but to free us from sin I became less interested and ended by scrapping it . . ." The point is vividly underscored in the same speech when he analyzes the coolness of his response to Christ. In Christian art he is confronted by a figure whose "sufferings, we are told, are undergone for our sake." And he thinks to himself: "I hope none of this has been undertaken for my sake, for I don't know what it's about." See "A Presidential Address to the Cambridge Humanists—Summer 1959," *University Humanist Federation Bulletin*, No. 11 (Spring 1963), pp. 4, 7. These statements indicate an important characteristic of Forster's psychology and one that explains why the conflict of good and evil in his fiction is decisive and why his characters are notably free of feelings of guilt. Their creator is equally decisive and equally free.

9. *Abinger Harvest*, p. 36; see also *Aspects*, pp. 102–4. Forster uses the phrase in distinguishing between fantasy where there is no right and wrong and those works into which the soul has entered and which, though they still treat the unusual, treat it mystically or humanistically. On his own definition, then, Forster's fiction is not fantasy.

10. Frye, p. 306.

11. This diffidence and modesty is still apparent in a statement Forster made in 1959: "One further note on the subject of Salvation. I used to be very keen on this and it figures in most of my early short stories, and a little in my novels up to *A Passage to India*, from which it has almost disappeared. It has now disappeared from my thoughts, like other absolutes. I no longer wish to save or be saved, and here is another barrier that has interposed between myself and revealed religion whether Christian or Pagan." Because it has disappeared from his thought, Forster is all the more likely to underestimate the role of salvation in the novels. The salvation he speaks of is not theological, for he had fallen away from believing even before writing the short stories. Salvation is very nearly synonymous with the insight of the eternal moment. What has been said above about the eternal moment applies here. The portrayal of salvation is more diffused in the novels but it is nonetheless decisive. See "A Presidential Address," p. 8, and note 8.

12. "'Amis and Amiles' at Weybridge," *Athenaeum*, July 25, 1919, p. 662. The phrase is used in praising the achievement of a play, put on by children, which was "deeply emotional because it did not mimic emotion." In this connection see also "Break-Up Day—New Style," *The Manchester Guardian*, December 8, 1920, p. 8. Another review, "*The White Devil* at Cambridge," *New Statesman*, March 20, 1920, pp. 708–9, shows Forster's dislike of the slickness used on the stage to gain what is supposed to be an illusion of realism. Such an illusion makes impossible the direct communication of any deeper reality the play might have. This attitude to realism in the theater indicates some of the grounds for his rejection of realism in fiction.

Critical Positions: Questions of Morality and Sexuality

Cosmos, Chaos, and Contingency

Alan Wilde*

Written with an exuberance that even the most sanguine of the later novels lack (perhaps one ought to make an exception of the still earlier conceived *A Room with a View*), *Where Angels Fear to Tread* testifies to Forster's faith, as he later recalled it, that a "new age had begun"[1] and to Leonard Woolf's that society "should [and would in the future] be free, rational, civilized, pursuing truth and beauty."[2] Clearly, there existed in the early years of the century a group, whatever its size, sharing common standards and aspirations and furnishing that community of belief upon which satire depends. Whether Forster's first novel conforms completely to Woolf's revolutionary fervor or indeed to his own optimism is another matter; and it may be best at this point to state ... that, however congenial to him throughout his career, satire proved a confining and often inadequate vehicle for his fundamental sense of life's complexity. Nevertheless, although it ultimately exposes the limits of what he was able to do with the form, *Where Angels Fear to Tread* obviously intends to be, and in some respects at least approximates the condition of, a satiric novel—holding up to ridicule as it does, through its controlled and witty verbal strategies, the triviality, complacency, and dishonesty of the lives exposed in its pages and, more importantly, presenting as the basis for its attacks a comprehensible and coherent world, embodied in the symbolically central figure of Gino Carella.

Gino and his city give a definite shape to the universe of *Where Angels Fear to Tread*, encompassing, as Philip sees it, everything between heaven and hell (p. 90) or between "the sun or the clouds above him, and the tides below" (p. 113). The novel's world may be mysterious and terrible, but it is ultimately limited and contained: an extrapolation (in Pierre Francastel's terms) from a "cube scénographique au centre duquel se déplace l'homme-acteur," "l'image d'une Nature dis-

*Excerpted from chapter two of *Horizons of Assent: Modernism, Postmodernism, and the Ironic Imagination* (Baltimore and London: Johns Hopkins Univ. Press, 1981), pp. 54–66, 67–68, 87–89, and reprinted by permission of The Johns Hopkins University Press.

tincte de l'homme, mais à la mesure de l'homme et de ses réactions."[3] Though he is seen by Caroline at one point as "greater than right or wrong" (p. 109), almost a transcendent force, Gino is very much of *this* world, conceived "à la mesure de l'homme," extending but also defining its boundaries.

In other words, Gino is the image of nature in the novel, and despite his occasional brutality (or because of it) a symbol of cosmos, of order. But his order is not Sawston's, and his function is not only to articulate the human limits of *Where Angels Fear to Tread* but to give its world a sense of dimension, to ratify its concern with views, which are as central to this as to Forster's other Italian novel. "Astride the parapet, with one foot in the loggia and the other dangling into the view" (p. 104), Gino exists, without being aware of it, in spatial and moral depth. He is part of the view, at one with, perhaps identical with, the phenomenal world and the world of value into which he merges. As contrasted with the superficial, morally conventional life of Sawston, Monteriano embraces, stretches, unifies (most notably at the opera), absorbing and accepting the melodramatic moments that are part of the texture of its life.

I've suggested already that in *Where Angels Fear to Tread* irony functions largely as a rhetorical weapon in the armory of satire. But the novel reveals as well another kind of irony: the perception of disparities or incongruities inherent in the very nature of existence and consequently resistent to the corrective thrust of satire. Furthermore, this other, disjunctive irony can be seen as the response to as well as the perception of a discontinuous and fragmented world, a world lacking order and coherence and, finally, meaning, as meaning is increasingly located not objectively in the cosmos but subjectively in the eye of the beholder. Longing to cross the gulfs and abysses that scar the landscape of modernist literature, the ironist (Francastel's "l'homme-acteur") is trapped in the dubious safety of distance and uninvolvement.

Gino stands outside this kind of irony. As the vehicle of Forster's satiric vision, he makes clear that the aim of the novel's satire is to break down barriers, to achieve through a sort of transparency or harmonizing unity a coherence that will make more radical ironies impossible. But Gino is less a solution than an ideal. Like his opposite number, Harriet Herriton, who has no view, no ability to see in depth, Gino is, for very different reasons, irrelevant to the whole problem of disjunctive irony. Absorbed in depth, as she is excluded from it, he has only a limited bearing on the problems raised by Philip, Caroline, and the narrator. Thus, though he continues to mediate Forster's satiric vision to the end of the novel, he comes to seem increasingly less effective as he is juxtaposed with these figures, who, standing on the periphery of the view, can recognize but cannot come to terms with the depth it is Gino's function to express.

Possibly unintended, these more recalcitrant ironies become apparent as soon as one moves to the more general level of moral inquiry on which much of the novel is conducted. So, in the principal normative statement of *Where Angels Fear to Tread*, the narrator contrasts "a sense of beauty and a sense of humour" with "human love and love of truth" (pp. 54–55), a suspiciously resounding collocation of what C. S. Lewis once called "the great abstract nouns of the classical English moralists."[4] Indeed, these abstractions, called upon to carry more conceptual freight than they can easily bear, produce in the reader a sense of slightly blurred vision, and one is hard put to specify the values they are meant to designate. Granted that Philip does in fact transcend the unpleasantness of his early laughter and the crudity of his youthful art-worship, still, more fundamentally, the trajectory of his short career reveals some puzzling insights into Forster's hypothetical ideal. That Philip's instruments in attaining truth are in fact an ingrained irony and what I've elsewhere called "the aesthetic view of life"[5] (that is, variants of what he presumably leaves behind), may be put down to Forster's own deliberate irony at the expense of the limited growth of his ironic protagonist. But it is more difficult to rationalize one's perception that love and truth are not, as Forster's formulation of the ideal suggests, coordinate but disjunctive.

Truth may be granted to Philip, if the word is meant to suggest his increase in self-knowledge and his ability, as the book ends, to "see round" the whole situation "standing at an immense distance" (p. 147). But the abortiveness of his love for Caroline seems, in the final analysis, less the result of circumstance or even of character than of Forster's failure to realize the implications of that love—or, indeed, of Caroline's for Gino. It is difficult to overlook a sense of distaste for sexuality, evident in Philip's thoughts and in Caroline's hysteria, more difficult still to avoid the conclusion that Forster has constructed a fable of impossibility: the offer of love *or* truth—but not both. What is at issue then is not simply the awareness of "the complexity of life" (p. 89), which Philip and Caroline share, but, more ambiguously, Forster's own notion of human relationships.

Early in the novel, the narrator describes, as a central feature of Italian life, "that true Socialism which is based not on equality of income or character, but on the equality of manners" (pp. 35–36). The passage goes on to envisage the possibility of a relationship as close as David's and Jonathan's, because free from "feminine criticism and feminine insight and feminine prejudice." My point is not, to return to Caroline for a moment, simply that her love is frustrated by her exclusion from this world of masculine camaraderie (as Lilia's to a large degree is), any more than it seems to me adequate to explain away her retreat in terms of the mores of 1905. The problem hinges, surely, on the word "manners," which suggests first and inevitably the drawing-rooms of Sawston.

The manners of Italy are very different of course: in the open-air world of the piazza, "in the democracy of the *caffè*," rooms and walls are dissolved, the domesticities of Sawston overturned, transparency and union achieved in "the brotherhood of man." But is the ideal proposed here any less artificial than the decorums of Sawston? "He will spit and swear, and you will drop your h's," the narrator comments, presenting, it would seem, a rather paltry end-product of socialism, democracy, and the brotherhood of man. It appears that we have been offered not a transcendence of but merely an opposition to Sawston, an inversion of its values; and, as a corollary, too feeble a structure to support the weight of the novel's satire.

In fact, it makes a good deal more sense to read the passage as a comment not on brotherhood but on sexuality, specifically homosexuality, and more concretely still, on a particular kind of homosexual relation. "He achieved physical sex very late," Furbank writes of Forster, "and found it easier with people outside his own social class"[6] Seen in these terms, everything in the passage falls into place: David and Jonathan, the destructive "feminine insight," and not least the (Italian) spitting and swearing and the more verbal, passive *h*-dropping of that "you" (Philip, Forster, or the English reader?) who deliberately, artificially remakes his manners to achieve (I am quoting Furbank again) "a kind of private magic . . . an almost unattainable blessing, for which another person was merely a pretext." What hope for Caroline, then, in a book where the unacknowledged truth is sex and in which sex is finally seen as antithetical to love?

I want to make clear my major point here, which is *not* that Caroline as a woman can find no fulfillment in the homosexual world of the piazza. Indeed this observation seems to me trivial as compared with what is implied by the opposition of character and manners. "Equality of manners" is the end-product of a reductive process, a stripping away of all that individualizes two sexual partners, a minimal, anonymous unity achieved by the suppression of complexity. But Caroline cannot forgo her complexity to join with Gino any more than she can retain it and love the disconsolate Philip; for if "equality of character" implies the possibility (and no more) of love, it also entails self-consciousness, division, and an irony more subversive than any implied by Forster's intended satire. If it is too simple to substitute sex for truth in Forster's formula, then truth needs perhaps to be seen as the incompatibility between love and sex: an ironic intuition of disconnection that shadows almost all of Forster's fiction.

There is, I'm aware, a danger of making too much of the passage I've been commenting on. And yet it seems to me that the total effect of the novel, as articulated in its various techniques, substantiates my reading of it. The predominance of air, light, and view notwithstanding, *Where Angels Fear to Tread* is a sad and chilly book, a novel whose tensions are held in check but not resolved. The sadness, no doubt, is intentional: a conscious and normative irony directed at the protagonists of the story, who have learned much but accomplished little. The lack of warmth and the sense of irresolution are another matter. Forster's signature is partly stylistic, partly narrative, and each of his techniques is in effect double. So the essentially paratactic style is at odds with the predilection for rhetorical figures and occasional high-sounding words and, too, with the addiction to inverted sentence order. The effect of this overlay of slightly old-fashioned elements on a predominantly simple syntax is to create a sense of a voice both fastidious and mannered, a combination which, for all the apparent intimacy of that voice, helps to keep the reader and the characters as well at a distance. Philip, we are told, "always adopted a dry satirical manner when he was puzzled" (p. 59), and the description suits Forster's tone too, if one allows for occasional modulations into enthusiasm and sentimentality.

As for Forster's notorious melodrama, the appearance of violent moments in the context of the book as a whole suggests, paradoxically, a quality of containment. The incidents themselves threaten to explode Forster's world, but the violence of imagination is constantly checked by the coolness of the treatment, by the disconcerting flatness with which even the most emotional incidents are described. This distance from the events (like that from the characters) makes for an understated power in the novel, but it also confirms, through its tonal and stylistic checks, Forster's resemblance to Philip. Viewing his fictional world aesthetically and (to use the word with all of its modernist resonance) ironically, Forster creates more light than warmth; and there is some question as to whether the novel itself manages to express the "human love" its author apparently desires.

The problem of "love of truth" is more complex still. The sexual question apart, it is clear from the start that the very search for truth is compromised by the blurred perspective Forster adopts in his pursuit of it. The stable foundations of satire contrast with the subjective, shifting ground on which disjunctive irony rests. And to acknowledge the transformation of the one into the other (or the uneasy balance between them) is to recognize that an apparently ordered world is about to give way: the objective standard of a solid, essentially unchanging world is threatened by the ambiguous, personal vision of a world in flux. In short, irony, unmoored from satire, becomes autonomous—a vision of the universe held together only in the troubled consciousness of the individual observer. Nevertheless, what is finally important about *Where Angels Fear to Tread* in Forster's career is that, at this stage, these two perspectives are able, however tenuously, however fragilely, to coexist, providing at least an aesthetic coherence Forster was not always able to achieve in his succeeding novels. My aim here, however, is not to pursue all of the byways in the development of Forster's irony. The high road leads to *A Passage to India*, where both the nature of the observation and the sense of control undergo a definitive change. In the metaphysical universe of Forster's final novel, modernist irony, absolute at last, is the dominant vision.

In *A Passage to India*, the humanized conception of a three-dimensional, orderly universe gives way to something vastly larger and less comprehensible. Space and time as well are defined no longer "à la mesure de l'homme" but in terms of infinity and eternity. And if the narrator comments at one point that "vastness [is] the only quality that accommodates them to mankind" (p. 141), it is because man has tried to make over even these ultimate abstractions into analogues of "Heaven, Hell, Annihilation—one or other of those large things, that huge scenic background of stars, fires, blue or black air" (pp. 197–98). But for Forster and for Mrs. Moore, who "in the twilight of the double vision" after the caves, "can neither ignore nor respect Infinity" (p. 198), there is behind the blue or black air only emptiness, silence, and indifference. Distances in Forster's final novel are incomparably greater than in *Where Angels Fear to Tread*; depth has become a bottomless abyss. Beyond the arches and vaults of the book, there is "that further distance . . . last freed itself from blue" (p. 3). Over and over, among the negatives that thread the novel together, the eye seeks rest in a perspective that offers no point of convergence but only "an impartiality exceeding all" (p. 34). With the dissolution of Forster's earlier cosmos, nothing any longer contains—except "the echoing walls" (p. 37), which drive the characters back into the uneasy worlds of their own consciousnesses.

Fielding's momentary belief "that we exist not in ourselves, but in terms of each other's minds" (*PI*, p. 237) may stand as a symbol for how the self responds to the de-anthropomorphizing of the universe. From the first chapter, where the views of Chandrapore form and reform with changes of perspective, the relativism of human perception asserts itself. In the land of the hundred Indias, truth is splintered; the pretension to it, the subject of the narrator's bitterest scorn. And the conception of love as rape and (in Mrs. Moore's disillusioned thoughts) as "centuries of carnal embracement" (p. 127) completes, notwithstanding the more hopeful relations of the novel, the reduction of "human love and love of truth" almost to the point of travesty. Forster's outlook has become, in short, ironic in a way that *Where Angels Fear to Tread* only begins to suggest. Which is to say that *A Passage to India* articulates a vision of life in which everything disappoints or deceives; in which appearances are equivocal and the possibility of a reality behind them at best a question; in which all things are subject to interpretation, depending upon how, where, and in what mood they are perceived; in which, at the extreme, meaning, no longer supported by value, is dissolved "into a single mess" (p. 220) and even the extraordinary is reduced to nothing.

The word "nothing" echoes through the novel, undermining, like the winds and airs in the middle section of *To the Lighthouse*, all pretension to human structure. But . . . I've called irony absolute in *A Passage to India* not primarily because of its despairing vision, which is common to all disjunctive irony, but because of its form. Central to Forster's novel is the unresolvable dilemma—not the disparity between right and wrong or real and pretended on which satire thrives, but the discordant and equal poise of opposites. So in Forster's meditation on unity, carried on through the description of the two well-meaning missionaries, the irony is only superficially at the expense of Mr. Sorley, who "admitted that the mercy of God, being infinite, may well embrace all mammals" (*PI*, p. 32). More fundamental and more unsettling is the awareness that inclusion and exclusion are alike impossible. It is, as I have suggested in my book on Forster, between these poles that the drama of *A Passage to India* takes place: the factitiousness of any attempt to impose order on the one hand and, on the other, the recognition of the unbounded as the chaotic. "In our Father's house are many mansions," but "We must exclude someone from our gathering, or we shall be left with nothing" (p. 32).

Nothing again; and inevitably one comes to the caves: "Nothing, nothing attaches to them"; "Nothing is inside them . . . if mankind grew curious and excavated, nothing, nothing would be added to the sum of good or evil" (*PI*, pp. 117–18). The use of the caves to symbolize the infinite and eternal is in itself ironic. The small, discrete, claustrophobic enclosures are made to represent their apparent opposite, the limitless, formless, agoraphobic universe both because men "desire that . . . infinity have a form" (p. 201) and because, as in the Kawa Dol, which is at the same time something and nothing, the extremity of opposition is identity. In the caves, immeasurable space and immeasurable time are flattened out in Mrs. Moore's horrified awareness that "everything exists, nothing has value" (p. 140).

With this sentence, we come to the heart of Forster's irony, as it manifests itself in his final novel. In the disconnection between existence and value; in the failure of simultaneity to entail relation; in the disappearance of the dimension that value and relation imply, there is a collapse of the book's various metaphorical "bridges" and a confirmation of its pervasive "gulfs." And there is a collapse too of that depth and of those views that shape the cosmos of *Where Angels Fear to Tread*. "Visions are supposed to entail profundity, but—," the narrator adds, "The abyss also may be petty" (*PI*, p. 198). The repeated emphasis on smallness, when what is at issue are the inconceivable reaches of the universe, has to do with the final reduction of meaning to a neutral coexistence in chaos. The amorphous and the illimitable come together when "the horror of the universe and its smallness are both visible at the same time" (p. 197). We are, in short, in a world of surfaces, where appearances, unresonant and reflexive, signify no meanings beyond themselves and where life, nonprogressive in its linear disconnection, "went on as usual but had no consequences" (p. 132).

The reduction of the metaphysical to the temporal and spatial dimensions of the caves parallels the transposition, accomplished through the mediation of consciousness, of the metaphysical into the psychological. Like the Anglo-Indians retreating from the implacable sun, the self, confronted with the silence of Forster's infinite spaces, folds in on itself. Viewed subjectively—and how else to view it when everything is "infected with illusion" (*PI*, p. 132)?—the universe dwindles into Mrs. Moore's cynicism and Fielding's solipsism.[7] If microcosm and macrocosm retain, conceptually and aesthetically, a metaphorical correspondence, effectively, self and world are disjoined. As J. Hillis Miller puts it: "When God and the creation become objects of consciousness, man becomes a nihilist. Nihilism is the nothingness of consciousness when consciousness becomes the foundation of everything."[8] In the shadow of the caves, the lesson of the Marabar is internalized, and causality gives way, with signification, to the terrified vision of simple contiguity: "Pathos, piety, courage—they exist, but are identical, and so is filth" (p. 140).

The perception of life as mere surface is a prefiguration of *The Life to Come* in the same way that the personal relationships of Forster's first novel look forward to those of his last. I'll return more fully to the question of depth and surface later on; but to a degree it bears on the human level of *A Passage to India* as well. The two paradigms of relating, mooted in *Where Angels Fear to Tread*, are here both clarified (to a degree) and polarized. Fielding and Adela, we are told, "spoke the same language, and held the same opinions, and the variety of age and sex did not divide them" (*PI*, p. 252); and of Ronny and Adela, the narrator similarly comments: "Experiences, not character, divided them" (p. 77). As defined by Adela's relations with the two men, "equality of character" comes to suggest an essentially static conception of character: predicated on the acceptance of the self; grounded on the belief in the possibility of rational understanding; and threatened both by the eruption of unacknowledged emotions and, more simply, by the conjunction of love and sex. Forster's strategy is to show that those who assume the stability of the ego are precisely those threatened by the depths of their own personalities. The intention, however, is not simply to expose the incompleteness of reason (Adela's imperious need to *know*) but, more profoundly, to test conventional notions of psychological depth (as he tests those of metaphysical depth in the caves) in order to reject them.

The point needs further explanation, involving as it does still another paradox. The relationships that dramatize "equality of manners" (Aziz's with Mrs. Moore, with Ralph, and with Fielding) are precisely those

that seem, in their acceptance of mystery, instinct, and intuition, to arise
from and to thrive on depth. But Aziz's friendships are not an answer to
Adela's inability to touch bottom; they suggest, rather, a revolt against
psychology, character, and the ego. Based not on being and knowing but
on acting and doing, they are a pushing away from conventional psychological depth toward a new kind of human surface, as yet only partly
realized in A Passage to India. In any case, one begins to see that Forster
repeatedly constructs his ideal fictional relationships (the earlier stories
and novels, particularly ... Maurice, provide examples too) in terms of
some initial abrasiveness—race, religion, class, age, nationality—which,
overcome, yields what is, in essence, not the acceptance of the self but
a creation of a new and desired self.

To a degree at least, the characters themselves consciously share
Forster's belief. Aziz thinks of Fielding and Mrs. Moore: "He loved
them even better than the Hamidullahs because he had surmounted obstacles to meet them" (PI, p. 134). And in his last ride with Fielding, he
turns aside his friend's attempt at personal conversation and begins deliberately, almost artificially, the political argument that leads to the assertion of friendship with which they part. The novel's ending is a
reminder, however, that the achievement of "equality of manners" depends not only on the transcendence of old patterns of relationship and
the transformation of the self but still more on a conception of the universe in which the self can find its fulfillment. Where there is existence
but no value and where, as Lawrence implied of Forster,[9] there remains
the desire to act on a belief no longer believed in, love, friendship, and
sex alike are futile.

It will be objected at this point, rightly, that I have arrived at the
end of the novel without more than a glance at its third, Hindu section.
So much has been written on the issue of "whether A Passage to India
reveals a pessimistic or optimistic view of the universe,"[10] that I am reluctant to stir the pot once again. Something, however, needs to be said
about the relation of "Temple" to the question of irony. Frederick Mc-
Dowell has written that the Indian essays in Albergo Empedocle and
Other Writings "weight the balance ... in favor of anti-rationalist, pan-
theistic, mystical, religious, and quasi-Hinduistic interpretations of the
novel."[11] And he notes, correctly I think, that the essays counteract Forster's remarks in The Hill of Devi. I am more willing than I once was
to admit that the desire for what Hinduism represents throbs through the
novel as the most perfect consummation of that transformation of the
self I've already referred to. And no doubt my concentration on the caves
has obscured the change in mood (signaled by the reappearance of
views) that part 3 represents.

Still and all, even before we arrive at "Temple," we are back on the
horns of a dilemma no less potent than, indeed related to, the inclusion-
exclusion paradox of part 1. If Mrs. Moore's perceptions as she travels

back across India and Fielding's as he returns to Venice represent a re-assertion of phenomenal reality independent of the transfiguring self, a return to depth; then Godbole and his Hinduism, already anticipated in Fielding's conversation with Aziz (*PI*, p. 265), are a denial of it. Forster's assertion that the Hindu festival represents the same thing as the scene in the cave "turned inside out"[12] seems to me to suggest not a disavowal but an alternate view of the meaning of the Marabar: a shift of perspective, which equivocally suspends questions of true and false. Throughout the novel, possibilities are mooted, but desire is not realization; and it is no easier for the reader to fix Forster's meaning than it is for Godbole to prolong his vision.

If I seem by now, in my attempt to question the legitimacy of reading "Temple" as a plunge into oneness, to be questioning as well my reading of "Caves," it is what I intend. The lesson of the criticism of the last fifteen years or so seems to me to be that, thematically considered, *A Passage to India* can be made to yield totally opposed and equally valid interpretations and that on this level no argument is ever likely to be accepted as final. I wrote some years ago, in a mildly existentialist reading of the novel, that, at its close, *A Passage to India* directs the reader back to life. It appears to me now that, more powerful than any suggestion of thematic open-endedness is the effect . . . of formal closure. In short, it is neither in the explication of its discursive content nor in the exegesis of isolated symbols that the key to the novel is to be found but in an examination of its pervasive and controlling technique.

Beginning with the opening sentence of the novel, in which, subtly but firmly, syntax establishes a dizzyingly ironic focus for the reader, Forster's strategy emerges. If Forster's cosmology undergoes a radical change between his first and last novel, the comparison of technique suggests an intensification rather than an alteration of basic approach. To put this another way, the collapse of Forster's earlier world seems to have called forth not a corresponding transformation in aesthetic form but, by way of compensation it would seem, a firmer sense of control. The result, predictably, is an enormous tension in the novel, manifest first of all in the style, whose still essentially paratactic structure supports and holds in check a texture that, in the density of its images and symbols, of its diction generally, is so much richer and fuller than that of the first novel and, too, so much more restrained. With the first view of Chandrapore, the urbane and cultivated voice of the narrator establishes his distance from the scene, the reductive tone expressing, along with the distance, a certain distaste. Matching the abundant stylistic qualifications—the careful *excepts*, *rathers*, and *thoughs*—the tone, for all its apparent casualness, is ultimately self-conscious, academic, fussy, almost precious in its attempt to produce "the coin that buys the exact truth [which] has not yet been minted" (*PI*, p. 12).

And so it is throughout the book. His tone verging at times on cynicism, the narrator continues to play down what is positive, to question what is taken for granted, to qualify what is whole. Laying out his narrative as a series of tableaux, discrete and contained despite the violence of the action they describe, he is the embodiment of artistic control surveying an incomprehensible world. Nothing within *A Passage to India* but *A Passage to India* itself is Forster's "self-contained harmony," which gives "us the illusion of perspicacity and of power" (*TC*, p. 57; *AN*, p. 44). Thus it is that, as one comes to "Temple," the ubiquitous irony of the novel plays over Hinduism, as over everything else, enforcing and at the same time questioning its own paradoxes. Forster's description, very near the end of the novel (and anticipating its "No, not yet," "No, not there"), of the "emblems of passage" expresses perfectly the attitude of aesthetic poise: "a passage not easy, not now, not here, not to be apprehended except when it is unattainable" (*PI*, p. 304). Like this fragment, the book as a whole achieves a stasis of equivocation: the accumulated negatives playing off against the imagination of desire. Suspended between the equally valid polarities of "nothing" and "extraordinary," *A Passage to India* is not so much open-ended as forever ironic in its simultaneous and equal assent to the contradictory possibilities man can entertain. If the fictional world of *Where Angels Fear to Tread* is chilly, *A Passage to India* is (like Virginia Woolf's *The Waves*) frozen, its "wintry surface" (p. 8) directing us, finally, back to itself through the extraordinary perfection of its art.

When Sir Richard Conway, surveying the remainder of his dull, country weekend, thinks to himself: "The visit, like the view, threatened monotony" (p. 97), he gives perfect expression to Forster's sense of ordinary existence in *The Life to Come*. Not the metaphysical terror of the caves but the monotony of "normal" life serves as the background of these stories, and their heroes, unlike Mrs. Moore or Fielding, who react by a movement inward, accept that monotony as an inevitable part of life's texture, while actively accommodating themselves to what are now seen (in a dramatic reversal of Forster's attitude in his last novel) as the intermittent pleasures of life's surface. At least, most of them do. Of the stories I am concerned with (those which, according to the dates offered in Oliver Sallybrass's admirable edition, were composed at about the same time as or later than *A Passage to India*),[13] three deal with love. Significantly, "The Life to Come," "Dr. Woolacott," and "The Other Boat" . . . are closer in feeling and strategy to Forster's earlier work. More ambitious and morally more ambiguous than the other five stories, they are also more obviously sentimental, sometimes, as in the opening of "The Life to Come," embarrassingly so. And in the first two at least, the attempt to render love leads to a style that is poetic by intention, yet curiously flat, thin, and conventional. More striking is the fact that each of these stories ends with death.

And although it is possible, given their orthodox psychology, to regard the endings as inevitable effects of causes specified in the stories, it is difficult to avoid the sense that what is being revealed more clearly still is a psychological pattern in Forster. If *Maurice* is predicated on a happy ending,[14] these stories express the more typical lure of failure in matters of homosexual love. Or, rather, not homosexuality as such but, as I've suggested, the conflation of love and sex. To combine the two is, in Forster's imaginative world, to invite, indeed to ensure disaster. To the last, as "The Other Boat" makes clear, Forster was unable to envisage the stability of complete human relationships in a universe of temporal and psychological change. What his imagination sought and intermittently found was a nondynamic world, freed from the impersonal determinations of causality as from the more subtle connections of love. It is, in part, the world to which the endings of many of the earlier fantasies (and of "Dr. Woolacott") unsatisfactorily point; it is also the world of the remaining five stories: "other kingdom" brought down to earth.

The deliberate avoidance of love in this second group has as its corollary the acceptance of sex as sex and for the moment. What Forster is after is described perfectly in "Arthur Snatchfold" as "the smaller pleasures of life," a one-time affair conducted "with a precision impossible for lovers" (p. 103). "Equality of character" gives way totally in *The Life to Come* to a series of unequal confrontations; and now that physical contact is out in the open, the abrasiveness I spoke of earlier is still more apparent. Indeed, the looser, freer structures of most of the sexual stories create, for the first time, a fictional world congruent with the asymmetric relationships they celebrate—one in which the new allegiance to surface is revealingly defined by means of the curious psychological discontinuity that marks their heroes. Even in "The Other Boat," Lionel, in the midst of his affair, forgets "any depths through which he might have passed" (p. 178). In the sexual stories this habit of mind is endemic: characters forget the men to whom they have been attracted, with whom they have had an affair, indeed by whom they have been raped—thereby ignoring or refusing the depth implied by memory and created by continuity of feeling. In all these stories, depth—spatial, temporal, and psychological—is inessential, inimical, or impossible: a force operating against the disequality of character that is now more than ever a positive good, a barrier not to be minimized or ignored but to be pleasurably overcome.

But the relationships achieved make for an "equality of manners" that needs to be further defined with reference to Forster himself. Furbank's comment: "He valued sex for its power to release his own capacities for tenderness and devotion, but he never expected an *equal* sexual relationship" (*TPF*, p. 62) indicates that equality is, in fact and paradoxically, inequality: a peculiarly limited, discrete moment, in which connecting becomes coupling and love, of course, sex. It is in the contact alone that the participants are leveled—equal in their enjoyment of their unequal pleasures. And so it is in the stories. Freed from senti- ment, if not from sentimentality, they represent a movement from For- ster's familiar "as if" to a very different "as it is": self joining with world in an unresonant acceptance of amoral pleasure. . . .

Taken together, the sexual stories in *The Life to Come* define the final stage of irony in Forster's work: an acceptance of contingency that is perhaps best illustrated, by its absence, in the figure of Count Wagha- ghren, the villain of "What Does It Matter?" and a man "unaccustomed to incidents without consequence" (p. 132). Obliquely, the description hints at the suspensiveness of Forster's irony and at the priapic ethos of the sexual tales. For Forster's late figures are, to repeat, men un- concerned with consequences; and the stories explore and celebrate, precisely, a world without causality, sequence, or depth. The results of this change of attitude, apparently so striking, need to be recognized and understood. In the movement from cosmos to chaos and, further, from the melancholy awareness to the feverish acceptance of surface; from redemptive moments to desperate snatches of pleasure; from "the power to love and the desire for truth" (p. 19) of "Albergo Empedocle" (and *Where Angels Fear to Tread*) to the truth of that discordant sex- uality heretofore at least partly concealed in Forster's fiction, what has most strikingly disappeared is the all-embracing ideal of connection set forth in *Howards End*. Along with the asymmetry of relationships comes, or seems to come, the acceptance of randomness and multiplicity as the very definition and condition of life and its satisfactions; and, in the light of Forster's earlier work, the acceptance is as radical as it is surpris- ing. . . . In *Howards End*, Helen Schlegel insists that "Death destroys a man; the idea of Death saves him" (p. 236). But Helen's conceptualiza- tion, her appeal to consciousness, is precisely what Forster rejects in *The Life to Come*. Not the idea of death but the death of the idea now saves; and Helen's statement of "the vague yet convincing plea that the In- visible lodges against the Visible" has no place in the surface world of Forster's final stories, where the anironic (the ideal that complements his irony), whether conceived in terms of sex or love, points inexorably in the same direction: toward death or the death of consciousness, the physical or psychological obliteration of the self.

The Life to Come is, then, . . . a set of variations on a theme. Although, as compared with much recent fiction, the book remains for- mally conventional (this is relatively true even of the more loosely or- ganized sexual stories), its vision is not. The point has some general importance, since it runs counter to the notion of a sharp break between modernism and postmodernism. It bears repeating that Forster and a sig- nificant number of his contemporaries as well come increasingly in the course of their careers to recognize (or to sense) the impasse to which their assumptions have brought them and are led to search out alternate ways of responding. The crisis point, therefore, needs to be located not after, but, more properly, before the war—in Lawrence's rethinking of "the old, stable *ego* of the character," in *Finnegans Wake*, in *Between the Acts*, in the ambiguous allegiances of late modernism, and, however much smaller its literary merit, in *The Life to Come*. If modernism represents, among other things, the imposition of the mind's structure on the external world, then Forster's stories are no longer modernist. Wylie Sypher's notion of "methexis" is relevant here. "The distance between life and art," he writes, "is no longer fixed or definable even as minimal.... There is participation as well as observation." And again: "The immediate occasion is sufficient unto itself.... If the significance is on the surface, then the need for depth explanation has gone, and the contingent, the everyday happening, is more authentic than the ultimate or absolute."[15] The self-confessed auto-eroticism of Forster's stories falls in its minor, narcissistic way precisely within this ethic of participation, although (and it should be said that Sypher is not discussing Forster) it hardly validates its interest or importance.

The excitement of Philip's anonymous contacts and of Helen's chance collisions translates, when these come to dominate Forster's fiction, into a way of life that is dispiritingly minimal and aleatory—like a good deal of the current art that goes by those names. Not that an allegiance to the phenomenal or to the suspensive necessarily implies a thinning out of either self or world. But in Forster's stories exactly that happens (explaining, perhaps, why Forster found himself unable any longer to deal with the more extended form of the novel). The dissolution of the self—not, as for the structuralists, in a web of language but in the peremptoriness of desire—leaves the self just as effectively a fiction. Hovering and havering in the world to which they have been abandoned, Forster's attenuated heroes are prescient of Beckett and the Surfictionists, and of the chaotic or baffling spaces of the *nouveau roman*. For all their violence, there is something exhausted about Forster's final stories. One has come a long way from the conceptual moments of the earlier fiction, which, however discrete in form, are intended to provide and enforce the opportunity for reflection and change. In the resolutely limited, sexual world of *The Life to Come*, moments exist for their own sake or for the sake of the minimal, limited activity generated by them. What Sypher, following Nietzsche, refers to as the "pathos of distance" (p. 128) gives way to a more pathetic capitulation to simple, disordered sensation.

Forster's stories, particularly after "The Life to Come" and "Dr. Woolacott," are a refusal of compromise in fantasy and a rejection of *Howards End*'s belief in the possible connection of life's antinomies. The injunctions of that novel give way at last, in the enervated suspensiveness of Forster's final work, not simply to the disjunctions that are in fact a feature of his work from the beginning but to something that is both more random and, oddly, more restricted as well. And if the stories become as a result more honest, at any rate less equivocal, still their values are sadly diminished, even reversed, in the process. No longer intent on the disappearance of the visible world, Forster abandons too the attempt to reconcile love and truth. Materializing Maurice's green-wood, so to speak, he creates a world in which the unexamined life is the only one worth living. Lionel March's murder of Cocoa in a final, sexual act is described in "The Other Boat" as "part of a curve that had long been declining, and had nothing to do with death" (p. 196). Fate, then, presumably, or, more accurately, inner necessity; but tending no less surely toward the literal or psychological extremity of death. If so, the curve is, mutatis mutandis, Forster's too, fictionally elaborated throughout his career in a movement from Philip's ill-understood desires to their realization in the impoverished relationships of *The Life to Come*. Like Lionel's, a barren climax; but also Forster's dubious passage to the contemporary scene.

Notes

1. E. M. Forster, *Goldsworthy Lowes Dickinson*, p. 97. My references to Forster's works derive from the Abinger Edition, edited by Oliver Stallybrass (London: Edward Arnold). The dates that follow are those of original publication and of the Abinger volumes: *Where Angels Fear to Tread* (1905; 1975); *Howards End* (1910; 1973), referred to as *HE*; *A Passage to India* (1924; 1978), referred to as *PI*; *Aspects of the Novel* (1927; 1974), referred to as *AN*; *Goldsworthy Lowes Dickinson* (1934; 1973); *Two Cheers for Democracy* (1951; 1972), referred to as *TC*; *The Life to Come and Other Stories* (1972).

2. Leonard Woolf, *Sowing* (London: Hogarth Press, 1967), p. 161.

3. Pierre Francastel, *Peinture et Société* (Paris: Gallimard, 1965), pp. 199 and 212.

4. C. S. Lewis, "A Note on Jane Austen," in *Discussions of Jane Austen*, ed. William Heath (Boston: Heath, 1961), p. 60.

5. Alan Wilde, *Art and Order: A Study of E. M. Forster* (New York: New York University Press, 1964), p. 11 and chapter 2, passim.

6. P. N. Furbank, "The Personality of E. M. Forster," *Encounter* 35 (November 1970): 62. Ed note.

7. Fielding, as we now know, was originally to have had the vision in the cave. See June Perry Levine, *Creation and Criticism: A Passage to India* (Lincoln: University of Nebraska Press, 1971), pp. 85–86.

8. J. Hillis Miller, *Poets of Reality* (Cambridge: Harvard University Press, 1965), p. 3.

9. See *The Collected Letters of D. H. Lawrence*, ed. Harry T. Moore, 2 vols. (New York: Viking Press, 1962), 2: 316–20.

10. Levine, *Creation and Criticism*, p. 119.

11. Frederick P. W. McDowell, "By and About Forster: A Review Essay," *English Literature in Transition* 15 (1972): 321.

12. See Wilde, *Art and Order*, p. 151, n. 8.

13. See Stallybrass's introduction and the dates on p. xii, which indicate that these stories run from 1922 to 1958. For convenience, I shall use the title of the

whole volume to refer to the eight homosexual stories that run from p. 65 to p. 197. The other five stories, written between 1903 and 1906, are not relevant to this discussion. The eight I do plan to examine can most conveniently be subdivided into "sexual stories" and "love stories."

14. See Forster's terminal note to *Maurice* (New York: Norton, 1971), p. 250.

15. Wylie Sypher, *Literature and Technology* (New York: Random House, 1968), pp. 102 and 240.

The Double Nature of Forster's Fiction: *A Room with a View* and *The Longest Journey*   Judith Scherer Herz*

Love is clearly the key word for Forster. More than any other, it binds together his writing, makes it a body, filled with a vital substance, both passionate and spiritual. Love is theory, love is practice, and sometimes in the fiction, it is difficult to distinguish between them. Love creates, love, indeed, *is* the beloved republic, but even as abstraction, as idea, it speaks of the experience of touch, the contradictions of desire, the need to connect.

In our reading we should leave a bit of our high-mindedness at the door. For that "petite phrase," that leitmotiv, love, that weaves its way through novel, essay, fantasy, biography, travel tale and bawdy tale is energy as much as idea, and sometimes more bloody than bloodless. Forster himself can be something of a misleading guide here. His reticence and propriety led him, for example, to suppress all but the vaguest reference to Lowes Dickinson's homosexuality in his biography of 1934 (while in the recently published autobiography Dickinson seems to talk of nothing else), and, evidently, led him to destroy those "sexy" stories which he thought more privately useful as an easing of his frustrations than successful as "works of art." The editor of the Ackerley letters speculates that Forster's not reviewing or even mentioning Ackerley's *Hindoo Holiday* until 1953 stemmed from real shock at its contents. "It was one thing to enjoy in a letter, the 'crafty-ebbing' details of the Maharajah's sexual behaviour, but quite another to see them in print."[1]

But he didn't burn all the stories. Reading them now, alongside all the novels, including *Maurice*, jolts one into realizing how much this sexual energy has been a component of Forster's fiction from the start, and how much the strategies invented to contain it—not necessarily to disguise it—are an important part of his accomplishment as a novelist.

*Reprinted from *English Literature in Transition* 21, No. 4, (1978), 254–65, by permission of the author and *English Literature in Transition*.

It is a point worth making, especially since this argument runs counter to several recent readings. Alan Wilde, for example, in a complexly argued essay claims that Forster's career moves toward an exhausted final stage, to a "peculiarly narrow and unresonant . . . world of triumphant sexuality."[2] This notion of stages is difficult to accept, particularly when it is so heavily moralized, so full of extra-literary "judgment." Forster is not betraying his earlier beliefs in his later "homosexual" fiction. Indeed, the heterosexual/homosexual distinction is quite artificial, suggested by the posthumous publishing but not by the fiction itself.

Forster's fictional career was, this essay will argue, all of a piece. At least as much as other writers he knew his motives and his methods. He was not a victim of his homosexuality at constant fictional cross purposes with himself, and, most important, he was in control in his fiction in both the tales and the novels, early and late. Obviously some fictions work better than others, but the best succeed because Forster was able to control and manipulate the tensions generated by the collision of surface plot and under plot. There is always another story beneath the surface of the story he is telling. Forster's ability to control the two in a complex range of attitudes and tones from ironic to lyric to comic to tragic was his greatest novelistic strength and should prevent us from accepting the now fashionable version of a Forster who, somehow more than others, was a victim of his difficult unconscious.

From first to last sexuality in all its guises is part of Forster's fictional world, but it is a contained energy. It forms the coil spring of the action as it does, for example, in "The Obelisk," a story which unfolds almost as if it were a diagram for the double plot structure. There the wife's story (the heterosexual "romance"), and the husband's story (the homosexual) contain the same characters, setting, events. But the stories absolutely oppose each other and because the wife's story finally includes the husband's (she "knows"; he doesn't), the comic punch line turns on itself and the wife is left with an awareness that the laughter cannot quite displace.

The very earliest of the strategies Forster developed to contain this sexual energy was the creation of a fantasy landscape. Often in Greece, sometimes in Italy, or even in an England inhabited by the semi-divinities, it is the place where one encounters one's true nature, where one is allowed one's real sexual identity, not the one so incongruously provided by the Peaslakes, the Tytlers and the Worters.

The clearest example of this process is in the early and very fine "Albergo Empedocle." The central relationships there foreshadow *The Longest Journey*, but here female destructiveness comes before marriage, and, in Harold's complete surrender to his dream of a greater Greek life, he is allowed a kind of triumph, although to all but the loving eyes of the framing narrator, Tommy, he has become totally lunatic. The story ironically develops the injunction of Mildred's Baedeker-born enthusiasm: "He must think and feel and act like a Greek. It's the only way. He must—well, he must *be* a Greek." But the Greek he becomes is not the sentimentalized effusion of Mildred's false imagination:

> "Did you also love better," she asked in a low voice. "I loved very differently." He was holding back the brambles to prevent them from tearing her dress as he spoke. One of the thorns scratched him on the hand. "Yes, I loved better too," he continued, watching the little drops of blood swell out.[3]

In "Albergo Empedocle," the other story is played out in a dream and, finally, in apparent madness. It is implicit in the narrator's love for Harold, but that love is never made to function fictionally, for Harold must inhabit his other kingdom, the fantasy world where he "loved better too."

Certainly the element of fantasy in the early stories is not in any reductive sense merely a coded sign for repressed homosexual desire. The contrasts of false and true, society and nature, past and present, England and Greece are resonant in these stories as well. But the primary release they describe is sexual and, as "The Story of a Panic" and "The Celestial Omnibus" make clear, the essential epiphany is boy with god.

In much of Forster's writing there is a constant recurring configuration—a divided universe, inhabited by a divided self. A late example and one that provides a nice retrospective link to *The Longest Journey* is "The Other Boat." The story connects Forster's writing chronologically as well, for it was begun in 1913, two years after Forster wrote in his diary, "will analyze causes of my sterility. . . . Weariness of the only subject that I both can and may treat—the love of men for women and vice versa,"[4] and was concluded in 1957–58, ten years after the early, first section had been published as "Entrance to an Unwritten Novel." It is clear why that novel stayed unwritten if novels were to be made and sold in the daylight world of the upper deck, for from the very first sentence, the relationship that matters, that connects all the details, the "finer undergrowth," is that between Lionel and Cocoa. From another point of view, of course, the novel did get written, for a good deal of *Passage to India* is implicit here. But, clearly, when Forster came to reconsider this material in 1957, he was no longer interested in the lame little dances of a Ronny and an Adela. (In fact, one could argue, he was not interested in them in *Passage*, either, that the binding relationship there is certainly Aziz/Fielding).

In "The Other Boat," the male/female separation holds absolutely. The highly detailed foreground action is made part of a larger, essentially mythic action in which the journey out is simultaneously felt as a descent into hell and ecstatic, mystical release. The story opens on a journey home from India, where from the mother's point of view, relationships don't matter, for the boat world is taken to be unreal. But it is precisely the unreal relationship that the story realizes, while the mother's world turns into shadow as she is doubly deserted, first by a husband gone native, and now by her son, a scandalous suicide in the Red Sea. In a sense she becomes a figure of the sea itself, so that Lionel's death can be seen as union with the mother as well as with the lover. She is a felt presence throughout the story, a kind of negative creation, a dimmer version of Mrs. Moore who provided in her death and burial at sea the paradigmatic version of this association.

For Lionel, the deck and cabin worlds are unreconcilable. They figure that split within, the sure knowledge of self, masked by the lie of self that leads inevitably to his death. As with Stephen and Rickie, the final union of Lionel and Cocoa occurs on the other side of death. Cocoa's body moves northward against the current, the undertow carrying it toward Lionel. They die in love to live in death, and in both fictions there is something of the same violence.

In the best of Forster's writing there is always a felt undertow. Two fictions move together in the same fictional space. Often one is true, the other a lie. Finally one or the other is displaced. This structure is visible from the earliest fantasies to the stories written late and read only to special friends. At base "The Story of a Panic" and both "The Other Boat" and "The Life to Come" reach the same conclusion, although the latter two move through tragedy to transcendence. In the other stories of the volume, the resolution of the dual structure takes a variety of forms, ranging from the comic release of the good joke consummately well delivered in "The Obelisk" to the ironic, comic yet savage unmasking in "Arthur Snatchfold." The point is, the main patterns and relationships of the homosexual stories are clearly present in the more familiar fiction. We perhaps can see these more sharply now as the recently published stories make us aware of their place in the full body of Forster's fiction. A good deal of his strength as a novelist thus depends upon the tension generated by the collision of two story lines, the surface heterosexual romance and the interior homosexual romance, and it is from this conflict, between what the plot claims as its main business and the suppressed inner narrative, that the novels take their energy.

Two novels that are usually kept quite separate in discussions of Forster, save for the critic's noting that they are both early, *A Room with a View* and *The Longest Journey*, illustrate this proposition very clearly. The surface of both—charming, casual, leisurely (in the sense of making a space to talk, to speculate along with the narrator)—is the thinnest skin stretched over the most turbulent inner action.

Both fictions deeply distrust marriage, and in *A Room with a View*, where the avowed intent is to get the young couple to the altar, or, at least, to the window together, this distrust sets up a powerful challenge to the primary action. From such a point of view one observes how little existence the couple has, how unconvincing in terms of romance their union is. It is, of course, the Reverend Beebe who casts the longest shadow over the action, and the major conflict of the second half of the book is essentially a symbolic one between him and Mr. Emerson over the soul of Lucy. The book is too subtle to mark out clear winners and losers in this contest. Purely in terms of plot, Emerson triumphs, but those who do not marry are for Forster clearly more interesting than those who do. Beebe and Cecil possess imaginative weight; George is little more than a disembodied series of kisses.

And yet, finally, Beebe is condemned. His celibacy, which is *almost* offered as a solution, turns out to serve religion and all the institutions that stifle instinct. We cannot forget, however, that it is his vision of Lucy that makes her worthy of being a heroine. It is Beebe who interprets her to us, who insists upon the process of discovery that finally casts her into opposition to him. But insofar as Lucy is Beebe's creation, his casting off at the end has an odd note of betrayal to it, the more noticeable as it is the counterpoint to the reinstatement of Charlotte Bartlett who up until this implausible last minute has been cast as the true enemy. Indeed, it is interesting to speculate why critics are so eager to accept Lucy's and George's desperate rehabilitation of her character and to pounce viciously on Beebe's "medievalism" at the same time. Perhaps it is the intuition that the novel's sympathies lie nearer Beebe's stern rejection of romance than either the logic of plot or the wishful readings of critics would allow.

In any event, the novel finally can contain this displacement, for the movement toward marriage provides the largest structure and is chiefly the source of comic energy. Set against the romance plot, however, are symbolic moments which render the characters totally in isolation from one another—Lucy playing Beethoven, George running naked through the woods. It is precisely in this last scene that Beebe could have emerged as a life supporting force and it is precisely at this moment that he fails. He bathes, too, but as he comes suddenly to realize the desires of his flesh, he makes himself deny desire.[5] For Beebe passion can be confronted only through the remove of art (Lucy's piano playing, not George's nakedness). He thus becomes part of a background of negation, an intentional sacrifice to comic romance. He must fail so Mr. Emerson can win and young love look out of its pensione window. But his vision still shapes our response. His absoluteness and final isolation render mechanical and somewhat trivial the conventional happy ending. We are left less with a feeling of elation or even completeness than with the uneasy question of why. Why the bother, why the fuss?— a feeling confirmed in Forster's account quite a few years later of their post-novel lives.[6] The Beebe plot provides the essential undertow. His presence tenses our response to the crucial events. It is Beebe who makes Lucy and George interesting.

It is quite an achievement in so early a novel—to take a tradition two hundred years in the forming and simultaneously accept and reject it. It reminds us that *Hamlet* and *Twelfth Night* were written at almost exactly the same time, although here, in the same fiction, "I say we will have no more marriages" sounds *sotto voce* as the couple embrace.

> ... given a few
> Incomplete objects and a nice warm day
> What a lot a little music can do![7]

What is shadow in *A Room with a View* is substance in *The Longest Journey*, a novel that has been oddly condescended to even by those who claim to admire it. The fullest reading and the one most in touch with its imaginative density is Stone's in *The Cave and the Mountain*. But his elaborate analysis is made to support the conclusion that "on the whole the book does not succeed; it tries to do too many things at once and struggles vainly, as Rickie does, to achieve an identity."[8] This conclusion is far from arbitrary; it arises out of the central premise of the entire discussion, that Forster was "doing what he did not fully understand he was doing." It is the sort of position that serves a critic very well since it allows him to reinvent the true book and explicate it to its minutest detail. And since it contains one obvious partial truth—the unconscious busily informing and just as busily subverting the daylight world of the rational, conscious self—and justifies our sometimes prurient, sometimes merely gossipy interest in the "real" life of the artist, it is often too readily welcomed as modish critical strategy.

Let us assume, however, that Forster knew what he was about, that his imaginative identification with Rickie did not violate the novel's integrity, and that he was aware of the implications of the choices he gave to his hero. Stone, for example, argues that Rickie had no alternative but to marry Agnes; it would have been suicidal not to. In this reading, Rickie becomes a specimen illustration of the mother-enslaved libido who will never grow up if he doesn't love a woman. A further assumption at work here is that Rickie is a flawed hero because of the latent homosexuality that he shares with his creator, leaving him paralyzed and confused about his choices and his author divided between ironic detachment and identification.[9] That Rickie is confused is clear enough and so is his inability to acknowledge his homosexuality, to find that registry office where the marriage of friendship to Ansell could be recorded. But Forster's analysis is complex and all too aware of the disastrous, even tragic, consequences of a blindness to self so readily reinforced by an even blinder society. The "registry office" is not merely metaphor for Forster. It refers to the need to find a context in the real world for such "marriages." The passage that more than any other serves as evidence for the confused author theory is the elaborately orchestrated response to the Gerald/Agnes embrace:

> The river continued unheeding. The phrase was repeated and a listener might know it was a fragment of the Tune of tunes. Nobler instruments accepted it, the clarinet protected, the brass encouraged,

and it rose to the surface to the whisper of violins. In full unison was Love born, flame of the flame, flushing the dark river beneath him and the virgin snows above. His wings were infinite, his youth eternal; the sun was a jewel on his finger as he passed it in benediction over the world. Creation, no longer monotonous, acclaimed him, in widening melody, in brighter radiances. Was Love a column of fire? Was he a torrent of song? Was he greater than either—the touch of man on a woman? It was the merest accident that Rickie had not been disgusted. But this he did not know.[10]

But the scene, comically played out among uneaten sandwiches, Mr. Pembroke's chatter, and preparations for lunch, makes better sense if we assume an undivided author who gave to Rickie a rhapsody purposely calculated to disguise his true response. It is Eros that is born, not Venus. Love is masculine, phallic, a column of fire, but it is necessary for Rickie's lonely and tragic journey that he mistake what he sees, that he fictionalize his feelings and not acknowledge, indeed not even know how to acknowledge, that his physical self has been touched by Gerald, as his emotional self by Ansell.

The surface story of the novel, Rickie's disastrous involvement with marriage and education, death as it turns out instead of life, is set against a series of complex and shifting interior relationships: Rickie/Ansell, Rickie/Stephen, Stephen/Ansell. These pairings and contrasts are not meant to illustrate some abstract notions of England's past and present.[11] As the characters come together, they play out a sexual drama which contains within it an intricate network of concerns. The novel is about the space we make significant—the room in Cambridge, the Wiltshire earth, the dell that is the best church. It wants to weigh and judge the uses of civilization. It is ambitious and serious, but what fuses it all imaginatively is Forster's interest at the very core of the novel in the lines of attraction and repulsion among his three chief characters.[12] Two of them, Rickie and Stephen, are almost a single character in symbolic terms, an identity that is mythically stated as accomplished fact (i.e. they together enact the Oedipus myth: one lame, the other cast out, one brought up amongst shepherds, the other playing out the fantasy of parent and child), and worked out in the novel as process, as becoming, as they move toward and away from each other more as lovers than as brothers.

How to make them intimate—that was Forster's chief difficulty in the novel[13]—an intimacy that was finally to be more symbolic than realized, but which we are asked to value, to believe to be far more real than, say, Rickie's marriage to the non-existent Agnes. What Forster was doing, and, this argument maintains, what he knew he was doing, was working out a complex, homosexual relationship that could not be consummated in the world of fiction or, for Forster, lived openly in the world of fact. The novel chronicles the evasions and disguises, compromises, small respites, even triumphs in this shifting set of relationships but in the interests of a story that has other, more acceptable relationships to describe (and acceptable labels—brother, friend—for the critical ones as well).

In this respect fiction and life are in close touch, where in the manner of Lowes Dickinson the homosexual temperament is more important than the homosexual experience. Or, to phrase the matter more precisely, the experience has to define itself against a tangle of confused, often unacknowledged and contradictory social norms and expectations, and, like any sexual experience, is mixed up with possession, disillusion and lust, while the temperament can be detached, idealized, made absolute. Forster's response in "My Wood," to Shakespeare's sonnet, "The expense of spirit in a waste of shame" (129), is illuminating here:

> Our life on earth is, and ought to be, material and carnal. But we have not yet learned to manage our materialism and carnality properly. They are still entangled with the desire for ownership, where (in the words of Dante) "possession is one with loss."[14]

It is, in fact, just this reading of the 129th sonnet that gives such urgency to the echo of the 116th in *The Longest Journey*:

> friendship—so strong it is and fragile. . . . Nature has no use for us. She has cut her stuff differently . . . a few verses of poetry is all that survives of David and Jonathan . . . He wished there was a society, a kind of friendship office, where the marriage of true minds could be registered. (p. 78)

The primary love relationship is between Rickie and Stephen, however. Ansell provided initiation and functions as a guide, but his role is more symbolic than dramatic. He encloses the book and provides it with its thematic "touchstones" (it is significant, for example, that Ansell instinctively and instantly responds to Stephen, and that they "play," the novel's surrogate form of physical contact). He gives it its conceptual framework, "A man wants to love mankind, a woman wants to love one man," but except for his critical entrance as Greek messenger at the peripeteia, his own life is not directly at stake in the novel's events.

But the lives of both Rickie and Stephen are in constant flux. In a scene whose language explicitly evokes the birth-of-love vision of the Gerald/Agnes embrace, their union is symbolically enacted:

> But they played as boys who continued the nonsense of the railway carriage. The paper caught fire from the match, and spread into a rose flame. "Now gently with me," said Stephen, and they laid it flower-like on the stream. Gravel and tremulous weeds leapt into sight, and then the flower sailed into deep water, and up leapt the two arches of a bridge. "It'll strike!" they cried; "no, it won't; it's chosen the left," and one arch became a fairy tunnel, dropping diamonds. Then it vanished for Rickie; but Stephen, who knelt in the water, declared that it was still afloat, far through the arch, burning as it would burn forever. (p. 309)

It is momentary contact only, destroyed by Rickie's foolish high-mindedness, his trying to possess, to make Stephen his own creation. Rickie is, after all, too timid to be a Greek (he got only a second class in the Classical tripos and Greek archaeology), whereas Stephen is a Greek from his first entrance into the novel, and emphatically consecrated as one by Ansell: "certain figures of the Greeks, to whom we continually return, suggested him a little . . . the conviction grew that he had been back somewhere—back to some table of the Gods" (p. 245).

For Rickie, the flame provides only a glimpse in the darkness of what might have been. Although his ghosts are placated, Mrs. Failing's "facile Ibsenism" seems momentarily to triumph, and, besides, there's no space in the plot and still less in the world it builds upon to bring that burning rose out of its dark tunnel. The dell had been violated (it was the landscape of the dryads, the world of not marrying, and it became, to its desecration, the scene for the decision to wed) and no registry office was found to record the truth and seriousness of friendship. For modern man, romantic love equals eternal ownership and the novel has exploded that supposed consolation without much remorse.[15] In an attempt at the end to be true to the vision of Ansell, Stephen is made to choose marriage impersonally, as something outside of himself. Thus, the final images of fertility are purely mythic—Stephen's house is now the shrine of the Demeter of Cnidus—and the primary relationships of the novel remain intact.[16]

What happened, then, when Forster allowed himself the luxury of writing the novel hidden beneath the surface of his other fiction? What occurred when Philip, Cecil, Rickie merge in the figure of Maurice in the novel that *The Longest Journey* could have become had Rickie moved upward to self acceptance rather than downward to disintegration? Unfortunately, Maurice's shorter journey occurs in a novel that lacks interior life, that lacks sub-surface in direct proportion as it lacks a containing fiction. The chronicle form of the novel is not a congenial mode for Forster whose habitual method does not allow for the continuous exploring of personality. Typically he sets and resets characters in a criss cross of relationships of persons, places and symbolic figures so that only aspects of characters are ever available at any one instance.[17] His usual structure is circular or spherical; movement is to or away from an enclosed interior space. In *Maurice*, however, the structure is paratactic, and although the boat house is symbolically such a dell-room-cave, it is only incidental and accidental in the design. In *Maurice*, he attempted to keep the whole character in constant focus. There is total illumination for the reader, although for the hero the process is more gradual. Our privileged view, however, is something given us gratuitously by the author who is lecturing through the novel rather than meditating in the shadows within.[18]

Rickie comes to exist as a result of a complicated structure of human relationships, Maurice only through one. In that sense the novel around Maurice is weightless, and, since the main action of the novel depends upon the conflict between self and society, the result is oddly unbalanced. There are no entanglements. The characters do not weigh on each other. There are marvellous moments, but too little density, no unknown.

To attack the ending, however, is absurd. In terms of the novel's premises, assumptions and formal strategies, the ending is absolutely consonant. Fantasy is fulfilled in the Green Wood of England. The Eustace of "Story of a Panic" has grown up, Gennaro is no longer half comic and half pathetic. There is no panic, only the sure notes of the pan pipes, celebrating a love that will not hide in evasions, nor book passage across the world, nor seek transformation to a world of mere vegetation. Why must there be tragedy? Why not the enacting on the most personal of levels of that fine doctrine of love?

But while one acknowledges this, it still seems evident that whatever the personal toll, and it must have been enormous, Forster's art needed the terrible tension that containing the homosexual imagination produced. The undertow is powerful; it propels Cocoa's body northward against the current. It moves the real lovers together, while on board, in propriety and decorum, romance and ownership maintain their sway.

Notes

1. Neville Braybrooke, ed., *The Ackerley Letters* (NY: Harcourt Brace, 1975), p. xxv.

2. Alan Wilde, "Desire and Consciousness: The 'Anironic' Forster," *Novel*, X (Winter 1976), p. 124. Wilde sees the essential contrast to be between "the 'stable' self" of the early novels and "the empty, static self of the sexual stories." This argument is an elaboration of his earlier article, "Depths and Surfaces: Dimensions of Fosterian Irony," *English Literature in Transition*, XVII:4 (1973), 257–74, where the position of attack ("bad art," the "devaluation of value," "evasion," etc.) is even more sharply maintained.

3. *The Life to Come*, ed by O. Stallybrass (Lond: Edward Arnold, 1972), p. 25.

4. Quoted by Stallybrass, p. xiv.

5. In a detailed and wide ranging article, written before the publication of *Maurice* and *The Life to Come*, " 'Vacant Heart and Hand and Eye': The Homosexual Theme in *A Room With a View*," *English Literature in Transition*, XIII:3 (1970), 181–92, Jeffrey Meyers argues that "Beebe's latent homosexuality has been released and he has fallen in love with George, and this will determine and explain his behavior throughout the rest of the novel" (p. 184). I think this is an essentially accurate statement (although too flat for the curves of Beebe's characterization), but I don't see this as a flaw in the novel. For Meyers concludes that there is a "negative strain in Forster's works . . . that undermines his power and effectiveness as a novelist and accounts for the spinster'sh and effete quality that sometimes obtrudes in his fiction" (p. 186). "Spinsterish" and "effete" are hardly literary designations. My argument, moreover, derives Forster's effectiveness, in part, from just this "strain."

6. "A View Without A Room," *Observer*, 27 July 1958, p. 15.

7. W. H. Auden, "The Sea and the Mirror," *The Collected Poetry* (NY: Random House, 1945), p. 360.

8. W. Stone, *The Cave and the Mountain* (Stanford: Stanford UP, 1966), p. 184.

9. This point of view is shared by a number of critics, notably John Harvey, "Imagination and Moral Theme in E. M. Forster's *The Longest Journey*," *Essays in Criticism*, VI (Oct 1956), 418–33 and Alan Wilde, *Art and Order* (NY: New York UP, 1964). Even the highly sympathetic recent reading of John Colmer, *E. M. Forster: The Personal Voice* (Lond: Routledge Kegan Paul, 1975) concludes that the disguising of homosexual love causes a flawed novel. Even reading with the aid of *Maurice*, Colmer argues, "does little to clarify the confusion of themes and symbols in the novel" (p. 83).

10. *The Longest Journey* (Norfolk, Conn: New Directions, nd), p. 52. All future citations from this edition will be made in the text.

11. For such an emphasis, see, in particular Stephen Spender, *Love-Hate Relations: A Study of Anglo-American Sensibilities* (Lond: Hamish Hamilton, 1974), pp. 173–76 and Elizabeth Bowen, "A Passage to E. M. Forster," in *Aspects of E. M. Forster*, ed O. Stallybrass (Lond: Edward Arnold, 1969), P. U.

12. In "Aspect of a Novel," *Bookseller*, (10 Sept 1960), 1228–30, the form in which Forster first published his introduction to the Oxford edition of 1960, he summarizes the novel as Ansell's and Stephen's failed attempt to save Rickie from Agnes. He also describes a scene omitted from the final version in which the Rickie/Stephen relationship has much more physical reality than it possesses finally.

13. "I had trouble with the junction of Rickie and Stephen. How to make them intimate." E. M. Forster, quoted by Furbank and Haskell in their *Paris Review* interview (1953), reprinted in *Writers at Work*, ed by Malcolm Cowley (NY: Viking P, 1959), p. 28.

14. "My Wood," *Abinger Harvest* (NY: Harcourt Brace, 1936), p. 25.

15. "But romantic love is also the code of modern morals, and for this reason, popular. Eternal union, eternal ownership—these are tempting baits for the average man" (*The Longest Journey*, p. 308).

16. In a recent study of marrriage plots, "Hierogamy versus Wedlock: Marriage Plots and their Relationship to Genres of Prose Fiction," *PMLA*, XCI (1976), 900–13, Evelyn Hinz makes the subsequent marriages of Stephen and Agnes evidence for the comic resolution, ("the novel ends with Agnes and Stephen happily married"), for the implied "good of society." This strikes me as quite lopsided for neither marriage balances the Rickie plot (indeed one is practically unaware of Agnes's marriage except for the mention at the end of "Mrs. Keynes"). Although Rickie certainly fails, the novel remains true to its central vision and does not measure his failure by society's norms: "The cries still call from the mountain, and granted a man has responded to them, it is better to respond with the candor of a Greek" (p. 302).

17. See Martin Price's discussion of Forster's handling of character in "People of the Book," *Critical Inquiry*, I (March 1975), 605–22.

18. Forster himself warns against the writer taking the reader into his confidence in *Aspects of the Novel* (Abinger Edition, Lond: Edward Arnold, 1974), p. 56. "It is dangerous, it generally leads to a drop in the temperature, to intellectual and emotional laxity."

The Flesh Educating the Spirit:
Maurice   Claude Summers*

Maurice is a significant achievement. Forster's most concentrated novel, it is resonant, subtle, sophisticated, and poignant. It dramatizes in deeply-felt human terms the most important recent conclusions of sexologists and psychologists—that homosexuality is a set of feelings, involving the connection and commitment one individual makes with another, and that such feelings predate sexual expression, sometimes by years—while at the same time placing this understanding in the concrete context of Edwardian England.[1] The social setting is important, for *Maurice* also explores the impact of self-awareness on social attitudes, and it is fundamentally a political novel. For Forster, individual growth is always measured in terms of sharpened insight into the nature of convention and repression.

Just as the heterosexual plot of *A Room with a View* articulates the ideology of the early English homosexual rights movement, so *Maurice* also reflects this ideology. Indeed, the later novel mirrors a significant debate within the Uranian movement, a loosely affiliated group of writers, artists, and philosophers dedicated to the goal of securing sympathetic recognition of the homosexual (or Uranian) impulse in a repressive society. The two most important ideologues of the movement were John Addington Symonds and Edward Carpenter. Both disciples of Whitman, they preached the love of comrades in numerous poems, pamphlets, and books. Symonds and Carpenter equally deserve credit as pioneers in sexual reform, but their styles and ideas are quite different, and *Maurice* pivots on the contrast between them. Whereas Symonds tended to be evasive and apologetic, Carpenter was open and visionary. Symonds implied the superiority of homosexuality to heterosexuality, finding the former more spiritual and less bound by material considerations; but Carpenter insisted on the equality of the two emotions, considering neither more nor less spiritual than the other. And while Symonds isolated homosexual love as a private experience and minimized physical passion, Carpenter forthrightly acknowledged the physical and linked homosexual emancipation with feminism, labor reform, and social democracy. For Carpenter, the homosexual experience provided an opportunity to question received ideas and to develop a radical critique of society itself.[2]

As Robert K. Martin has demonstrated, *Maurice* enacts a dialectic between these two main branches of Uranian thought.[3] The novel opposes not heterosexuality and homosexuality, but two versions of homosexuality, one associated with Symonds, the other with Carpenter. This

*Reprinted from chapter six of *E. M. Forster* as abridged by the author (New York: Frederick Ungar Publishing Co., 1983), pp. 141–80, by permission of the author and Frederick Ungar Publishing Company, Inc.

dialectic is reflected in the very structure of the book, which divides
into two parallel sections, the action of each half mirroring the other
with significant differences. The first half (comprising Parts One and
Two) is devoted to the Maurice-Clive relationship. It traces a false
vision of "superior" homosexuality that is platonized and sublimated in
the manner of Symonds. The second half of the novel (encompassing
Parts Three and Four) is devoted to the Maurice-Alec alliance, and it
tracks Maurice's salvation through a Carpenterian homosexuality that
includes physical love and that leads Maurice to reject class barriers and
social conventions. Maurice finally comes to embrace the political consequences of homosexuality and to adopt the radical perspective on
society conferred by the outlaw status of the homosexual in 1913.

Appropriately, the most significant literary influence on Forster's
novel is the work of Victorian England's most famous homosexual outlaw, Oscar Wilde. Sentenced in 1895 to two years' hard labor for homosexual activities and subjected to the cruelest of humiliations, Wilde
became the era's most conspicuous martyr to sexual ignorance and intoler-
ance. His long letter from Reading Gaol, De Profundis, informs Maurice
at every turn.[4] The frequent echoes of De Profundis serve to incorporate
Wilde's work into the very texture of Forster's novel and help establish
Wilde's martyrdom as the historical reality that all considerations of
the social and political consequences of homosexuality must confront.
Wilde's insistence in De Profundis on the transcendent value of self-
realization and on the redemptive potentiality of suffering—its ability
to transform perspective and to deepen character—shapes the development of Forster's hero. Moreover, Wilde's rejection of society and his
expectation of solace in nature help explicate the retreat into the greenwood at the end of Maurice, a conclusion that has troubled many critics.

What is most impressive about Maurice is its superb artistry. Full
appreciation of its subtlety depends on several readings. Indeed, Maurice demands the reader's engagement in a process of interpretation
and reinterpretation. The novel's "double structure," in which the second half (Parts Three and Four) recapitulates the first (Parts One and
Two) with crucial differences, is complemented by an elusive narrative
technique that combines the point of view of the focal character with
frequent though cryptic authorial intrusions. The effect of this sophisticated technique is to force the reader to experience first-hand Maurice's
bewilderment and pain and exhilaration and muddle, thus contributing
to the book's peculiar poignancy. Only later, on rereading the first section in light of the second, is the reader able to place the early events
of the novel in context, thereby correcting his or her original responses;
and only through this process of reinterpretation can the reader detect
irony in the narrator's apparent endorsement of a particular perspective.
Much of the novel's pleasure resides in the subtle exposure of unexpected dimensions and unsuspected ironies.

In the "Terminal Note," Forster writes that in his hero, "I tried to

create a character who was completely unlike myself or what I supposed
myself to be: someone handsome, healthy, bodily attractive, mentally
torpid, not a bad business man and rather a snob. Into this mixture I
dropped an ingredient that puzzles him, wakes him up, torments him
and finally saves him." Like Lucy Honeychurch of *A Room with a View*,
Maurice Hall is a very ordinary person who moves painfully from muddle to clarity, from conventionality to heroism. The journey of Forster's
hero is from ignorance to truth, from dream to reality, from internal obscurity to the "light within," and from comfort to joy. The "vast curve"
of Maurice's life includes a progress to a relationship in which the flesh
educates the spirit and develops "the sluggish heart and the slack mind
against their will."

The dominant imagery in the novel is that of light and darkness,
ascent and descent, sleep and wakefulness. This imagery is crystallized
in the recurrent metaphor of the "Valley of the Shadow of Life," sur-
rounded by the lesser mountains of childhood and the greater ones of
maturity. The metaphor itself—an ironic reversal of the biblical "valley
of the shadow of death" (Ps. 23:4)—may have been suggested by Wilde's
comment in *De Profundis* that "I have hills far steeper to climb, valleys
much darker to pass through" (p. 30). In the "Valley of the Shadow of
Life," Maurice Hall falls asleep, awakens, and finally scales the constrict-
ing mountains to emerge—after periodically slipping back into the abyss
of the obscured "I"—into the full light of self-awareness. The emphasis
throughout the novel on Maurice's torpor probably reflects Carlyle's
description of life on earth as somnambulism, a state that underlines the
difficulty of asking the crucial but unanswerable question, "Who am I;
what is this ME."[5]

At the very center of *Maurice* is this paradoxical insight about the
loneliness of the human condition: the achievement of self-knowledge
depends on communion with another. "To ascend," Forster writes of
his hero, "to stretch a hand up the mountainside until a hand catches it,
was the end for which he had been born." Thus, Maurice's search for
his own identity is necessarily bound up with his need for a friend. This
need is expressed in the two dreams he has at school, which Forster
says, "interpret him." The first dream is of George, the garden boy, "just
a common servant," whose name he whispers as a charm against his fear
of the shadowy reflections in the looking-glass. In the dream, George
runs toward him, naked, bounding over obstacles. Just as the two meet,
Maurice awakens, filled with disappointment. Maurice's attachment to
his playmate is apparent when he bursts into tears, overwhelmed by "a
great mass of sorrow," upon learning that George has left his mother's
employment. Only later, after his encounter with Alec Scudder, whom
he at first also regards as just a common servant, does Maurice realize
"very well what he wanted with the garden boy." And only then is he
able to accept without fear "the land through the looking-glass."

The second dream is one in which "Nothing happened. He scarcely saw a face, scarcely heard a voice say, 'That is your friend,' and then it was over, having filled him with beauty and taught him tenderness." This dream haunts the novel and establishes the ideal against which Maurice's struggles toward fulfillment are measured: "He could die for a friend, he would allow such a friend to die for him; they would make any sacrifice for each other, and count the world nothing, neither death nor distance nor crossness could part them, because 'this is my friend.' " Maurice at first attempts to convince himself that the friend of his dream is Christ, then he thinks that perhaps the friend is a Greek god. He finally accepts the fact that "most probably he was just a man." He gradually comes to regard Clive Durham as the friend "who was more to him than all the world." But the dream achieves fleshly reality only in the person of Alec, whose name appropriately means "Help."[6] The morning after their first night together, Maurice asks the young man, "Did you ever dream you'd a friend, Alec? Nothing else but just 'my friend,' he trying to help you and you him. . . . Someone to last your whole life and you his." He finally recognizes Alec as "the longed-for dream."

Forster's vision in *Maurice* is a humanist one in which "man has been created to feel pain and loneliness without help from heaven." As in Arnold's "Dover Beach," the world of the novel is a land of dreams in which human love offers the only help for pain. This view of human isolation gives urgency to Maurice's plight and depth to his search for a communion of body and soul. The relationship with Clive, the development of which is one of the major achievements of the novel, is a necessary but preliminary step in Maurice's growth. Maurice responds to Clive's sincere intellect and superior knowledge. Soon Maurice's heart is lit with a fire "never to be quenched again, and one thing in him at last was real." The young men's debates about religion constitute a courting ritual. Maurice's pose as a theologian is simply a ploy to engage his friend's interest. He has no answer when Clive attacks his "tenth-hand" opinions, questioning whether it isn't improbable that genuine belief could be imparted by parents and guardians. "If there is [a belief for which you would die] won't it be part of your own flesh and spirit?" Clive asks, echoing Wilde's remark that belief "must be nothing external to me. Its symbols must be of my own creating. . . . If I may not find its secret within myself, I shall never find it: if I have not got it already, it will never come to me" (pp. 32–33). These debates also provide the first concrete evidence of how Maurice's homosexuality can shape the curve of his life, saving him from a hollow existence fed on catch-words like that of his father, who "was becoming a pillar of Church and Society when he died." Forster adds: "other things being alike Maurice would have stiffened too."

Although Maurice loses the debates, "he thought that his Faith was a pawn well lost; for in capturing it Durham had exposed his heart." When the two embrace after their return to Cambridge from the long vacation, Clive declares his love, assuming that Maurice has understood the implications of the *Symposium*, which he had asked his friend to read. Maurice's shocked response—"a rotten notion really"—causes Clive to sever his links with the young man, suggesting in an icy note "that it would be a public convenience if they behaved as if nothing had happened." This break forces Maurice into a frenzy of self-examination: "It worked inwards, till it touched the root whence body and soul both spring, the 'I' that he had been trained to obscure, and, realized at last, doubled its power and grew super-human. . . . New worlds broke loose in him at this, and he saw from the vastness of the ruin what ecstasy he had lost, what a communion."

The pain of Clive's rejection and the introspection it provokes lead Maurice to an important step toward maturity. He determines not to "deceive himself so much." He accepts the fact that "He loved men and always had loved them. He longed to embrace them and mingle his being with theirs." He rejects the judgments of the world and determines no longer to be fed upon lies. He haunts the bridge leading to Clive's quarters; and one night, "savage, reckless, drenched with the rain, he saw in the first glimmer of dawn the window of Durham's room, and his heart leapt alive and shook him to pieces." Just as he springs into the room, he hears Clive call his name. Part One of the novel thus ends with Maurice's achievement of manhood and of communion.

Part Two of the book begins with the new dawn of the communion between Clive and Maurice and ends with the darkness of Clive's repudiation of their relationship. For two years the young Uranians enjoy "as much happiness as men under that star can expect." Their relationship is modeled on Clive's interpretation of the *Symposium*: "The love that Socrates bore Phaedo now lay within his reach, love passionate but temperate, such as only finer natures can understand." The elitism of Clive's assumptions here—and when he tells Maurice "I feel to you as Pippa to her fiancé, only far more nobly, far more deeply . . . a particular harmony of soul that I don't think women have ever guessed"—reflects his snobbishness and misogyny and the apologia of Symonds. The relationship is one in which Clive "educated Maurice, or rather his spirit educated Maurice's spirit." It is doomed to failure, as Forster hints early in the book when he describes the bridge leading to Clive's room as "not a real bridge: it only spanned a slight depression in the ground." Maurice's ascent from the Valley of the Shadow of Life requires a helping hand extended from greater heights than Clive has achieved. The Maurice-Clive relationship is limited, for it is based on distrust of the body and on a bookish—hence false—hellenism.

Clive's distrust of the body and contempt for his sexuality are deeply rooted in his subconscious. They result from his having internalized the Christian prohibitions that he outwardly rejects, and they are reflected as well in his extreme reaction to Maurice's understandable shock at his declaration of love. Clive requests his friend not to mention his "criminal morbidity" to anyone and tells him, "It is a lasting grief to have insulted you." For all his vaunted hellenism, Clive's emotional life has been shaped by his early Christian conviction that homosexuality is an abomination. Even on the apparently idyllic expedition into the Cambridgeshire countryside, Clive's distrust of the body is manifest. His refusal to undress in order to swim in the dyke is analogous to Mr. Beebe's failure to participate fully in the homoerotic bathing scene in *A Room with a View* and similarly signifies self-repression. In contrast, Maurice disrobes, shouting "I must bathe properly." As Robert Martin has noted, this scene in its entirety is wryly ironic, concealing a note of warning beneath its surface of ecstatic prose. The lovers' reliance on a machine—like the Wilcoxes in *Howards End*, "They became a cloud of dust, a stench, and a roar to the world"—signals an "opposition between nature and the products of an industrial society,"[7] and establishes an important point of contrast between Maurice's false communion with Clive and his real one with Alec, who is consistently linked with nature and the natural.

Clive's self-imposed repression is equally apparent when he flushes crimson at Maurice's adulation on his first visit to Penge. "I think you're beautiful," Maurice tells him in the Blue Room, the color of which symbolizes the spiritual and cerebral nature of Clive's love.[8] "I love your voice and everything to do with you, down to your clothes or the room you are sitting in. I adore you." Clive responds tepidly, "Those things must be said once, or we should never know they were in each other's hearts," but insists that their love, "though including the body, should not gratify it." This arrangement initially satisfies Maurice, largely as a result of Clive's "hypnotic" power over him. But Maurice later comes to regret that he had never fully possessed Clive even in their hour of passion and to reject his friend's doctrine that the "less you had the more it was supposed to be."

The conflicting attitudes of the young men toward their sexuality are cast into bold relief by their reactions to the moment they spend in bed together on the eve of Clive's departure for Greece. Clive has already begun to develop heterosexual attractions and to regard his homosexual attachment as something dirty and shameful. As an antidote to these feelings, he asks Maurice if he may join him in bed. The encounter proves unsatisfactory to each, but for tellingly opposed reasons: "They lay side by side without touching. Presently Clive said, 'It's no better here. I shall go.' Maurice was not sorry, for he could not get to sleep either, though for a different reason, and he was afraid Clive might hear the drumming of his heart, and guess what it was." Maurice is sexually excited by the closeness of his lover and fears that Clive may disapprove; in contrast, Clive is confirmed in his disgust at the notion of physical contact with his friend.

The limitations of the Maurice-Clive relationship are also evident in its failure to provoke a searching analysis of their society and their roles in it. The young men are aware of the hypocrisy around them, yet they fail to question the fundamental assumptions of their society. Both are misogynistic and utterly conformist save for their Wednesdays and weekends spent together. Although Clive professes to believe that fertility is not the goal of love—"For love to end where it begins is far more beautiful, and Nature knows it"—he does not challenge his family's expectations that he will dutifully beget an heir for Penge. And although he thinks of himself as "a bit of an outlaw," he acquiesces in the assumption that he will succeed his late father as a Member of Parliament. The young men placidly step into the niches that England has prepared for them, Clive as country squire and Maurice as "suburban tyrant" and successful stockbroker. "Society received them, as she receives thousands like them," Forster writes, adding: "Behind Society slumbered the Law. They had their last year at Cambridge together, they travelled in Italy. Then the prison house closed. . . . Clive was working for the bar, Maurice harnessed to an office."

This concept of society as a prison house probably reflects Wilde's comment in the letter to Robert Ross quoted in the preface to *De Profundis,* "I know that on the day of my release I shall be merely passing from one prison into another" (pp. vi–vii), as well as Wordsworth's idea in the "Intimations" ode that "Shades of the prison-house begin to close / Upon the growing boy" (ll. 67–68). Forster's adaptation of these views in the novel both exposes the shallowness of the Clive-Maurice relationship and anticipates the result of the social analysis occasioned by the Alec-Maurice liaison. That analysis will lead Maurice to reject the life of respectability for a life of freedom, to sacrifice a spurious safety for the struggle that "twists sentimentality and lust together into love."

Even Clive's hellenism is conventional, distorting ancient ideals as thoroughly as does Maurice's Greek Oration at Sunnington. Just as the Oration wrenches Greek ideals toward exercise and bodily health in order to glorify the contemporary obsession with war, so Clive distorts the Greek ideal of moderation into abstinence in order to justify his conventional distaste for sexuality, a distaste rooted in Christian rather than classical thought. Although Clive condemns the Dean's suppression of references to Greek homosexuality on the grounds of "pure scholarship," his own classicism is equally partial. The "harmony of soul" that he proposes is purchased at the expense of the physical and the ecstatic, and it causes him to ignore the Dionysian spirit latent in Maurice. This potential is suggested by the consuming "frenzy" Maurice experiences when he first falls in love with Clive. As Forster comments then, "A slow nature such as Maurice's appears insensitive, for it needs time even to feel. . . . Given time, it can know and impart ecstasy." The potential for Dionysian ecstasy is implicit as well in Maurice's "good head" for liquor and in his fur-clad appearance "like an immense animal."

Precisely because Clive's hellenism is artificial and disproportionate, it finds no sustenance in the Greek ruins that the young man visits in a "childish and violent" attempt to preserve his attraction toward Maurice. One of the novel's most revealing ironies is that Clive's tenuous classicism is so utterly routed by the faint stirrings of his incipient and unwilled heterosexuality. The elaborate intellectual edifice he constructs to justify his homosexual tendencies crumbles at the onset of his growing physical attraction toward the opposite sex. Clive defines himself exclusively in terms of his soul and denies his body, yet his change is a result of the body's "inscrutable" will, a "blind alteration of the life spirit" that resists rational explanation. Clive's conversion to heterosexuality vividly illustrates the power of the physical, even in someone who has struggled so long to repress it, "not realizing that the body is deeper than the soul." Clive is exposed as shallow and hypocritical by the eagerness with which he embraces the "beautiful conventions" that earn social approval and by the cruelty with which he denies the reality of Maurice's love for him in the pivotal confrontation scene that ends Part Two. This scene marks the termination of the long day of spiritual communion between Clive and Maurice and announces the dawn of "the full human day" that Clive believes the love of women promises him.

This promise, however, is belied by the evidence of the confrontation scene itself, which in a series of subtle contrasts reveals the insipidity of Clive's heterosexuality, while simultaneously implying the potential of Maurice's sexuality for stimulus and growth. Structurally, this scene is parallel to the encounter between Clive and Maurice that concludes the novel. Both confrontation scenes are set at night and in darkness. At the end of Part Two, however, Clive's way is lit by street lamps, while at the end of Part Four, Maurice's walk is guided by evening primroses; and the scene in Part Two takes place indoors, whereas the novel's final scene is out of doors. These differences signify the limitations of Clive's triumph here—its connection with the artificial and the societal. They also help explicate Maurice's fuller triumph at the end of the book when he departs into "the darkness where he can be free."

Throughout the bleak final scene of Part Two, Forster exposes the shallowness of Clive's passion and foreshadows the depth of Maurice's future commitment to Alec. For instance, as Clive awaits his friend's arrival, he appreciates the Hall women for the first time. But significantly he finds them reminiscent "of the evening primroses that starred a deserted alley at Penge," the very place where Maurice will eventually encounter Alec and bid farewell to Clive. Clive is particularly attracted to Ada, whose voice is similar to Maurice's. He regards her as a "compromise between memory and desire," thus establishing a telling contrast with Maurice's earlier hope for a life without compromise and his later choice of such a life. The knowledge that he might arouse Ada's love lights Clive's heart "with temperate fire," thus recalling the fierce fire "never to be quenched again" that love had ignited in Maurice's breast and that will finally be sustained by Alec's matching ardor. Most pointed of all is the contrast between the appearances of the two young men when Maurice arrives, looking "like an immense animal in his fur coat," to find Clive bandaged like an accident victim, having happily "submitted his body to be bound" by the sisters. This contrast of animal vitality and voluntary repression crystallizes the differences between the former lovers and foreshadows their fates. Moreover, the scuffle between Maurice and Clive over the key to the Halls' dining room anticipates Alec's later message to Maurice, "I have the key," a reference to the boathouse at Penge, where the lovers will meet at the end of the novel to begin their lives in the greenwood.

The immediate impact of the confrontation with Clive devastates Maurice. Clive not only affirms the reality of his heterosexuality, for which he cannot be blamed, but, more culpably, he also coldly rejects the legitimacy of his former attachment. "I was never like you," he tells Maurice. To deny one's experience is, in the words of Wilde's *De Profundis*, "to put a lie into the lips of one's life. It is no less than a denial of the soul" (p. 37). Clive's rejection of his past here exposes him as a hypocrite and questions the sincerity of the quality by which he defines himself, his soul. By characterizing romantic love between men as unreal, Clive also attacks the very basis of his friend's identity, for only through his love did Maurice become a "real" person. The love affair terminates with an ugly scuffle and with Maurice sobbing, "What an ending . . . what an ending." The repeated phrase alludes to Wilde's account of his despondency during his first year of imprisonment when he "did nothing else, and can remember doing nothing else, but wring my hands in impotent despair, and say 'What an ending, what an appalling ending!'" (pp. 121–22). Significantly, however, the force of this allusion in *Maurice* is positive. It promises a new perspective; for Wilde—having grown as a result of his suffering—continues, "now I try to say to myself, and sometimes when I am not torturing myself do really and sincerely say, 'What a beginning, what a wonderful beginning!'" (p. 122). This allusion suggests the possibility that, like Wilde, Maurice will also profit from his pain.

On the surface, however, this appalling ending is bleak, leaving the former lovers enveloped in darkness, both literally and metaphorically. Maurice extinguishes the electric light and sits gloomily alone, while Clive goes out into the night, exchanging "the darkness within for that without." But Clive's promised dawn will culminate in a sexual relationship "veiled in night" and in a marriage marked by deception and ignorance; his deep-rooted distaste for "the reproductive and digestive functions" will continue to limit his communion with others. Maurice, on the other hand, will achieve wholeness of being; he will discover "the light within" and embrace the evening's external darkness as a refuge against ignorance and hypocrisy. The false climax at the end of Part Two thus ironically mirrors the triumphant climax of the novel itself. It is actually a new beginning.

Maurice's new beginning is painful indeed: he "returned in a few hours to the abyss where he had wandered as a boy." As a result of

Clive's defection, his life is barren and empty. After abandoning the temptation to suicide, he continues a dreary existence for some time, "proving on how little the soul can exist." Forster poignantly conveys the pain of Maurice's grief, but central to the novel is the meaningfulness of suffering. *Maurice* dramatizes Wilde's contention that suffering is not a mystery but a revelation: "One discerns things one never discerned before. One approaches the whole of history from a different standpoint" (p. 52). Thus, in his loneliness Maurice comes to a firmer understanding of his position in society: "He was an outlaw in disguise." Even in the depths of his despair, he fleetingly entertains the possibility that "among those who took to the greenwood in old time there had been two men like himself."

Maurice's regeneration begins with the stirrings of lust. On the very morning that he learns of Clive's engagement, he is awakened to desire. He glimpses the nude body of Dickie Barry, his young houseguest whom he rouses from a late sleep. He discovers Dickie "with his limbs uncovered. He lay unashamed, embraced and penetrated by the sun. The lips were parted, the down on the upper was touched with gold, the hair broken into countless glories, the body was a delicate amber." This vision of Eros leads Maurice momentarily to abandon himself to joy and then to reproach himself bitterly. Significantly, Maurice faces his predicament with a new frankness: "His feeling for Dickie required a very primitive name. He would have sentimentalized and called it adoration, but the habit of honesty had grown strong." Still, Maurice finds his newly awakened passion deeply troubling, and his resistance to his body's natural responses leads to a vicious assault on a railway passenger whose "disgusting and dishonorable old age" Maurice fears may prophesy his own. This resistance culminates in a desperate hope for punishment and cure. At the same time, however, Maurice's awakening to physical desire represents "the flesh educating the spirit." It promises the ultimate attainment of the "fresh mode of self-realization" that Wilde speaks of in *De Profundis*: "the mode of existence in which soul and body are one and indivisible: in which the outward is expressive of the inward" (pp. 27, 53).

Maurice's internal contradictions are brilliantly juxtaposed on his visit to Penge, where "he seemed a bundle of voices . . . he could almost hear them quarreling inside him." At Penge he both pursues his appointment with the hypnotist and confirms "his spirit in its perversion," as Lasker Jones will later diagnose the result of his "sharing" with Alec. Penge itself functions as a double symbol in the novel, representing the duality within Maurice. As a dilapidated country house, it symbolizes the Philistinism of the English upper middle classes; but, located on the Wiltshire border, Penge is also part of the English countryside, embodying the solace of nature and the natural. Penge thus epitomizes the novel's contrast of the indoors and the outdoors, the values of society and those of nature, the life of respectability and the life of the earth.[9] It is the setting both of the Durhams' snobbery, in which Maurice initially joins, and of Alec's natural responsiveness to life, in which Maurice eventually participates. Its dichotomies may best be represented by Anne, whose maiden name—Woods—signifies a naturalness that her upper middle-class upbringing has stifled through the deliberate inculcation of sexual ignorance. Interestingly, Anne functions as an unconscious agent of connection for Alec and Maurice, being responsible for Alec's employment at Penge and for drawing Maurice's attention to him at a pivotal moment. Presided over by Clive, "whose grievances against society had passed since his marriage," Penge is at once a citadel of oppression and a stimulus to Maurice's growth.

That stimulus is provided most forcefully by Alec, whom Maurice notices as he drives through the park to begin his visit at Penge. Throughout his stay, he is vaguely aware of the undergamekeeper, though in his snobbishness Maurice denies full humanity to the lower classes. Maurice's class consciousness precludes an early union, but that is what each subconsciously desires. On his first two nights at Penge, Maurice gazes from his bedroom into the rainy night longing for a companion, only later to learn that Alec, filled with a similar yearning, had been waiting on the lawn for his call. Maurice first acknowledges Alec's individuality when he temporarily leaves Penge for his appointment in London. He offers Alec a tip and is outraged when the young man refuses it. Although Maurice's fierce reaction may seem petty, based as it is on a misinterpretation of Alec's independence as impertinence, it it actually more liberal than Archie London's condescending attitude that "When servants are rude one should merely ignore it."

As his carriage leaves Penge, Maurice looks out the window at the dog roses that border the lane and suddenly recognizes Alec:

> Blossom after blossom crept past them, draggled by the ungenial year: some had cankered, others would never unfold: here and there beauty triumphed, but desperately, flickering in a world of gloom. Maurice looked into one after another, and though he did not care for flowers the failure irritated him. Scarcely anything was perfect. On one spray every flower was lopsided, the next swarmed with caterpillars or bulged with galls. The indifference of nature! And her incompetence! He leant out of the window to see whether she couldn't bring it off once, and stared straight into the bright brown eyes of a young man.

This recognition shocks Maurice into an awareness of Alec's beauty and anticipates the perfection of their eventual union. As James Malek remarks of the passage, "This initial association of Alec with nature and perfection leaves a lasting impression and colors our response to him throughout the remainder of the novel."[10] Placed immediately before

Maurice's consultation with the hypnotist, the vision of Alec's perfection also renders ironic Lasker Jones's attempt to implant in Maurice's subconscious his own palely conventional aesthetic and erotic responses.

After his interview with the hypnotist, Maurice returns to Penge, convinced that "he wasn't the same; a rearrangement of his being had begun." But he is wrong to credit Lasker Jones with the alteration. The credit belongs to Alec, whom he encounters several times that momentous night in the darkness of the deserted alley starred with evening primroses. The change in Maurice is evident when he returns from a stroll outdoors with his head all yellow with pollen. The evening primrose pollen expresses Maurice's Dionysian potential, a potential implicit in his preoccupations as he strolls through the alley and encounters Alec: "Food and wine had heated him, and he thought with some inconsequence that even old Chapman had sown wild oats. . . . He wasn't Methusaleh—he'd a right to a fling. Oh those jolly scents, those bushes where you could hide, that sky as black as the bushes!" As he goes indoors, expecting to resume his life as "a respectable pillar of society who has never had the chance to misbehave," he bumps into Alec, fittingly a Pan figure.[11]

This encounter sharpens Maurice's mind, making him consciously aware of Alec as an individual, a "fine fellow," who "cleaned a gun, carried a suitcase, baled out a boat, emigrated—did something anyway, while gentlefolk squatted on chairs finding fault with his soul." Maurice attacks the clergyman Mr. Borenius's legalistic religion, telling him, "that may be your idea of religion but it isn't mine and it wasn't Christ's," thus echoing Wilde's assertion that Christ "exposed with utter and relentless scorn" the "tedious formalisms so dear to the middle-class mind" (pp. 110–11). As Maurice goes to bed that night, his brain—wreathed with a "tangle of flowers and fruits"—works more actively than ever. He sees commonplace objects with a new clarity and he redefines darkness as something to be desired: "not the darkness of a house which coops up a man among furniture, but the darkness where he can be free." Conscious of the irony of having paid a hypnotist to imprison him in a "brown cube of such a room," Maurice drifts off to sleep, dimly aware of alternatives. "There was something better in life than this rubbish," he thinks, half-asleep, "if only he could get to it—love—nobility—big spaces where passion clasped peace, spaces no science could reach, but they existed for ever, full of woods some of them, and arched with majestic sky and a friend. . . ." This dream of perfection, of harmony with nature and communion with another, achieves the promise of reality.

Maurice's sleep-walking cry "Come!" is answered by Alec, who scales a ladder into the Russet Room: "someone he scarcely knew moved towards him and knelt beside him and whispered, 'Sir, was you calling out for me? . . . Sir, I know. . . . I know,' and touched him." This consummation, beautiful in its tenderness and simplicity, parallels the communion of Maurice and Clive at the end of Part One. But the sharing of Maurice and Alec in the Russet Room promises the fuller relationship for which both long, a union of body and soul, of the flesh educating the spirit.

Part Four of the novel chronicles the achievement of this promise and the completion of Maurice's journey toward self-realization. Beginning with the bright dawn of a new relationship and ending in the darkness of a confrontation scene, Part Four recapitulates Part Two. But whereas the dawn of Part Two is what Wilde describes as one of the "false dawns before the dawn itself" (p. 116), the new daybreak proves genuine. Similarly, the darkness in which Part Four concludes is the protective cover of the greenwood in which Alec and Maurice discover freedom, not the interior darkness of the earlier climax. And in the confrontation scene that ends the novel, Maurice triumphs unambiguously, having truly earned a new beginning.

Maurice's self-realization is accomplished as the result of a struggle between his real self and the obscured "I" of his social self. When he descends from the scene of communion with Alec "to take his place in society," his suburban gentleman's class consciousness battles with his longing for fulfillment. His life disturbed "to its foundations," Maurice alternates between his conventional distaste for "social inferiors" and his desire for comradeship. As he and Alec play cricket together that morning, Maurice meditates on the possibilities of their union: "They played for the sake of each other and their fragile relationship—if one fell, the other would follow. They intended no harm to the world, but so long as it attacked they must punish, they must stand wary, then hit with full strength, they must show that when two are gathered together majorities shall not triumph." But this reverie of liberation is interrupted by the arrival of Clive, the apostle of class loyalty to whom "intimacy with any social inferior was unthinkable." Suddenly sick with fear and shame, Maurice returns to his home, seeking security rather than joy.

But even as Maurice struggles against his deepest instincts, his flesh continues to educate his spirit. That night his body yearns for Alec's: "He called it lustful, a word easily uttered, and opposed to it his work, his family, his friends, his position in society." But, Forster adds, "his body would not be convinced." In a childish and violent expedient analogous to Clive's trip to Greece, Maurice telephones Lasker Jones for another consultation. This time, however, he is unable to enter a trance. He leaves the hypnotist's office curiously relieved. Walking home, he observes the King and Queen passing through a park. He unthinkingly bares his head in a gesture of respect. Then he suddenly despises these symbols of society, seeing them as victims of the very values that oppress him. This insight gives him a new perspective: "It was as if the barrier that kept him from his fellows had taken another aspect. He was not afraid or ashamed anymore. After all, the forests and the night were on his side, not theirs." This new insight radically alters his previous image of himself wandering "beyond the barrier . . . the wrong words on his lips and the wrong desires in his heart, and his arms full of air."[12]

Maurice's acceptance of himself and his outlaw status here presages his final liberation. He gains new insight into the inequities and limitations of his society. He suggests to his aunt "that servants might be flesh and blood like ourselves." He questions the ethics of his profession, despising his clients' choice of comfort rather than joy, of "shelter everywhere and always, until the existence of earth and sky is forgotten, shelter from poverty and disease and violence and impoliteness; and consequently from joy." He determines himself to seek the "life of the earth" and to accept the struggle that may make possible the attainment of love. He evaluates his own past actions, concluding that he erred grievously in trying "to get the best of both worlds." In a society that criminalizes him and falsifies his experience, he must embrace his outlaw status and be true to himself. Thus, when he receives a threatening letter from Alec, containing many words, "some foul, many stupid, some gracious," he agrees to a meeting. "Both were outcasts," he thinks, "and if it came to a scrap must have it without benefit of society." Maurice's point here reflects Wilde's painfully earned confession from Reading Gaol: "The one disgraceful, unpardonable, and to all time contemptible action of my life was to allow myself to appeal to society for help and protection" (p. 135).

The meeting of Alec and Maurice in the British Museum is one of the novel's most delightful scenes. Maurice quickly realizes that Alec's attempt at blackmail "was a blind—a practical joke almost—and concealed something real, that either desired." The extortion attempt is a reaction against Maurice's mistrust and condescension, a reflection of pain at having been neglected and a sign of interest. As the two men spar, they are interrupted by Mr. Ducie, who as always gets "the facts just wrong" as he tries to remember Maurice's name. When Maurice tells the school master that his name is Scudder, the identification of the young men is complete. As Maurice will shortly realize, "In a way they were one person." Maurice succeeds here in winning Alec's love by approaching him as an equal: "Not as a hero, but as a comrade." He "stood up to the bluster, and found childishness behind it, and behind that something else." By suffering, Maurice has learned to interpret the suffering of others. He has absorbed Wilde's lesson that "behind sorrow there is always a soul" (p. 133).

Forster's account of the lovers' communion in the hotel—the mixture of "tenderness and toughness" in their sharing—beautifully affirms Maurice's success in grasping the lessons that the flesh teaches the spirit. Tellingly, the night of passion in a "casual refuge" that protects them momentarily "from their enemies" is made possible by Alec's insistence that Maurice cancel the formal dinner party "of the sort that brought work to his firm." The cost of the joyful night thus anticipates the price of "the safety in darkness" that the escape to the greenwood will exact. That retreat requires mutual sacrifice, as Alec acknowledges when he protests that Maurice's vaguely formulated plan "Wouldn't work. . . . Ruin of us both, can't you see, you same as myself." But balanced against the loss of the young men's careers, family ties, and respectability is the prospect of being numbered among those few who, according to Wilde, "ever 'possess their souls' before they die" (p. 82). When Alec fails to appear for the departure of the *Normannia*, he surrenders his security and distinguishes himself from "the timorous millions who own stuffy little boxes but never their own souls." The mutual sacrifices of the lovers give the lie to Mr. Borenius's assumption that "love between two men must be ignoble," and their compensation is one familiar in Forster's novels: "They must live outside class, without relations or money; they must work and stick to each other till death. But England belonged to them. That, besides companionship, was their reward."

After Maurice's confrontation with Clive in the deserted alley at Penge, "where evening primroses gleamed, and embossed with faint yellow the walls of night," Maurice and Alec depart for the greenwood. The final chapter recounts Maurice's repudiation of Clive's influence, "the closing of a book that would never be read again." This ending is a necessary preliminary to the self-confessed outlaw's new beginning with Alec. When Maurice disappears into the night, having elected a life "without twilight or compromise," he leaves behind only "a little pile of the petals of the evening primrose, which mourned from the ground like an expiring fire." Symbolic of the fire that Clive's love originally inspired within Maurice's breast, the dying petals signify the death of Maurice's love for Clive and the enormity of Clive's loss in failing to appreciate his friend's potential for Dionysian ecstasy. Ironically, however, though Maurice wrestles free of Clive's influence, the country squire who smugly denied the reality of homosexual love will never escape the memory of his incomplete passion. Maurice will continue to haunt all his days and nights to come, mocking his timidity and rebuking his hypocrisy: "To the end of his life Clive was not sure of the exact moment of departure, and with the approach of old age he grew uncertain whether the moment had yet occurred. The Blue Room would glimmer, ferns undulate. Out of some external Cambridge his friend began beckoning to him, clothed in the sun, and shaking out the scents and sounds of the May term." Clive's fate is aptly summed up in Wilde's description of men who desire to be something separate from themselves, such as a Member of Parliament. Such a person, Wilde writes, "invariably succeeds in being what he wants to be. That is his punishment. Those who want a mask have to wear it" (p. 119).

Maurice and Alec's retreat into the greenwood has frequently been scorned by critics as sentimental and unconvincing. Actually, however, the ending is neither. Alec and Maurice have earned their happiness through suffering and sacrifice; and despite their differences in back-

ground and education, they are well-matched. There is nothing sentimental in the notion of hard-won happiness earned through mutual trust
and support. This happiness is bought at a high price, but their willingness to pay such a toll is what finally enables Maurice and Alec to transcend the artificial barriers that separate them. Still, the ending is flawed.
"The problem," as James Malek explains, "is that Forster succeeds more
completely on the general level than on the particular. There is no doubt
about the value or rightness of the lovers' decision. Nor, on the level
of the particular, do we doubt their ability to follow through, but we
have not been prepared for the specific form it might take, nor is it
easy to imagine since Maurice has talked of it in very general terms."[13]
The vagueness of the lovers' future life together probably reflects a
compromise between Forster's original vision of two men roaming the
greenwood and his post-war realization that "Our greenwood ended cata-
strophically and inevitably," as he remarks in the "Terminal Note." Although the escape into the "big spaces . . . arched with majestic sky and
a friend" is too vaguely formulated and too broadly generalized, it is
nevertheless essential to the novel's vision.

The escape into the greenwood expresses Forster's radical critique
of his society while it also conveys his humanist faith in personal relationships. The ending of *Maurice* is influenced by the conclusion of *De
Profundis*, a moving coda in which Wilde looks to nature for healing
and wholeness: "Society, as we have constituted it, will have no place
for me, has none to offer; but Nature, whose sweet rains fall on unjust
and just alike, will have clefts in the rocks where I may hide, and secret
valleys in whose silence I may weep undisturbed. She will hang the night
with stars so that I may walk abroad in the darkness without stumbling,
and send the wind over my footprints so that none may track me to my
hurt: she will cleanse me in great waters, and with bitter herbs make
me whole" (pp. 150–51). Like Wilde, Forster has no faith in reforming
society. Even in the "Terminal Note" of 1960, Forster remains pessimistic about social reform, remarking that "Since *Maurice* was written there has been a change in the public attitude here: the change from
ignorance and terror to familiarity and contempt." In his novel "Dedicated to a Happier Year," he shows how the "four guardians of society—
the schoolmaster, the doctor, the scientist and the priest" all condemn
the homosexual.[14] Thus, Maurice and Alex must utterly reject society,
whose injustices they perceive as a result of their homosexuality. But
unlike Wilde's, Forster's pessimism is tempered by belief in personal relations. Hence Maurice and Alex together accept England's air and sky
as their birthright, facing the world unafraid, showing that "when two
are gathered together majorities shall not triumph." The escape into
the greenwood thus simultaneously renders a summary judgment against
society and endorses the possibility of the flesh educating the spirit,
even in the midst of repression.

Maurice is a book of haunting beauty, tracing the painful journey of its hero from bewilderment to self-realization. It is preeminently a political novel, for Maurice's education through suffering culminates in a sweeping indictment of his society, an indictment that results directly from his awareness of the political implications of the homosexual experience in a hostile world. At the same time, however, the book transcends the political by affirming the possibility of alleviating the loneliness endemic to the human condition. The communion of flesh and spirit achieved by Alec and Maurice may isolate them from "the congregation of normal men," but it promises help in a universe in which "man has been created to feel pain and loneliness without help from heaven." Forster's most undervalued work, *Maurice* is a worthy addition to the canon of a superb artist.

Notes

1. See Alan P. Bell, Martin S. Weinberg, and Sue Kiefer Hammersmith, *Sexual Preference: Its Development in Men and Women* (Bloomington: Indiana University Press, 1981). On the homosexual milieu of Edwardian England, see Ira Bruce Nadel, "Moments in the Greenwood: *Maurice* in Context," in *E. M. Forster: Centenary Revaluations*, ed. Judith Scherer Herz and Robert K. Martin (Toronto: University of Toronto Press, 1982), pp. 177–90.

2. For an account of the Uranian movement and Symonds's and Carpenter's roles in it, see Brian Reade's introduction to *Sexual Heretics: Male Homosexuality in English Literature from 1850–1900* (London: Routledge & Kegan Paul, 1970). Although he applies the term *Uranian* too narrowly to designate only a group of pederastic poets, see also Timothy d'Arch Smith, *Love in Earnest: Some Notes on the Lives and Writings of English 'Uranian' Poets from 1889 to 1930* (London: Routledge & Kegan Paul, 1970).

3. Robert K. Martin, "Edward Carpenter and the Double Structure of *Maurice*," *Journal of Homosexuality* 8 (Spring/Summer 1983): 35–46.

4. My quotations from *De Profundis* are from the version published in London by Methuen in 1905 and are cited parenthetically by page number. Owing to the Ransome libel action, which was heard in April 1913, Wilde and *De Profundis* were much in the news in the year Forster began work on *Maurice*.

5. Thomas Carlyle, *Sartor Resartus*, ed. Charles Frederick Harrold (New York: Odyssey, 1937), pp. 53–54.

6. See "Alexis" in "A Pronouncing Vocabulary of Common English Given Names," in *Webster's New Collegiate Dictionary* (Springfield, Mass.: Merriam, 1959), p. 1131.

7. Martin, "Edward Carpenter and the Double Structure of *Maurice*," p. 40. See also Kathleen Grant, "*Maurice* as Fantasy," in *E. M. Forster: Centenary Revaluations*, ed. Herz and Martin, p. 200.

8. Forster's use of the Blue Room as the scene of Maurice's exchange with Clive fittingly links their relationship with the apologia of Symonds, whose collection of essays is entitled *In the Key of Blue*. Certainly Forster intends a contrast between the spiritual communion in the Blue Room and the later physical communion in the Russet Room. As Bonnie Blumenthal Finkelstein writes, "Maurice's cool, platonic affair . . . in the Blue Room . . . is finally superseded by a more complete, hot, passionate, and physical affair in the Red" (*Forster's Women: Eternal Differences* [New York: Columbia University Press, 1975], p. 172).

9. On this point, see Norman Page, *E. M. Forster's Posthumous Fiction*, ELS

Monograph Series 10 (Victoria, B.C.: University of Victoria, 1977), pp. 93–94; and Martin, "Edward Carpenter and the Double Structure of *Maurice*," p. 41.

10. James S. Malek, "Tackling Tribal Prejudices: Norms in Forster's Homosexual Fiction," unpublished essay, p. 38.

11. See Alan Wilde, "The Naturalisation of Eden," in *E. M. Forster: A Human Exploration*, ed. G. K. Das and John Beer (New York: New York University Press, 1979), p. 202.

12. This incident may have been inspired by an 1838 letter from Thomas Carlyle to his mother. See *New Letters of Thomas Carlyle*, ed. Alexander Carlyle (London: John Lane, 1904), I, 119.

13. Malek, "Tackling Tribal Prejudices," p. 38. On the flawed ending of *Maurice*, see also Stephen Adams, *The Homosexual as Hero in Contemporary Fiction* (New York: Barnes & Noble, 1980), pp. 116–19.

14. Glen Cavaliero, *A Reading of E. M. Forster* (London: Macmillan, 1979), p. 137.

The Major Novels

Howards End: The Sacred Center John Edward Hardy[*]

Howards End is a novel of integrity. No other term will serve at once to indicate its structural unity and to define its theme—thus to suggest the peculiar interdependence of structure and theme that is realized, or achieved, here as in few works of modern fiction.

First, the novel is in a very obvious way concerned with the problems of personal integrity. This is one of the many rather old-fashioned aspects of E. M. Forster's thought: he does not take the view of the human person suggested by the other, currently more acceptable, derivatively technical term, "integration"—as in "integration of personality," "social integration." He does not regard the person as simply the product of his experiences. The persons to be encountered in this book are not so much personalities, in the usual modern sense of the word, as they are, precisely, characters. They are conceived as beings whose actions are something which not only can be accounted for, but for which they are accountable. The quest for the wisdom of self-knowledge—Margaret Schlegel's development is the most instructive example—is emphatically a quest for responsibility. The person is defined, defines himself, in and by his responsibilities.

And this conception of character, this notion of integrity, what we mean when we say that a person is or is not a man *of* character, or that he *has* character or hasn't, is also the source of Forster's emphasis, so unusual in the novel of the twentieth century, on plot. There is a thoroughly modern, a rich and complex system of symbolic motif in the book. But this has a secondary, supporting function. The essential order is the order of action, intelligible as consequence of human intention—and, where it turns on coincidence, as in the embarrassing reappearance of Jacky at Evie's wedding, suggesting only, further, that intention need not be always conscious and specific, that the limits of man's

[*]Excerpted from chapter two of *Man in the Modern Novel* (Seattle: Univ. of Washington Press, 1964), pp. 34–39, 43, 46–51, by permission of the author and the University of Washington Press.

foreknowledge do not excuse him from the responsibility of moral fore-
sight. The coincidences of this novel are quaintly conspicuous, perhaps
because it is one in which the action is not, as in most modern fiction,
all coincidence.

But it is not so easy to define the active principle of the integrity.
The motto "Only connect . . . ," its provocative incompleteness, clearly
indicates the problematical character of the work. Connect what, we
are to ask, with what? And how? The novel pictures a civilization in
which everything is disconnected—past from present, country from city,
culture from economic reality, morality from manners, institutions from
human need, purpose from technique, reason from impulse, the unseen
from the seen, masculine from feminine, man from nature, man from
man. How, if at all, are the rifts to be healed? Lionel Trilling wants to
refer everything to the "class war" and the battle of the sexes.[1] But
these concepts are hardly comprehensive, although both are, in a
sense, central. With due allowance for the ironic fact, which Mr. Trilling notes, but fails to make very much of, that all the major characters
really belong to different ranks of the middle class, the concept of class
struggle will serve well enough to define the conflict between the Wilcoxes and Leonard Bast. But that is finally to be resolved by the com-
bined influences of the Schlegel sisters' personalism and the nature
mysticism which is embodied (or, perhaps it would be more accurate
to say, disembodied) in the first Mrs. Wilcox. Nor will it do simply to
interpret Margaret's humbling of Henry Wilcox as the triumph of the
feminine over the masculine. No formula of this kind, socioeconomic
or sociopsychological, will cover the whole range of issues raised by the
novel.

With sly casualness—"One may as well begin with Helen's letters
to her sister"—Forster goes to work at once on the theme of disconnection. There are the letters, communications which do not communicate,
that in their very style, however charmingly self-ironic the air of distrac-
tion, discover Helen's own despair of getting through, even before we
see their effect on Margaret and Mrs. Munt. The correspondence, then,
is abruptly terminated in the "anti-letter" of the telegram—which be-
latedly confesses at once the folly both of love and of writing. Both,
we get the impression, love and letters, are simply out of date; in the
age of "telegrams and anger," it is no good trying to cultivate those
antique arts. There is Margaret's and Aunt Juley's talk of the "engagement" of Helen and Paul. The word is richly and variously ironic in the
situation. Not only are these two not engaged in any specific and formal
sense—Margaret, against her better judgment, allows herself to be
carried along by Aunt Juley's meddling excitement—and are not going
to be; but by the time Mrs. Munt appears on the scene at Howards End,
if not before, it is fairly apparent that the only kind of engagement

likely to occur between the two families, the two worlds, of Schlegel and Wilcox, is a battle engagement, not a betrothal.

Now, of course, at the same time that he is showing us the conditions of conflict, Forster is carefully planting hints as to the nature and means of possible resolution. The opening sentence of Helen's first letter —"It isn't going to be what we expected"—applies not only to Howards End, the house and place, but to the whole situation of the novel. It is fair warning against any kind of oversimplification. Even at first glance it is apparent, for example, that Mrs. Wilcox may be an unpredictable element, that in her case the so easily reversible attitudes of the volatile Helen toward "Wilcoxes" in general are probably irrelevant. And on a second reading, when we have seen the promised engagement and marriage after all fulfilled, the Wilcox and Schlegel worlds after all joined, although not in the persons of Paul and Helen but of Henry and Margaret, we will detect how this was foreshadowed in the opening pages. The surprise development was really inevitable. It is through Mrs. Wilcox's mysterious agency that Henry and Margaret are brought together, as in a sense it was also by her that Paul and Helen were separated. And the final episode of the novel, with the cutting of the hayfield and Mr. Wilcox's revelation concerning the destroyed will of his first wife, returns us smoothly to the characterization of her in Helen's first letter. There, her chief distinguishing feature is her immunity from the hayfever that afflicts all the other members of the family.

But the dominant impression in the first four chapters, to be redeemed but slowly and with frequent reversals thereafter, is one of disorder and division, of a profound uncertainty of motives and values which can only be overcome by the Schlegels as well as by the Wilcoxes, after this first skirmish, by retreating from the issues of conflict, behind hastily re-erected and already patently inadequate barriers of moralistic formulae. The Wilcoxes have their strident slogans of "soundness" and "progress." But hardly less spurious, hardly less a slogan, if not so pompously asserted, is the central article of the Schlegels' faith—that belief in the supremacy of "personal relations" to which they return with all the greater fervor after the brief period of doubt created by the first "Wilcox episode." "I know that personal relations are the real life, for ever and ever," says Helen upon her return to Wickham Place; and "Amen!" echoes Margaret; and the overtones of self-mockery do not conceal the pietism of the avowal.

On the far horizon is the threat of international conflict. The time of the novel's main action is one in which old Ernst Schlegel's hope for a re-emergence in Germany of the "mild intellectual light" of pre-Bismarckian idealism, about which we are told at the end of Chapter IV in the sketch of the sisters' childhood, has been long since abandoned. The stereotypes of national character are hardening, the rival, imperialistic chauvinisms of Germany and Great Britain—the book appeared only four years before the beginning of World War I—more and more loudly, intransigently defining themselves. Closer to the center is the opposition of the families, the Schlegel and Wilcox worlds of idea and attitude—a conflict whose theme extends itself into the area of the German-English opposition on the one hand, and, on the other, with the introduction of Leonard Bast, into that of the "class war." Still deeper are the frictions between the sisters, between Henry Wilcox and his son, between Mrs. Wilcox and her husband and children, which are discovered and exacerbated in the trials of the two families' encounters. And, finally, at dead center, the source of all the rest it is suggested, is the disturbance within the individuals, the sickening uncertainty or ambiguity of purpose, pull of the idea against the passion—in short, the disunity of the self.

When they set out on their successive projects, as they might be called—to "connect" first with the Wilcoxes, then, briefly failing that, with Leonard Bast, and finally to connect the connections, bring Wilcoxes and Basts together—what the Schlegel sisters are really seeking is self-justification. Suspended, so to speak, as they are, above or beyond common life and common loyalties, with their mixed German and English heritage, the two elements of which tend simply to neutralize each other, economically classless, a species of charming drones who live effortlessly on the income from obscurely defined, for the most part "foreign" investments, they are in a sense compelled to seek perfection of the inner life, the life of private sensibility. There is, literally, nothing else for them to do. But they are beset by anxieties about the isolation to which they are thus condemned.

The question is not whether the inner life is worth sustaining—they are never in any doubt on that point—but whether it can be entirely self-nourishing. They suspect, from the rather compelling evidence of Tibby's case, that the life of pure self-containment is not very easily distinguishable from one of simple self-indulgence. Again, the insistent repetition of the word "engagement" in the opening chapters suggests the theme. Helen may quickly have to abandon, as an obvious absurdity, the idea of becoming engaged to Paul, but both she and Margaret very definitely retain the need to be *engagé*. In other words (they are in more ways than one comparable to Ursula and Gudrun Brangwen at the beginning of Lawrence's *Women in Love*), they suspect that the person, the truest, inner person, is somehow able to know or discover himself only in his relations with other persons, in the discovery of other inner lives.

"Personal relations, for ever and ever." But the trouble is that they find very few others, if any, who are either willing or able to enter into such relations—i.e., which according to the implicit definition of the terms are truly relations, and at the same time truly personal. And when it appears, thus, as with the Wilcoxes, that one's concept of "person" must exclude a considerable number of "people," exclude them from all possibility of the establishment of personal relationships, then the reiteration of the formula begins to take on a note of desperation. It risks becoming, as we have observed, mere slogan—as impersonal, despite the words, as any other slogan. Schlegels risk becoming as insincere, as self-deceptive, as Wilcoxes. . . .

Since Trilling's book on Forster, critics have generally recognized in Howards End, the house, a symbol of England itself, and in Margaret's coming into possession of it, thwarting after all the efforts of Charles Wilcox and his father to set aside the will of Ruth, a symbol of hope for England's future—for a future, that is, informed by the past, preserving tradition. It should also be apparent that Margaret's having the place is the reward of her willingness to give it up, her indifference to it merely as possession, as property, expressed when she throws the keys to the house on the ground before Henry. The clear implication is that true possession is of the spirit, that the "house" will survive so long, and only so long, as the pattern of integrity in personal relations among the inhabitants is maintained. The implication is that so long as this is done it will not matter if the building itself is obliterated by the tide of suburban development which Helen, in the final chapter, sees creeping inexorably toward them from London. But, does it matter?

K. W. Gransden has noted the significance of Ruth Wilcox's answer to Margaret's comment that a house "cannot stand by bricks and mortar alone."[2] The first Mrs. Wilcox replies, "It cannot stand without them." There is, in fact, a persistent note of misgiving on Forster's part about this. It is more than nostalgia. The opening description of the house at Howards End begins the statement of a large and complex architectural metaphor which is extended throughout the novel. Buildings, and the design of them, the architectural character of a civilization, would seem to be in Forster's mind fundamentally related to its character of manners and morals. The question would seem to be raised whether, when an effective sense of this relationship is lost—when it really no longer shall matter that a city should "rise and fall in a continual flux," waves of building replacing one another as indifferently as the undulations of the sea—we shall not also have lost the essence of civilization. . . .

But, again then, where is the hope? For the book does have, essentially and finally, the look of comedy. The answer, I think, is to be found in re-examination of the proposition we had seemed obliged to abandon —i.e., that the house as such, the building, stands for something beyond itself; it is the house spiritual, not the house physical, that can and must be preserved.

What it stands for, to put the matter as succinctly as possible, is the value of the extrapersonal. The novel, it has been observed, is a novel much about death. Gransden has pointed out the importance of the Wilcoxes' fear of death. (The episode of the little girl and her cat, of

Charles's flight from the scene, rather farcically dramatizes the theme which is more seriously elaborated elsewhere.) They are embarrassed and baffled by death, they flee it, try to hustle it out of sight. The whole anxiety of their kind to keep things moving, to keep the shape of the civilization constantly changing, can be interpreted just as this frenzy of flight from the intolerable fact of death. They strive, as it were, to bury death itself, under the life-appearance of change. But, it is implied, of course there is no possibly adequate understanding of life to be built upon a denial of death, no real acceptance of life without acceptance of death. And the continuing service of Ruth Wilcox to her husband after death, somewhat to redeem him from Wilcoxism, the effect of her refusal to "stay buried"—leaving the note that wills the house to Margaret, reincarnating herself as it were in the second wife, who with her bouquet of weeds is spookily mistaken for Ruth by old Miss Avery—is, in the final paradox, to keep Henry reminded that she *is* dead. Her presence, mysteriously identified with the house itself, survives to remind Henry, and Margaret and Helen too, that life continues and must be pursued beyond concern for any particular form, embodiment, of it; that there are values in life beyond the claim of, beyond our sympathy for, our responsibility to, any individual person; in brief, that the ultimate life values, as I have said, are extrapersonal.

This implicit, extrapersonalist doctrine is certainly not to be identified with the progressivist "realism" of Wilcox. That, and the moral blindness, blindness to self, which it engenders, stand unequivocally condemned in Margaret's climactic speech to Henry on his inability to see the connection between his own sin with Jacky and Helen's with Leonard—between his responsibilities to Margaret and hers to her sister. Henry, as "Wilcox," must be and is broken. ("... to break him was [Margaret's] only hope.") But neither, then, is the extrapersonalism something which results, or is to be derived, from the marriage of Schlegelism to Wilcoxism—even from a marriage in which the former properly asserts its superior position. To see this, as many critics have done, as the essential "connection" proposed by the novel is the worst possible oversimplification. Here is the ultimate significance of the fact that the marriage of Margaret and Henry is in itself a sterile union. The final hope lies in something that transcends both the Wilcox progressivism and the Schlegel personalism, and also any compromise between these two opposed sets of values—anything like that mere "formula, both rational and patriotic, which should preserve the best qualities of each kind of outlook and condemn the worst," that Gransden sees Forster "trying to work out" in the novel.[3]

The implication has been rather embarrassing to a number of readers, who want to see the novel as purely a novel of manners and of social morality, but there is no blinking the fact that what we are witnessing in the last chapter is a fertility ritual. The mower is "encompassing with narrowing circles the sacred centre of the field" as the chapter opens; at the end, Helen, with baby on arm, rushes into the house to hurrah the harvest—"'The field's cut!' [she] cried excitedly.... 'we've seen to the very end, and it'll be such a crop of hay as never.'" Nothing could be plainer. "Circles," a "sacred centre," baby, bumper crop. The transcendent extrapersonalist principle to which Forster makes his final appeal is, purely and simply, the fertility principle.

There is no other way, than by taking very seriously the symbolism of her wisp of hay, to account for the mysterious power that Ruth Wilcox—herself so significantly devoid of personality, so nearly inarticulate, unintellectual, to the embarrassment of the Schlegel sisters' clever London friends—exercises over the lives of the others. It is the same power that redeems the merely impersonal fanaticism of Helen in her affair with Leonard Bast. Thereby, she had as we have seen violated both him and herself; but the rape produces a child, and in the end this is to make all the difference, to reconcile all three parties, Schlegel, Wilcox, and Bast, as they could not have been by any other means. His fatherhood redeems also the absurdity of Leonard himself. The merely satiric comedy of his murder—at the hands of a Wilcox wielding a Schlegel sword, the case of books, which had been his undoing in life, toppling over on him as he clutches at them in death—is raised, in the sequel, to high comedy. The son of farming people, Forster is careful to have told us, reduced to anonymity by the competitions of urban life, Leonard Bast unwittingly "comes home" at last to Howards End, and leaves his heir to repossess the land.

It is essential to the dignity of the proceedings, however, that Leonard should die not knowing that he was to have become a father. For in the end, as embodiment of the extrapersonal values, the baby must be presented as no one's in particular—not Leonard's, not even, exclusively, Helen's. He is referred to, repeatedly, just as "baby." Helen does not want him, as she admonishes Tom, "cut into two or more pieces" by the mower. But this only ironically points up the theme of sharing, of the common, ritual participation that involves the whole group in the final scene at the farm. The baby, sent out with Tom to play in the hayfield, belongs like Howards End itself to everybody.

The fertility principle transcends even the particular, sexual shortcomings of the characters. Lionel Trilling complains that the ending of the novel is not an "entirely happy" one—"this rather contrived scene of busyness and content in the hayfield; the male is too thoroughly gelded, and of the two women, Helen confesses that she cannot love a man, Margaret that she cannot love a child."[4] But, aside from the implicit, mere inaccuracy of the reference to Helen's "confession"—she does not say that she cannot love *a* man, in the sense of *any* man, but only that she finds herself forgetting Leonard—the criticism, it seems to me, fails to accommodate Forster's own obvious awareness of the incongruities in the situation. The triumphant, feminist liberalism of the Schlegels, for all the moral insight it yields, is openly acknowledged to be a sterile force in society. Especially as it is embodied in Margaret—with her meager figure, her face "all teeth and eyes," as Leonard Bast sees her during their first conversation—it is man-destroying, sex-destroying. Insofar as it is dedicated simply to "breaking" Wilcox, it can promise, ultimately, only its own extinction. It is pretty precisely Forster's point, I think, that the Schlegels have come very close to self-extinction. They have to be rescued by something beyond their rational view of themselves and their responsibilities, even beyond the power, still so dryly fastidious, of their moral intuition.

To come back once more to the question of Forster's attitude toward the house itself—how important is it that the place should, in physical fact, survive? The answer is implicit in this emphasis, in the final chapter, on what is going on in the field rather than in the house. It is a relatively simple answer. The house is worth keeping intact, so long as it can be kept. Houses last, can and should be made to last, longer than individual human lives, longer even than families. That is their unquestionable value, to the defeat of Wilcox notions of property rights. But it would be worst folly to suppose that "as long as can be" is forever. (There is fair warning, at the very outset, of what happens when one attempts to deny altogether the fact of decay and change; it is what has happened to the cathedral at Speyer—"ruined, absolutely ruined, by restoration; not an inch left of the original structure," the thing destroyed by the very effort to preserve it. There is a telling appropriateness in the fact that the sisters should have met the Wilcoxes on this expedition. For the progressive conservatism of English Wilcox, at least with respect to the destruction of buildings if not otherwise, comes in the end to exactly the same thing as the work of the German restorers.) Howards End is the house; but it is also the wych elm, and the meadow. The house endures. But there is one thing still longer enduring—namely, the land itself. And it is there, in the field, that the drama of human survival finds its valid and final, "sacred centre."

I am not sure that it is altogether a convincing answer. *Cold Comfort Farm* may well, and maybe rightly, have prevented by now our taking this sort of thing—anti-intellectual antics of jaded intellectualism, Bloomsbury gone a-haying—with ultimate seriousness. Certainly, there are distressing lapses of psychological probability that perhaps account for the embarrassing effect of the conclusion and are not to be explained away by such an argument as I have brought against Trilling's complaint. The crucial sexual encounters, which prepare the way for the ritual of fertility, are put rather awkwardly offstage. Forster knows very well how to handle the rich comedy of Henry's courtship of Margaret. But the old affair with Jacky, absolutely essential to the moral argument of the book, is a rather unlikely contrivance. A man like Henry could, no doubt, have gone casually if guiltily to bed with such a woman, once or twice. But Forster unmistakably insists on its having been something more than this. And, if it is difficult to imagine these two repeating the act very often, it is all but impossible to think of Helen and Leonard at it even once. Again, they have to, for Forster's purposes; one understands that. But, as created personalities, persons, in the fumbling flesh, one must critically wonder how they could manage it.

But, entirely convincing, entirely satisfactory or not, I insist it is a clear answer. This novel, although not his most ambitious—that, obviously and rather painfully, is *A Passage to India*—is Forster's most careful performance. Anything that it fails to provide must simply be asked of another author.

Notes

1. Lionel Trilling, *E. M. Forster* (Norfolk, Conn.: New Directions Books, 1943).
2. K. W. Gransden, *E. M. Forster* (Edinburgh: Oliver and Boyd, 1962).
3. Ibid., p. 55.
4. Trilling, *E. M. Forster*, p. 135.

Howards End: Fiction as History   Peter Widdowson

Despite the discernment and subtlety, the irony, the antipompous and sceptical tentativeness of *Howards End's* style and manner, there is a resolute controlling mechanism which makes the novel "prove" Forster's conception; the material is cut and sewn to the approved design.[1] Paradoxically, Forster was well aware of the problems of the over-patterned novel, and although he is criticising Henry James in terms of aesthetic, rather than moral, control, his comments in *Aspects of the Novel* suggest something of his own tendency:

> It is this question of the rigid pattern . . . Can it be combined with the immense richness of material which life provides? Wells and James would agree it cannot. Wells would go on to say that life should be given the preference, and must not be whittled or distended for a pattern's sake. My own prejudices are with Wells. . . . That then is the disadvantage of a rigid pattern. It may externalise the atmosphere, spring naturally from the plot, but it shuts the doors on life, and leaves the novelist doing exercises, generally in the drawing room. (*AN*.164–5)

*Excerpted from chapter five of *E. M. Forster's Howards End: Fiction as History*, Text and Context Series (Published for Sussex Univ. Press by Chatto and Windus, 1977), pp. 94–99, 106–13, and reprinted by permission of the author and the Scottish Academic Press Limited.

If Forster's prejudices were with Wells' ostensible openness to life, his practice was equally close to the didactic realism of Wells' fiction. But Forster might have added that pattern does not just exclude life, but can actually falsify the "life" it is treating.

Howards End, however, is a complex work, and there remains a major complication: the novel is, of course, by no means unequivocally a "fable" or a "romance." As critics from Virginia Woolf onwards have noticed,[2] the novel is a mixture. The problems develop when the expectations of a realistic novel are aroused, and in *Howards End* they certainly are. The conversational opening of the novel: "One may as well begin with Helen's letters to her sister" (5), with the letters appended, immediately suggests a novel aiming at verisimilitude. Forster continues throughout to be specific about time and place. The references to Tariff Reform, Imperialism, female emancipation, the NEAC, Augustus John, suburban spread and so on, quite clearly establish the scene as Edwardian England between about 1908 and 1910. Equally carefully established—if sometimes not very knowledgeably—are the social matrices of the various characters: their heredity, class, attitudes, work, houses, etc. The Basts' "background," for example, is attempted in considerable detail, and the treatment of their flat reads more like Arnold Bennett or H. G. Wells than "romance":

> The sitting-room contained, besides the arm-chair, two other chairs, a piano, a three-legged table, and a cosy corner. Of the walls, one was occupied by the window, the other by a draped mantleshelf bristling with Cupids. Opposite the window was the door and beside the door a bookcase, while over the piano there extended one of the masterpieces of Maud Goodman. (46)

Great care is taken, also, with the characterisation and the dialogue. The former is, admittedly, done largely through the narrative voice, but then this, rather than the dramatic mode, has been the norm for most of the realist tradition. It is particularly strong in the cases of the Wilcoxes and the Schlegels, and when Forster does present a dramatic "scene," the dialogue is generally handled in a masterly way and is entirely convincing both in the comic and the serious vein. Margaret's luncheon party for Mrs. Wilcox (Chapter IX) is a good example of the former, and Henry's "confession" to Margaret about his affair with Jacky Bast, of the latter:

> "Did Helen come?" she asked.
> He shook his head.
> "But that won't do at all, at all! We don't want her gossiping with Mrs. Bast."
> "Good God! no!" he exclaimed, suddenly natural. Then he caught himself up. "Let them gossip. My game's up, though I thank you for your unselfishness—little as my thanks are worth." . . .
> "It is not good," said Henry. "Those things leak out; you can-

not stop a story once it has started. I have known cases of other men—
I despised them once, I thought that *I'm* different, *I* shall never be
tempted. Oh, Margaret—" He came and sat down near by, improvis-
ing emotion. She could not bear to listen to him. "We fellows all come
to grief once in our time. Will you believe that? There are moments
when the strongest man—'Let him who standeth, take heed lest he
fall.' That's true, isn't it? If you knew all, you would excuse me. I was
far from good influences—far even from England. I was very, very
lonely, and longed for a woman's voice. That's enough. I have told
you too much already for you to forgive me now." (229)

What Forster is so good at doing in scenes of this sort, is making a
"thematic" concern take on the *timbre* of an actual conversation: the
revelation here, in the tones and postures of Henry's speech, of what
Helen has earlier identified as the "panic and emptiness" at the heart
of "Wilcoxism," is brilliantly achieved. But even when the characterisation is weak—as in the case of the Basts—it is rather because Forster
does not *know* about them, than because he is not *trying* to make them
"convincing." The very amount of effort he clearly puts into describing
them suggests this.

Finally, one further aspect of the "realistic" texture of large sections of *Howards End* is the wry wisdom of the authorial comment.
Except in certain ways, which I will explain in a moment, this is both
common to the realistic tradition and, in Lionel Trilling's apt word about
Forster's wisdom, indelibly "worldly."[3] For example:

> The two men were gradually assuming the manner of the committee-
> room. They were both at their best when serving on committees. They
> did not make the mistake of handling human affairs in the bulk, but
> disposed of them item by item, sharply. . . . It is the best—perhaps the
> only—way of dodging emotion. They were the average human article,
> and had they considered the note as a whole it would have driven
> them miserable or mad. Considered item by item, the emotional con-
> tent was minimised, and all went forward smoothly. (93)

Such passages are the result of observation and reflection, the quality
which makes Forster's essays so continuously stimulating. They imply
the "realism" he admires in Margaret Schlegel: "a profound vivacity,
a continual and sincere response to all that she encountered in her
path through life" (11). It is precisely this complex and ironic perception of life which opposes the more rhetorical or vision-controlled passages, so that despite their common theme, each calls into question the
other's validity.

There would be little excuse in labouring what is perhaps an obvious point about Forster's realism, were it not that several aspects of
the novel run counter to it and that the novel as a whole implicitly rejects it in favour of "vision." The "precarious synthesis" that David
Lodge mentions, of realism, romance and allegory . . . , is upset by For-

ster's conflicting needs.[4] On the one hand, he wishes to propagate a vision—which he partially recognises to be exclusive and insecure—and for which he needs myth, pattern, symbolism: "contrived" or "fabulous" modes. On the other hand, he must try and convince us of the "reality" of the vision: one can scarcely hope to make "England" credible if one ignores England. And for this he needs all the paraphernalia of realism, since the danger of plain fable, because of its manifest artificiality, is the option it grants the reader simply to disregard its "moral." But because the vision itself is partial, the realistic bolstering of it never really becomes credible; it is too closely tied to the symbolic and mythic elements and is too regulated and selective. Forster's eye is first and foremost on the "vision," and the "realism" exists, therefore, in terms of that. The mixed mode of *Howards End* is never quite synthesis. As Virginia Woolf remarked: "Elaboration, skill, wisdom, penetration, beauty— they are all there, but they lack fusion; they lack cohesion; the book as a whole lacks force. His gifts in their variety and number tend to trip each other up." (*CEI*.348). Those critics who have attempted to justify Forster's "romance" or "visionary" apparatus, in this novel at least, as appropriate to his didactic purposes, fail to recognise that the partial realism involves not just questions about literary coherence or "decorum," but also questions about the validity of the "vision" itself. A vision or a fable has to be absolute, totalising and assured; tiny fragments of doubt, or chinks through which an alternative world can be perceived, are likely to smash its all-embracing completeness. It must exist totally within the artificial but absolute walls of its convention. Forster's liberal vision is, almost by its nature, tentative and uncertain; "realism" creeps in, the certainty of the world of the fable is questioned, and the realistic elements in the novel set up a clamour for more *proof*, more application of vision to world. The walls have been breached and when such fissures appear an affirmation has to be made in symbolic or mythical terms. This uncertainty is significantly less evident in the earlier novels where the social satire is firmly contained within the terms of the moral vision—Life against non-Life. But in *Howards End*, where the vision is to comprehend a social reality—England—the strains begin to show. The correlation between liberal dilemma and fictional form is most apparent here; just as the insistent realities of the real world undermine the liberal position so that it must begin to doubt itself, so the realistic elements in the novel call in question the self-sufficiency of the fable, and thus the validity of the vision.

Were this paradox—vision juxtaposed with reality—the novel's intended subject, consciously realised and explored in the characters and the action, then the novel would be less questionable, less synthetic, less "finished." There would be no need for the "positive" ending which reveals intensive structuring on behalf of the controlling idea. But the paradox is not a "subject" *within Howards End*; the *whole novel* is constructed to confirm the uncertain absolute of the vision. From the beginning, it is geared to proving the *idea*, and prove it it does. The novel attempts, to borrow Margaret's thoughts quoted at the beginning of this chapter ["Looking back on the past six months, Margaret realized the chaotic nature of our daily life, and its difference from the orderly sequence that has been fabricated by historians" (*HE*.101).], to reflect "the chaotic nature of our daily life," but it is finally bound by the "orderly sequence" of Forster's vision and its narrative formulation. In the search for harmony, for "connection," narrative and stylistic contrivance is used to justify them against other, more realistic, elements that the novel's world itself contains.

It is to these "contrivances" that we must now turn. There are two features in particular I wish to consider which help to create the fictive "completeness" of *Howards End*—the plot and the narrative voice; and a third in passing, the use of symbolism. In the first case, it is what may be called the controlled contingency of the plot which is most obviously used to make certain that the right things happen and that the vision is given substance. . . . The search for completion and harmony demands contingency; and Leonard's death and Charles' imprisonment successfully resolve problems which have been created by more sensitive and realistic perceptions in other parts of the novel. Forster had attempted to establish solidly the types of which the Wilcoxes and the Basts are examples. With the Wilcoxes he was particularly successful but (like the reality they represent) they became increasingly difficult to accomodate in the vision. The key line in the passage above is: "She did not see that to break him was her only hope."[5] The only way to pull Henry (his important economic resources and the house) into "connection," and so realise the vision, was to "break" him, to make him a shuffling, enfeebled, old man. One way of achieving this (for it is Forster's problem as much as Margaret's) is to send Charles to gaol on a manslaughter charge. It is necessary for the victory of the vision, and thus it is necessary in the plot. Henry's obtuseness, which blocks Margaret's attempts to expand his spirit and "connect," is exorcised by the final smash. What sort of victory this constitutes for the vision's values, it is hard to say. Henry's spirit is not expanded, as Margaret earlier hoped . . . it is merely broken. And it is broken, we must realise, by *the logic of the Wilcoxes' own attitudes*, not by the efficacy of Margaret's: Charles *must* attempt to sort out the family crisis in his tough, masculine way; he *must* horsewhip Leonard; and, having contributed to his death, "the law, *being made in his image*, sentenced him to three years' imprisonment." Margaret's liberal-humanism, except in a circumstantial way, has nothing to do with "breaking" Henry; and Charles, the most consistent, recalcitrant and virulent "Wilcox," is, like Leonard, simply removed, *hors de combat*. The vision goes its own way, but it is *given* certain essential free passes, with the result that neither the Basts nor the Wilcoxes are really included in "Liberal England." Forster is almost recognising this when he allows Margaret to say, looking back over "the black abyss of the past": "They had crossed it, always excepting Leonard and Charles" (313). And when she finally possesses Howards End, she muses: "There was something uncanny in her triumph. She, who had never expected to conquer anyone, had charged straight through these Wilcoxes and broken up their lives" (318). "Uncanny" indeed and Forster himself obliquely supplies the explanation in his remarks on "endings" in *Aspects of the Novel*: "there is this disastrous standstill while logic takes over the command from flesh and blood. . . . No wonder that nothing is heard but hammering and screwing. . . . The novelist has to labour personally, in order that the job may be done to time" (102–3). What remains at the end of *Howards End* as a result of the personal labour of the novelist, the hammering and screwing, is the situation—achieved but unrealised—which is necessary for the success of the original "vision": an emasculated Mr. Wilcox, a motherly Helen, a Margaret approaching the numinous spirituality of Ruth Wilcox, and "the child," unformed, unknown to the reader, to be taken on trust as the ultimate and rightful "heir" of England. All we know is that he does not, significantly, suffer from hay-fever.

My last remark introduces a second aspect of Forster's "fictional" technique, his symbolism. I do not intend to describe the significance of the separate symbols themselves in any detail—much of that is explicit in the description of *Howards End's* pattern and theme discussed above; I merely wish to indicate the way in which Forster *uses* symbolism. Symbolism can act as an intensification of objective situations, as verbal signs of an already existing state of affairs; Dickens and Shakespeare tend to use it in this way. It can also be archetypal, either anthropological or literary. In both of these cases, it is referential to more or less objective and commonly accessible phenomena. However, it can also be a private language, given internal currency by reiteration and context, but with a largely personal infrastructure. This sort of symbolism helps to *create* pattern, to point up significances and to express areas of experience which seem to evade prosaic statement. It also gives a kind of "public," "objective," status to essentially private and individual perceptions. It is here, of course, that the potential dangers lie: objects and actions can be given significance that they do not necessarily have, or they may be the products of a dream, imprecise and arbitrary but imbued with an aura of definition and certainty. This, I believe, is what Forster effects in *Howards End*, by his use of houses, hay, and hay-fever, the wych-elm, country and city, and so on, and indeed by the entire symbolic action of the book. George H. Thomson[6] has argued that Forster does not borrow existing myths and symbols, as the modernists do, to impose order on flux; rather that he creates his *own* highly charged mythology and symbolism. But the argument is incomplete: Forster, we may agree, *does* create a personal symbolism but he uses *that* to impose pattern and order on his material. The question is: What is the significance of such symbols? Howards End is a house; why should it

be "England," except that Forster requires it to be so? And why does
he require it to be so? Because it evokes a highly subjective vision of
what he would like England to be: "it was English, and the wych-elm
that she saw from the window was an English tree" (192). "London,"
in the same terms, clearly fails to be "English." So many of the symbols
in the book are, in effect, personal beliefs given an "objective" significance but beyond the terms of the "vision," they help to define nothing.
Hay, for example, is an iterative symbol in the book, but it merely distinguishes those of the Mrs. Wilcox camp (the "inner-life" characters)
from those who are not—the other Wilcoxes and Tibby, all of whom suffer from hay-fever. It has no inherent significance, and its resonance
is nil; it merely becomes schematic short-hand. We know, at the end,
that Helen's son does not suffer from hay-fever, which means that he
is one of "the right sort"; but what his merciful freedom from hay-fever
tells us about the future of England, it is more difficult to say.

In his essay, "Ibsen the Romantic" (1928), Forster suggests that the
power of Ibsen's symbolism springs from the fact that "it is in the exact
place which its surroundings require" (AH.84), and that "a connection
is found between objects that lead different types of existence; they
reinforce one another and each lives more intensely than before" (83).
Forster's own symbolism is both more artificial and less resonant than
Ibsen's. Interestingly enough, it is with Ibsen that Virginia Woolf com-
pares Forster when she is discussing his symbolism, ("In this combination of realism and mysticism his closest affinity is, perhaps, with Ibsen"),
but she suggests that where in Ibsen's work the sudden symbolic
radiance of the ordinary object hits us with absolute certainty, in Forster's "we are puzzled, worried. What does this mean? we ask ourselves.
What ought we to understand by this? And the hesitation is fatal. For
we doubt both things—the real and symbolical" (CEI.346–7). Virginia
Woolf suggests, wrongly I think, that it is because he is too much the
realist. Rather, it seems to me, it is because the "vision" demands a
kind of expression which realism cannot accommodate. Nevertheless, she
is absolutely right to point out the mutually damaging effect of the
mixed modes of the book.

My overall point, however, is that the vision, at its most equivocal,
requires just such an indefinite and insubstantial symbolism to find expression. Forster's remark . . . about the "tragedy" of life being "that
no device has been found by which these private decencies can be trans-
mitted to public affairs," is revealed in its literary form by his own
practice here. Private values are given public application by the use of
symbolism, and this is nowhere better revealed than in the whole action
of the novel which, as we have seen, is itself symbolic. The process of
"connection" and inheritance which is the basic movement of the book
is perfectly acceptable at the individual and personal level, but it is intended to contain much wider public significance and to be about the
fate of England. It is at this level that the system of "connections" breaks

down. Private solutions are not inevitably public solutions, as Forster was well aware: "But in public who shall express the unseen adequately?" he asks in *Howards End.* (77) He might have answered that novelists, with their "illusion of permanence" for Love at the end of their books (*AN*.62–3), attempt it, and especially if they employ an affirmatory symbolism like his own in *Howards End.* The problem is that the gap between the symbolic expression of his vision and the situation to which it is supposed to refer is too great, even for fictional "transmission."

One further example of Forster's private symbolism will lead us to the last major feature of the fictional embodiment of the vision. It is Helen Schlegel who uses the phrase "panic and emptiness" to describe the inner life of the Wilcoxes, and it is Helen who is supposed to programmatise Beethoven's Fifth Symphony in Chapter V. "Panic and emptiness" and "the goblin footfall" are, however, used as motifs in the novel as a whole. It is as though the novelist has borrowed the private musings of one of his characters, and turned them into an objective symbolism. But it raises a larger point than this: the identity of the narrative voice itself in *Howards End.* Helen clearly "thinks" the interpretation of the symphony. The passage is encapsulated by references to her, and in the middle Forster's stage-direction: "Her brother raised his finger" (33) confirms that Helen is still the registering consciousness. And yet the recurrent use of phrases from it in other parts of the novel, *outside* Helen's consciousness, together with the last sentence of the passage: "and that is why one can trust Beethoven when he says other things," which is clearly the narrative, and not the dramatic voice, implies that it is Forster speaking too. Now if there is an unclear distinction between dramatic and narrative voices, then the overall tone of a book becomes personalised. Leavis noted the tendency in Forster's style many years ago: "Mr. Forster's style is personal in the sense that it keeps us very much aware of the personality of the writer, so that even where actions, events and the experiences of characters are supposed to be speaking for themselves the turn of phrase and tone of voice bring the presenter and commentator into the foreground."[7] The problem here is that if characters like Helen and Margaret, who are supposed to be living their lives autonomously, are no more than cyphers in the pervasive subjectivity of the novel, then the ostensibly objective support they should give to the visionary idea is again diminished. They are intended, after all, to make the vision "real," but if they are indistinguishable from the narrative voice and the controlling vision, they are *only* real within its own terms, and the self-fulfilling tendency we have noticed before again obtrudes. Like Hardy's characters, as Forster saw them, they are too controlled by the demands of the vision to develop into free individuals who would confirm the reflections of the narrative voice. George Eliot, in her novels, is the wise woman who steps in to comment but her role is clearly defined and separate—an intelligent interpreter of the scene she surveys. Jane Austen holds the ironic veil firmly between herself and the characters she purports to identify with. But in Forster's case, subject and object, action and commentary are blurred, so that everything in the novel seems to be controlled by the novelist's own ideas.

This is especially so in the case of Margaret, who is certainly nearest to representing Forster although she is presented as an autonomous character who is supposed to develop in the course of the book. There is, of course, immediately a problem of verisimilitude here: how can a character who "grows" throughout a novel, be at the same time a consistently reliable mouthpiece? In a sense, there is no problem: Forster and Margaret are so close, that the latter's "growth" is merely a confirmation of the vision and even when she is "judged" by the author (as, for example, over the "trap" for Helen) it is entirely within the code of values to which she herself adheres. Time and again there is an ambiguity as to which "voice" is speaking. For example, when Margaret takes Mrs. Wilcox Christmas shopping, we have the following piece of reflection:

> How many of these vacillating shoppers and tired shop assistants realized that it was a divine event that drew them together? She realized it though, standing outside in the matter. She was not a Christian in the accepted sense; she did not believe that God had ever worked among us as a young artisan. These people, or most of them, believed it, and if pressed, would affirm it in words. But the visible signs of their belief were Regent Street or Drury Lane, a little mud displaced, a little money spent, a little food cooked, eaten, and forgotten. Inadequate. But in public who shall express the unseen adequately? It is private life that holds out the mirror to infinity; personal intercourse, and that alone, that ever hints at a personality beyond our daily vision. (77)

Initially, Forster enters Margaret's mind and offers her reflections on the Christmas scene but by the end of the passage the tone is clearly that of the narrator. This movement effectively turns the private responses of an individual character in a particular situation into statements which purport to be general truths. In this case, London and the Christmas shoppers ("these people") are implicitly judged as being without "private life," not, finally, by Margaret, but by Forster himself. The London which is supposedly being strained through Margaret's consciousness is treated by the author as though it were the objective reality, and because his consciousness is almost identical to hers, London appears as it has to appear for the personal values of the vision to be confirmed.

This is the constant tendency of the novel: a vision affirmed by Art. The life that Forster might observe would scarcely support his vision of "England"; but before the Great War, for a man of Forster's persuasion, there was still the possibility of believing in Liberal England victorious. For Forster, as for Margaret, (again their voices blend) Howards End and its wych-elm were potent evidence of the truth and viability of the vision: "Their message was not of eternity, but of hope on this side of the grave" (192). The fact that for public expression "their message" required fictional manipulation is only further evidence of how complex an historical construct *Howards End* is.

At the very end of the novel, occurs the following well-known passage:

> "There are moments when I feel Howards End peculiarly our own."
>
> "All the same, London's creeping."
>
> She pointed over the meadow—over eight or nine meadows, but at the end of them was a red rust.
>
> "You see that in Surrey and even Hampshire now," she continued. "I can see it from the Purbeck Downs. And London is only part of something else, I'm afraid. Life's going to be melted down, all over the world."
>
> Margaret knew that her sister spoke truly. Howards End, Oniton, the Purbeck Downs, the Oderberge, were all survivals, and the melting-pot was being prepared for them. Logically, they had no right to be alive. One's hope was in the weakness of logic. Were they possibly the earth beating time?
>
> Because a thing is going strong now, it need not go strong for ever," she said. "This craze for motion has only set in during the last hundred years. It may be followed by a civilization that won't be a movement, because it will rest on the earth. All the signs are against it now, but I can't help hoping, and very early in the morning in the garden I feel that our house is the future as well as the past." (316)

In a sense, this passage contains the essence of the whole novel: the conscious ambivalence of Forster's recognition of imminent breakdown and, at the same time, the affirmation of the vision ("the earth beating time"), despite that recognition. But it also acts as a commentary on the mode of the novel as a whole: Margaret's "hope" in "the weakness of logic" is reflected in the "weakness of logic" in the fabric of the book. And that, in its turn, is symptom and sign of the weakness of logic in the vision. Paradoxically, the structural weaknesses are the result of the intense control exercised by Forster, and by the very completeness of the "connections." Time and again, to achieve them, Forster has to fall back on "illogical" fictional devices which claim exemption from the laws of probability while their medium purports to be the phenomenal world of Edwardian England. But Forster, before the war made his Georgian utopianism totally untenable, could attempt to effect a solution which diminished the reality of his world while still employing techniques which cause that world to be inescapably intrusive. There is a constant tension, therefore, between the sketchy, under-realised, but potent "reality," and the fictional attempts to realise the "vision." And this results from the tension between an admission that "it is impossible to see modern life steadily and see it whole" (152), and the affirmation that "in these English farms, if anywhere, one might see life steadily and see it whole" (250). The former represents the realistic perception, the latter the contrived resolution. As the liberal-humanist world-view lost potency, so did the cosmography of the realistic novel seem to become redundant. For Forster, in the pre-war days of Liberal England, it could not substantiate the visionary dream; for later writers, in the post-war world, it could not express a seemingly unreal reality. The emphasis is, of course, very different, but the implication is the same: traditional realism was the expression of an assured and self-confident liberal-humanist world-view. The primary ambivalence of *Howards End* is its uncertainty of form. It is this tension which confirms its "historical" significance, symptomatic as the novel is of the "liberal crisis"—ideological and literary.

Notes

1. Page references to the following works appear in brackets in the text, with the abbreviated title where necessary. E. M. Forster, *Abinger Harvest*, 1936 (Edward Arnold "Pocket Edition," 1946), referred to as *AN*; *Howards End*, 1910 (Penguin Books, 1961), referred to as *HE*. Virginia Woolf, "The Novels of E. M. Forster" in *Collected Essays*, Volume One (The Hogarth Press, 1966), referred to as *CE.I.* Ed. note.

2. Other critics who have been concerned with the duality of mode in Forster's work are: F. R. Leavis, *The Common Pursuit*, Chatto and Windus, 1952; Lionel Trilling, *E. M. Forster*, Hogarth Press, 1944; J. B. Beer, *The Achievement of E. M. Forster*, Chatto and Windus, 1962; C. B. Cox, *The Free Spirit*, Oxford University Press, 1963; Alan Wilde, *Art and Order: A Study of E. M. Forster*, New York, 1964; Frederick C. Crews, *E. M. Forster: The Perils of Humanism*, Princeton, 1962; George H. Thomson, *The Fiction of E. M. Forster*, Wayne State University Press, 1967. The problem with several of these works is that they are "positive" readings, and attempt to explain away, or justify by special pleading, the tensions in Forster's work. Wilde's essay on *Howards End*, Cox's, and the end of Crews', however, tend to support my reading of it.

3. Lionel Trilling, *E. M. Forster*, Hogarth Press, 1944, p. 22.

4. See David Lodge, *The Novelist at the Crossroads and Other Essays...*, Routledge, 1971. Ed. note.

5. The reference is to a passage quoted by Widdowson from page 311 of the novel. Ed. note.

6. In *The Fiction of E. M. Forster*, Wayne State University Press, 1967. The whole of this book is such special pleading that it tends, unfairly, to confirm one's sense of Forster's aesthetic and ideological uncertainties.

7. F. R. Leavis, *The Common Pursuit*, 1952, p. 275.

"A Universe . . . not . . . Comprehensible to Our Minds": *A Passage to India*

Frederick P. W. McDowell*

THE "DOUBLE VISION" AND THE TENTATIVE HINDU SYNTHESIS

A Passage to India is important for its social and political implications and for its revelations of Forster's luminous intelligence. Nevertheless, the book's appeal is primarily aesthetic, symbolic, and philosophic. Forster's creative imagination, as it illuminated the elemental aspects of humanity, results in this novel's richness. Forster saw his book as metaphysical rather than social in impact since he "tried to indicate the human predicament in a universe which is not, so far, comprehensible to our minds."[1] The book exists chiefly as a vibrant aesthetic entity which comments implicitly upon issues that are universal in their significance. In its approach to the transcendent *A Passage to India* reaches romance and prophecy, but it does so without sacrifice of social verisimilitude.

The "double vision," which bridges the extremities of existence, expresses Forster's main preoccupation in *A Passage to India*. He conjoined opposites as he had done earlier; but in *A Passage to India* the mediation is more an ongoing process for which only tentative resolutions exist. The exertions of the individual's will are important; so is the quality of the individual's mind and sensibility. For the superficial individual, guided only by his intellect, the possibility of attaining unity will not occur, or it will seem unimportant. Only an individual with developed powers of intuition can grasp the polarities of experience and see them in their true relationships.

When such polarities are continually present to the consciousness, truth is paradoxical. So throughout the book Forster stresses the complex qualities of ultimate reality and of God, and his attitude toward nature and the primitive is also complicated. He communicates the ambivalence of the Marabar Caves and the Gokul Ashtami festival; and he conveys, too, the elusive quality of Godbole, the individual who most often expresses a convoluted view of reality or dramatizes it in his conduct. Mrs. Moore is, moreover, at once a woman who is repelled by life in India and one who grasps its essence.

Godbole's Hinduism takes us beyond good and evil to a cosmic force more often passive than positive and always unpredictable. At Fielding's party Professor Godbole explains that his song is a lament

*Excerpted from *E. M. Forster* (Boston: Twayne Publishers), pp. 106–21. © 1982 and reprinted with the permission of Twayne Publishers, a division of G. K. Hall & Co., Boston, and of the author.

for the God who does not come; and, in reply to Mrs. Moore, he explains further that no song exists that celebrates His certain coming. Following the disaster at the Marabar Caves, Godbole is even more explicit, if still exasperating, to Fielding. "Absence implies presence," Godbole says, though the two are not the same. Yet absence is not "non-existence," so we can say, "Come, come, come, come," in the hope that at some time the Divine may descend. Just as absence and presence are related, so are good and evil as aspects of the Divine. Both together, not either one separately, express the total universe. To desire the one without acknowledging the power of the other is to falsify. In the Caves Mrs. Moore is, unwittingly, the victim of simplified notions. She is immobilized because she finds God in His absent aspect when she had been too eager for God in His present aspect. Godbole, on the other hand, knows God's presence in "Temple" because he is less anxious to find Him and because he perceives that God will inevitably soon again be absent from him. Godbole is, in short, mystically more sophisticated than his English counterpart, Mrs. Moore.

Evil is not to be desired but to be endured, since its presence presupposes also the existence of good which will in its turn dominate. Good and evil are also universal human characteristics. When an evil act is performed, everyone has done it, Godbole asserts. So, if Adela were affronted in the cave, everyone who knew her shares complicity, whether or not he was present. Even Adela is in part guilty, as she sometimes senses when she heeds her deepest instincts instead of her intellect.

Godbole is a reconciling agent, wise but passive, intense yet indifferent. His mien suggests an imperturbable confidence, the result both of effort and of effortless vision: ". . . his whole appearance suggested harmony—as if he had reconciled the products of East and West, mental as well as physical, and could never be discomposed."[2] He also has a preternatural insight which none of the other characters possesses, except in part Mrs. Moore. Like his fellow Hindus, Godbole continually seeks the unseen, a chief aspect of the Hindu temperament as Forster elsewhere described it: "The Hindu is concerned not with conduct, but with vision. To realize what God is seems more important than to do what God wants. He has a constant sense of the unseen—of the powers around if he is a peasant, of the power behind if he is a philosopher, and he feels that this tangible world, with its chatter of right and wrong, subserves the intangible."[3] One who beholds the beatific vision can, like Godbole, die to the world and refuse to act in conformity to social pressures; one who beholds the horrific vision can, like Mrs. Moore, die to the world, refuse to help her friends, and long for her own death.

Mrs. Moore, who misunderstands her vision at the Marabar, dies before she can see it in perspective. Alone, she is unable to reach the reality symbolized by the Hindu temple where all life forms merge: "life human and superhuman and subhuman and animal, life tragic and cheerful, cruel and kind, seemly and obscene."⁴ At the temple's apex is the sun which expresses the unity underlying these forms and the unity to which they aspire. It is the underside of this unity that Mrs. Moore encounters in the Caves; and it is only in death that she attains the knowledge of all sides of it.

Her stature increases when she, at death, is transformed into an Indian presence with powers similar to, and possibly exceeding, Godbole's own. In mythic terms she becomes a goddess who saves Aziz at the trial, who brings the truth to Adela, who brings healing rains and fertility to the parched land by the sacrifice of her life, and who reconciles East and West through her surviving influence in the minds of Aziz and Godbole and in the personalities of her children, Ralph and Stella. This redemptive aspect of Mrs. Moore is consistent with her mystical sensitivity in the first pages of the book; but she must endure a spiritual crucifixion before she can exert transcendent power. She is buried in the ocean before she becomes a Hindu goddess, just as the image of Shri Krishna must be thrown into the Mau tank before He can exert His remaining strength. As one critic suggests, Mrs. Moore atones for the rape of India by her countrymen through saving the life of an Indian accused of assaulting an English woman.⁵

Godbole does not figure greatly in the action, but he is the chief source of truth as the representative of the most comprehensive world view in the novel, that of Hinduism. Hinduism enables Godbole to divine the complex relationships between himself and an unseen power beyond the here and now. Fact to Hinduism is less important than the intangible, as Forster had seen in 1914: "Greece, who has immortalized the falling dust of facts, so that it hangs in enchantment for ever, can bring no life to a land that is waiting for the dust to clear away, so that the soul may contemplate the soul."⁶ Forster's own allegiance was divided: as a scion of G. E. Moore, Grecian fact remained for him an indispensable component of the spiritual life, but as a visionary, sensitive to the mystical philosophy of Plotinus and that of the Orient, the lure of the Hindu venture into the spiritual world also exerted its spell.

If Godbole provided him with some of his standards, still Forster did not accept Hindiusm uncritically. Its philosophical drift interested him more than its external aspects; like Mrs. Moore's children, Ralph and Stella, he was drawn to Hinduism but unconcerned about its forms. On balance, Hinduism meant more to him than either Islam or Christianity. In *The Hill of Devi*⁷ he commended Islam for its order and criticized Hinduism for its disorder. But in the 1960s he could disparage Islam for its "orderliness."⁸ In the novel he asserted that "the shallow arcades" of the mosque do not take us very deep into religious mysteries nor does Islam's primary belief, "There is no God but God"; and he referred scornfully to the "poor, talkative Christianity" that had been Mrs. Moore's solace before she entered the Marabar Caves.

Forster revealed a still more positive affinity with Hinduism when he described himself on "nearer nodding terms with Krishna than with any other god," and when he perceived the power of Hinduism over skeptical temperaments such as his own: "it has caught sceptics at all times, and wrings cries of acquiescence and whispers of hope."[9] In Hinduism Forster found an encompassing reality that could unify the world and bind together animate and inanimate life, an impersonal spiritual force with which one might identify mystically, and a belief in love as a binding spiritual and moral value—a "love in which there neither was nor desired to be sensuality, though it was excited at the crisis and reached ecstasy."[10]

THE MARABAR CAVES: "ILLUSION...
SET AGAINST THE BACKGROUND OF ETERNITY"

The Marabar Caves embody the neutral substratum of the universe and lack positive attributes.[11] Just as Hinduism takes us philosophically to a plane beyond good or evil, so the Caves exist physically—insofar as natural objects can—in a void, having been created before space and time began. They contain, therefore, a primordial reality, basic to all later differentiations of being, animate or inanimate, in space or time. Godbole intuitively knows this truth about the Caves, but at Fielding's tea party he senses that his Moslem and Occidental audience would not understand him if he were now to describe it. Godbole realizes that in the Caves one may have perceptions which reach "straight back into the universal, to a blackness and sadness so transcending our own that they are undistinguishable from glory."[12] In these words, whereby Forster express the concern of Melville and other prophetic writers, he characterizes the intuitions of Godbole, the formidable negations experienced by Mrs. Moore in the Marabar, and the affirmations she fails to find there.

If the inmost Caves were to be excavated, nothing would be added to the sum of good and evil, Forster explains; yet good and evil, and all other polarities, are in the Caves.[13] The reality the Caves enclose can extend in a negative or a positive direction as circumstances or the powers of the individual permit. They were created before pestilence or treasure, Forster says; but pestilence and treasure, and all such contrarieties, develop from them.

The Caves and Hills are genuinely extraordinary and their meaning is elusive. Close at hand they present "a nasty little cosmos"; at a distance, they seem finite and romantic and breathe a promise of spiritual renewal. Everything in the world possesses equal value, the Caves assert through their confounding echo; and there is nothing special, then, about man and his aspirations. If man is equal to all other beings, he has no special value in himself but is as valuable as all other manifestations of existence, valuable as a wasp, a snake, or a sun-burnt rock. He is not necessarily at the apex of a great chain of being nor a little less than the angels. Godbole knows that the world was not made for man, but Mrs. Moore's Christianity does not allow her to see that far.

Fearsome as the Caves are in their aboriginal darkness, when a light is struck the beauties of the reflected light are like "exquisite nebulae." What had seemed completely dark is the source of light; and the Caves, with their rough exterior surface, possess hidden beauty. The struggling of the flames within the granite walls to reach the source of light on the outside is symbolic of the efforts of Godbole, Mrs. Moore, and some of the others to let their human fires merge with a divine fire. And the radiance increases as image and flame seemingly touch each other and "kiss" before they expire, just as the soul expires when in Hinduism it merges with the world soul to achieve its Nirvana.

The powers of nullity are too strong for the English women to withstand at the Marabar. The Caves overwhelm them, saddling Mrs. Moore with disillusion and Adela with delusion. There, the eternal and the infinite lack beauty and sublimity, and become ugly and sinister. The unseen achieves expression not only in the unsettling echo but in such a phenomenon as the cheeping of the mangy squirrel outside Aziz's house before the picnic. During the hot weather at least, the infinite has no link with exaltation, aesthetic or spiritual. The two women feel isolated from other people and from each other; and the Caves intensify and bring to focus their latent frustrations: Mrs. Moore's doubts about her usefulness as a human being and Adela's misgivings about sex and love.

The concept of eternity becomes equivalent in the Caves to an "undying worm," and this worm or serpent is full of crawling maggots. Insofar as the serpent is a phallic emblem of the life principle, it is contorted and twisted in the Caves; life, as seen from the perspective of the Caves, recoils on itself and has no purposeful motion. Even Shri Krishna, a life-god in Hinduism, had once appeared as a fearsome serpent to churn the seas in order to form the objects of creation and to interchange them so as to cause them to lose their individuality.[14] To Mrs. Moore, life, seen purposefully, retreats before the echo's expression of chaos, disorder, and negation. As yet, she has no power to see that chaos and disorder betoken life as well as death, and imply, by their very existence, the existence of their opposites. Men can endure only so much of the negation that Mrs. Moore finds in the echo before they retreat into the self, where they are apt to find all too little strength. The echo muffles Mrs. Moore's spirit, just as a direct view of God might have blinded her.[15]

The unseen is sinister only when it confronts one starkly. If, as Fielding says, "the echo is always evil," that which the echo emanates from need not be. If one penetrates the echo, he may not be totally reassured; but he will, likely as not, find a reality that is more than negative. But reality remains hidden and can only be grasped evanescently, even by the adept. Preparatory to her visit to the Caves Mrs.

Moore sees the universe as a series of receding arches with an echo beyond the last arch, and then a silence. The silence is evidently Eternity, impassive but not hostile; the echo in its reverberation is more malign than the silence. The wise man accepts the universe as it is; and he sees that its apparent evils, if overpowering, need not be permanent. Arch and echo are expanding and retracting images that connect the individual, sometimes against his will, with an Eternity more ominous than reassuring. Yet the existence of the Eternal, however veiled to human eyes, argues for a measure of stability and meaning in a chaotic universe.

Fielding and Adela do not understand the mysteries inherent in the Hills or the terrors inherent in the Caves, but they do have glimmers of perception. The Anglo-Indians, who have none at all, are unequal to India and think, for example, that its irrational energies can be controlled by numbering the Marabar Caves with paint to distinguish one from another. The antagonism between Ronny and his mother, particularly after Aziz's arrest, indicates his failure to comprehend the irrational forces that now sway her.

Ronny is not at home anywhere in India, in mosque, caves, or temple ("Mosque," "Caves," and "Temple" are, in fact, the titles of the three successive divisions of the novel). He is symbolic of the rootless Anglo-Indian officials who lack not only Mrs. Moore's mystical awareness, but Fielding's graciousness and humanity, Adela's sincerity, and Aziz's dedication to the personal. Those who attend Fielding's tea party would not be misfits in the "Mosque," but they would not understand (except for Godbole) the full implications of "Caves" or "Temple."

The Caves comprise the sum total of all experience—the locus of community activity and of burial rites, the womb and tomb of all existence, an archetype of the great mother and of annihilation.[16] In the Caves one can discern the upward swirl of aspiration and the downward pull of fact, the life in the unconscious and the failure of the mind to comprehend this life. The Caves include, besides, all the rhythms of existence, especially the most basic, that of life versus death. It is sometimes difficult to disentangle the life from the death principle. One implies the other, just as absence asserts presence, and evil, good. The Caves, which embody death as well as life, are of "very dead and quiet" granite; and Mrs. Moore receives one part of India's message, the disabling echo, in "that scoured-out cavity of the granite" (208). Rock is refractory, although as Forster implies elsewhere (247), stones, as well as plants and animals, feel perhaps the pain of the universe and are potentially sentient. In *Alexandria* Forster had said that for the Neoplatonist all things are parts of God, including the stones;[17] and he had implied, therefore, that some mystics had achieved a completeness greater than Godbole's. In Hinduism "completeness" matters, not "reconstruction," which may be too human in implication (286).

But even Professor Godbole cannot assimilate stones to his vision of cosmic unity though he can merge with Mrs. Moore, whom he only dimly remembers, and the wasp. The stones signify the difficulty in his attaining completeness of vision rather than, as one critic asserts, an inability to attain it.[18] Another fact emerges: the negations of the Marabar cannot be assimilated to a philosophy less inclusive than that symbolized by the Caves and Hills. Hinduism, alone of the religions presented, has the comprehensiveness to absorb such realities.

As many of the most perceptive commentators have suggested, the Caves relate to Hinduism. The presence of caves in Hindu myths and rituals, the correspondence between illusions (such as those experienced in the Marabar) and the Hindu veils of Maya, the similarity of the echo sound to that of the mystic syllable "om," and the presence of flame and serpent imagery alike at the Marabar and in Hindu scriptures link the Marabar Caves to Hinduism. One need not assert that Mrs. Moore has a Hindu vision there; rather she undergoes, as Forster said, "the vision . . . with its back turned."[19] The revelation to her is less a repudiation of Hinduism, however, than an apprehension of the negative aspect of its primal reality.

If the Caves embody a life principle however contorted or disguised or remote from us, they also suggest the death principle. After too great an exposure to the forces let loose at the Marabar, the characters return to Chandrapore in a train that seems dead though it moves; and all the people in it are like corpses. The Hills are seen as gods, and the earth is a ghost in comparison. So, as dwellers on the plain, we find that our mundane lives and values become illusory before the cosmic truth concentrated in the Hills; in their vicinity, "everything seemed cut off at its root, and therefore infected with illusion" (140).

Forster also agreed with a statement which he quoted in a review and which stressed the insignificance of our lives when compared to the transcendent: ". . . for in Indian art, as in Indian philosophy, all life, even the life of the gods, is an illusion or play set against the background of eternity."[20] Such a juxtaposition of meaning and nothingness is too difficult for Mrs. Moore and the non-Hindus in the novel to grasp entire. The dispelling of illusion and the confronting of a first Reality should, for the initiated, eventuate in knowledge and insight rather than in the disillusion suffered by Mrs. Moore. All of Mrs. Moore's spiritual constructs—love, beauty, piety—now lack abiding force for her at the Marabar. They are man-made, abstract formulations, irrelevant to the amoral, primordial essence of things, revealed both in the Caves and in Hinduism.

The Hills—and by implication the Caves which they cover—overwhelm by excess; they lack the "proportion" seen even in the most rugged hills elsewhere and deflect the aspiration for a comprehensible certitude. The Caves and the negations undergone there by the Western visitors are crucial. But the Caves open out to the Shri Krishna birth festivities and provide for their exuberance the most solid possible base.

Just so the cave, with its suggestion of mystery and the elemental, is at the heart of the temple. But the cave is also subsumed by the entire temple which flaunts a multifaceted, inclusive rendition of outward forms. The antecedent matrix of being, contained in the Caves, is assimilated into the total structure of creation. It is never lost, however, and we must be prepared to acknowledge its violent, primitive effects. If Hinduism has inclusiveness, it is not orderly: "Ragged edges of religion ... unsatisfactory and undramatic tangles ... God si love" (316).

This amorphousness permits Hinduism to absorb disillusionment and apathy, as well as creativity and joy—both the experiences that transfigure life and the knowledge that these experiences are also illusions that perish. If the ceremonies possess "fatuity," they also possess "philosophy."[21] In its widest reaches Hinduism would annihilate sorrow for all: "not only for Indians, but for foreigners, birds, caves, railways, and the stars; all became joy, all laughter; there had never been disease nor doubt, misunderstanding, cruelty, fear" (288). Truly, as Forster said in 1914, in the Hindu view of things "the divine is so confounded with the earthly that anyone or anything is part of God."[22] If the Caves induce in the unprepared individual a dynamic nihilism, the Temple festivities induce in the prepared individual a sense of cosmic unity and of dynamic life.

A "BEWILDERING ... ECHOING CONTRADICTORY WORLD"

The structure of the novel illustrates its paradoxical content. Many readings, however, stress a "triadic" structure of thesis, acting upon antithesis, to produce a synthesis; and this kind of progression is not absent from the book.[23] The rational, sentimentalized views of God, such as the Moslem Aziz and the Christian Mrs. Moore express in "Mosque," crumble when an indifferent cosmos subdues Mrs. Moore and Adela Quested in "Caves." In turn, the spiritual lethargy induced by the Marabar and the evil forces of division let loose there yield partly in "Temple" to the mystical strengths of Hinduism, its emphasis upon love, and the breadth of its philosophy. Each section of the novel is, moreover, associated with one of the three principal seasons of the Indian year.[24] Still, the novel charts primarily the dualities of life as they exist in uneasy conjunction with one another rather than the transmutation of them into something else. All contrasting objects and mental states merge into the Unity underlying the universe, but they do not usually become something else midway in the process.

The motion of the novel is cyclic rather than linear; dialectical opposites are not resolved and continue indefinitely to exert their strength. Forster is at once preoccupied with a timeless unity and with the concrete manifestations of that unity in time. So at the end Aziz distrusts, then accepts, a cyclic explanation of his life; and he realizes that little enough has been resolved through his sufferings. His encounter with

Ralph Moore induces a fear that the Mosque-Caves cycle may start again. He dreads the prospect but perceives that he cannot avoid the inevitable.

The dispelling of drought and suffering by the monsoon rains organizes the novel in terms of a cyclic fertility ritual, as Ellin Horowitz and other critics have suggested; and Mrs. Moore is, as we have seen, the god who must be sacrificed in order that the healing rains descend. In this cyclic pattern the progress is from affirmation to negation to qualified affirmation. Nothing is canceled. The forces of division and unity still exist, but in "Temple" they reveal themselves in a double aspect, as temporal and eternal. Temporal discordances will in time yield to a merging of hitherto abrasively active dichotomies.

In "Temple" the affirmation is tentative and hard-earned. Mrs. Moore's assertion, "God is Love," in "Mosque" had been too complacent. The Hindu version of this same principle, "God si Love," is more flexible; the fact that the Hindu recognizes mundane chaos is implied in the misspelling of the verb. For the Hindu, love is more abstract, more transcendental, more removed from the individual's desires and ideals than for the Christian or the Moslem. Though infinite love is the basis for the Hindu religion, the Hindu regards "love" apart from the order and the precise formulations of the Western or Islamic mind.

Love for the Hindu is an experience at once more immediate and more remote, less fastidious and more far-reaching, than for other men. For Godbole, and indeed for Mrs. Moore in her mystical moments, love extends to the wasps and, by implication, to all forms of animate life; and Godbole would include the inanimate, the stones of India, if he could manage to do so. The progression of the book is from light to darkness to modified light; the fact that illumination once existed implies that it may come again: "Hope existed despite fulfilment, as it will be in heaven" (303).

The nature of God Himself, as the Hindu envisages it, is complex. In "Temple" Godbole is standing in the presence of God but removed from Him, at the other end of a carpet which distances Him from His worshipper. God, in short, exists; but He is difficult to know. All statements about Him are alike true and untrue: "He is, was not, is not, was" (283). God has not yet been born when the Shri Krishna ceremonies begin; He will be born at midnight, but He was also born centuries ago; He can never be born, perhaps, because, as the Lord of the Universe, He has always existed and transcends all human endeavors to encompass Him in creed or in ritual. At the height of the festivities He is thrown into the water; but He can't be thrown away. Such are the ambiguous rituals that the Hindu observes, such the certainties and uncertainties inherent in all spiritual proceedings. The God to be thrown away and all other such images and symbols are, Forster says, "emblems of passage": "a passage not easy, not now, not here, not to be apprehended except when it is unattainable" (314).[25] In any event, God transcends the categories that we can formulate for Him.

Nature, another manifestation of the unseen, is scarcely amenable to the understanding. The Ganges River seems glamorous in the moonlight to Mrs. Moore when she first visits India, but she recoils when she learns that crocodiles inhabit it. Now the river seems both terrible and wonderful. "The "jolly" jungle scenery at Mau also conceals a deadly cobra, as Aziz and Fielding go on their final ride; the scenery, though it "smiles," places, as it were, a "gravestone on any human hope" (321). If nature is apparently indestructible, she is yet undergoing slow change and erosion; and gradually the plain will engulf the hills which are of "incredible antiquity" and "flesh of the sun's flesh" (123).

Nature is not only an imponderable force but a vital, animating one, as Forster's personification of the Hills and his use of the pathetic fallacy in describing them indicate. The Hills both "lie flat" and "heave"; they "creep forward" to the city and "leap" to beauty at sunset; they thrust "fists and fingers" up to the sky; inside, the walls of the Caves are skin to the fists and fingers; and the foothills are "knees" to the other hills. The surrounding caves and boulders proclaim that they are alive; and when the intruders to the "queer valley" leave, "stabs" of hot air pursue them. If Grasmere is more manageable and more romantic than India, it is also less real and alive. Mrs. Moore, when she comes to India and sees the moon in all its splendor, thinks how dead and alien it had seemed to her in England.

The punkah wallah (fan attendant) at the trial is a symbol of India's natural vitality. Under his impassive influence Adela becomes aware of more than her own sufferings and is receptive to the double vision which awakens in her when the crowd outside the court chants its version of Mrs. Moore's name, "Esmiss Esmoor." The punkah wallah, as an embodiment of the Life-Force, contrasts with "the serpent of eternity" known in the Caves; Adela understands neither one fully, though each one disturbs her radically. The resplendent Indian who in "Temple" wades into the Mau tank during the tempest to consign the palanquin bearing Shri Krishna's image to the waves is, like the punkah wallah, an emblem of primitive strength.

The truth is that India is both a muddle and a mystery, but a mystery that can only be reached through muddle. So the Temple ceremonies are "a triumph of muddle," though they suggest certain transcendent truths. To those who experience her superficially, India seems vast and amorphous, a country where life abounds but where discernible purpose is absent: "There seemed no reserve of tranquillity to draw upon in India . . . or else tranquillity swallowed up everything" (78). To those who can penetrate the outward confusion, she proves to be a mystery and purveys certain truths. India's very size and multiple cultures prevent anyone from understanding her easily, let alone completely. The Indian countryside is too vast to admit of excellence; only from the remotest perspective, from the moon for instance, would India acquire at last a firm outline.

At the same time, categories in India are rigid and defeat the attempts made to bridge them: so "the bridge party" is a failure, and the picnic at the Marabar a fiasco when Aziz "challenged the spirit of the Indian earth, which tries to keep men in compartments" (127). The country is divided between Moslems and Hindus who do not understand one another; and even Hinduism fragments into a hundred dissenting sects. The numerous inflexible distinctions found in Indian life reinforce the impression of disunity and multiplicity produced by the landscape, the confused social patterns, and the many civilizations of the subcontinent.

Aziz's desire to encompass "the vague and bulky figure of a motherland" (268) in his conversation and in his poems is mostly false, therefore, since his idea of the diversities and of the unity to be found in India is inadequate. For the Moslem, India can be perplexing; so Aziz's dead wife looks out from her portrait on a "bewildering ... echoing, contradictory world" (117), and Aziz in Mau dismisses the Hindu festival as remote from any sanctities of his own. The Indian culture and the Indian mind also baffle the rationalistic Westerner, leaving him "with the sense of a mind infinitely remote from ours—a mind patriotic and sensitive—and it may be powerful, but with little idea of logic or facts; we retire baffled, and, indeed, exasperated."[26] At no point, moreover, are the Westerners so confused, disturbed, and fascinated as by Godbole's impromptu song at Fielding's tea party.

There is something equivocal and difficult about life in India that the sands of the Suez Canal and the Mediterranean countries wipe out as soon as one leaves the waters of the Orient. The Mediterranean civilization has escaped "muddle" and attained a true harmony, "with flesh and blood subsisting" (282). From such a "norm" we depart as soon as we leave the Mediterranean, particularly if we leave it to the South where the "monstrous" and "extraordinary" are most likely to confront us, in India and the Orient in general. Western humanism is unable to explain India; it is too selective and too easily abashed by the stubborn facts. In India new categories are difficult to impose, intellectual discriminations are often impossible to make, the unaided powers of the mind are insufficient to comprehend a land so diverse. In India, as Forster says in *The Hill of Devi*, "everything that happens is said to be one thing and proves to be another" (93). In the East the harmonies of Western art and religion are replaced by the dissonances of Hindu music, the teeming "world-mountain" of the Indian temple, and the sounds and confusions of the Gokul Ashtami rituals. On the other hand, the forms of Occidental art are reassuring to the Western European; but, satisfying as they are for him, they yet represent only a partial view of reality.

The Gokul Ashtami festival represents a "frustration of reason and form" and a "benign confusion"; the participants reveal a "sacred bewilderment." No one knows precisely what happens, "whether a silver doll or a mud village, or a silk napkin, or an intangible spirit, or a pious resolution, had been born" (290). In "Temple" Forster made aesthetic use of chaos similar to Emily Brontë's use of it in *Wuthering Heights*.[27] Since, in Forster's view, Brontë implied more than she said, she had had recourse to "muddle, chaos, tempest" to enable her characters to achieve through it the greatest degree of expressiveness for their superhuman experiences. So only in confusion can the Hindu religious rituals and the collision of the boats in the Mau tank during the tempest attain their ineffable implications. For the Eastern sensibility, vitality is surely more important than beauty. The Eastern mentality senses that the disorder of the universe presupposes an ultimate order; the conventional Western moralist or religionist would impose his own order upon the universe instead of responding to the strong chaotic currents within it which go beyond mere negation or mere affirmation.

Notes

1. "Forster's Programme Note to Santha Rama Rau's Dramatized Version," (1960) Abinger Edition, ed. Oliver Stallybrass (London: Edward Arnold), p. 328.

2. Forster, *A Passage to India* (New York: Harcourt, Brace, 1958, Harbrace Modern Classics), p. 72. Page references in parentheses refer to this edition. Ed. note.

3. Forster, "The Gods of India" (1914) in "*Albergo Empedocle' and Other Writings by E. M. Forster*," ed. George H. Thomson (New York: Liveright, 1971), p. 221.

4. Forster, "The World Mountain," *Listener* 52 (December 2, 1954): 978.

5. Ellin Horowitz, "The Communal Ritual and the Dying God in E. M. Forster's *A Passage to India*," *Criticism* 6 (1964): 81.

6. "The Age of Misery," "*Albergo Empedocle*," p. 213.

7. Forster, *The Hill of Devi* (New York: Harcourt, Brace, 1933), p. 127. Ed. note.

8. K. Natwar-Singh ed., *E. M. Forster: A Tribute. With Selections from his Writings on India* (New York: Harcourt, Brace and World, 1964), p. xii.

9. "The Blue Boy," *Listener* 22 (1957): 444; "A Great Anglo-Indian" (1915), "*Albergo Empedocle*," p. 213.

10. Forster, "Indian Entries from a Diary," *Harper's Magazine* 224 (February 1962): 51.

11. All commentators agree that the caves are central to the novel. Pessimistic interpreters of the novel, with whom I disagree (Frederick Crews, *E. M. Forster: The Perils of Humanism*. Princeton: Princeton University Press, 1962; Alan Wilde, *Art and Order: A Study of E. M. Forster*. New York: New York University Press, 1964; Reuben A. Brower, "The Twilight of the Double Vision: Symbol and Irony in *A Passage to India*" in *The Fields of Light: An Experiment in Critical Reading*. New York: Oxford University Press, 1951, pp. 182–98), maintain that the negations embodied in the caves are never neutralized, whereas the [following] critics

all feel that the caves represent only the negative pole of reality, at times an overwhelming aspect of experience but still a partial one: James McConkey, *The Novels of E. M. Forster* (Ithaca: Cornell University Press, 1957); Gertrude M. White, "A Passage to India: Analysis and Revaluation" *PMLA* 69 (1953): 641–57; Louise Dauner, "What Happened in the Cave? Reflections on *A Passage to India*" *Modern Fiction Studies* 7 (1961): 958–70; Glen O. Allen, "Structure, Symbol and Theme in *A Passage to India*" *PMLA* 70 (1955): 934–54; A. Woodward, "The Humanism of E. M. Forster" *Theoria* 20 (June 15, 1963): 17–33; Ellin Horowitz, "The Communal Ritual and the Dying God in E. M. Forster's *A Passage to India*"; Wilfred Stone, *The Cave and the Mountain: A Study of E. M. Forster* (Stanford: Stanford University Press, 1966); George H. Thomson, *The Fiction of E. M. Forster* (Detroit: Wayne State University Press, 1967); Michael Spencer, "Hinduism in E. M. Forster's *A Passage to India*" *Journal of Asian Studies* 27 (1968): 281–95; Malcolm Bradbury, "Two Passages to India: Forster as Victorian and Modern" in *Aspects of E. M. Forster: Essays and Recollections Written for His Ninetieth Birthday January 1, 1969*, ed. Oliver Stallybrass (London: Edward Arnold, 1969; New York: Harcourt, Brace and World, 1969); Benita Parry, *Delusions and Discoveries: Studies on India in the British Imagination 1880–1930* (Berkeley and Los Angeles: University of California Press, 1972). Ed. note.

12. *Aspects of the Novel* (New York: Harcourt, Brace and World [1956], Harvest Books), p. 143. Page references in parentheses refer to this edition.

13. Attempts to identify the caves with evil exclusively or to restrict otherwise their meaning represent oversimplifications: see Glen O. Allen's identifying them with intelligence or rationality.

14. Forster, "The Churning of the Ocean," *Athenaeum* (May 21, 1920), pp. 667–68.

15. Benita Parry in *Delusions and Discoveries*, pp. 286–99, suggests that Mrs. Moore's negative vision in the caves is essentially Jainist, emphasizing pessimism, asceticism, and renunciation. Later she passes beyond Jainist limitations, Parry asserts, to become a redeemer as a Hindu deity.

16. Dauner and Stone regard the caves from this standpoint.

17. *Alexandria: A History and a Guide* (Garden City: Doubleday, 1961, Anchor Books, 1961), p. 71.

18. McConkey, p. 141.

19. Angus Wilson, "A Conversation with E. M. Forster" *Encounter* 9 (November 1957), p. 54.

20. "The Art and Architecture of India," *Listener* 50 (September 10, 1953): 421. The quotation is from the book reviewed, Benjamin Rowland's *The Art and Architecture of India* (London: Penguin, 1953).

21. *The Hill of Devi*, p. 169.

22. "The Gods of India," "*Albergo Empedocle*," p. 222.

23. See Allen who identifies "Mosque" with emotion, "Caves" with intellect, and "Temple" with love. See Stone's discussion of "triads," pp. 311–317.

24. The life of the goddess Vishnu furnishes a pattern for the events chronicled in the book and follows the same "seasonal" organization. See Stone, p. 309n.

25. This statement answers Crews's judgment in *E. M. Forster: The Perils of Humanism*, p. 142, that unity cannot be attained. It can be sporadically experienced, but through disorder rather than through logic and harmony. Hinduism does not so much sacrifice the values of humanism (Crews, p. 150) as go beyond them.

26. Forster, "The Indian Mind" (1914), "*Albergo Empedocle*," p. 207.

27. *Aspects of the Novel*, p. 145.

What Happened in the Cave?
Reflections on *A Passage to India*

Louise Dauner*

A Passage to India is E. M. Forster's best known and most popular novel; yet it remains a work which, more than thirty years after publication, still leaves us with a vague sense of frustration. Forster *is* elusive, sometimes through subtlety, occcasionally through infirm control of structure, and, notably, as in *A Passage to India*, through ability to seize upon and fully realize the potentials of an archetypal symbol—here, the Marabar Caves. Thus, though critics agree that the caves are the central symbol of the novel, interpretations of their meaning are widely diverse. Furthermore, we are still, literally and metaphorically, in the dark as to what really happened to Adela Quested in the cave; and yet this episode is the structural core of the novel.

Perhaps we may arrive at some illumination in these matters if we explore what the caves themselves imply. I wish therefore to examine the caves viewed as natural phenomena or nature symbols, and as archetypes or psychological symbols. Then we may attempt an interpretation of Adela's experience in the cave, the synaptic point for plot and story.

The differentiation between plot and story is, of course, Forster's. In a Forster work the story, which may be thought of as lying beneath and extending beyond the consummation of the plot, is the "real thing." In the story, which is an insight or a "perception," lie symbolic representations of experience upon which Forster has a firm intuitive grasp, no matter how loose at times may be his control of plot. To use the word *intuitive*, however, is to touch the heart of the difficulty; for Forster belongs to that small group of writers—one thinks within the last century of Melville, Hawthorne, D. H. Lawrence, and Dostoevsky—whose deepest wisdoms transcend temporal and racial boundaries because their insights derive not so much from the conscious mind as from what Jung calls the Collective Unconscious, that source for creativity which gives rise to a vision of genuine primordial experience common to humanity. Rex Warner, in his *E. M. Forster* (1950), locates the sources of Forster's power in "a combination of vision and nightmare," as particularly apparent in *A Passage to India*. Thus an exegesis of a Forster work which focuses only upon the patterns structured by the conscious mind, the plot, and which relies only upon the techniques and terms of conventional literary analysis must leave undefined perhaps the deepest significances, which reside in the story, and which may be carried by symbolic elements such as the caves. Concepts and insights which derive

*Reprinted from *Modern Fiction Studies* 7 (Autumn 1961), 258–70, by permission of *Modern Fiction Studies*, © 1961, by Purdue Research Foundation, West Lafayette, Indiana, 47907.

from non-literary but pertinent systems of knowledge such as archeology and Jung's analytical psychology should provide appropriate means for an exploration of the story. Before such an attempt is made, however, it is well to note briefly representative interpretations of the meanings of the caves.

Lionel Trilling, basing his interpretation upon the psychic and emotional changes wrought by the caves upon Adela and Mrs. Moore, calls them "wombs." Gertrude White calls them "the voice of evil and negation . . . of Chaos and Old Night. . . . The answer that they give to the problem of oneness is an answer of horror and despair, whether on the human or the universal level." William York Tindall sees them as including "the primitive, the unconscious, and the sexual." To Austin Warren they suggest "eternity, infinity, the Absolute." Glen O. Allen considers them 1) as representing a kind of religion, "a devotion to reason, form, and the sense of purpose as the *sine qua non* of right behavior and attitude"; 2) as equating to "the ultimate identity of Brahma and Atman"; and 3) as representing, in Mrs. Moore's and Adela's experiences of them "the inadequacy of the Christian and the intellectual points of view." And James McConkey suggests that the symbol of the caves, though still a mystery, may be read on one level as representing, in their emptiness, "the absolute Brahman" in Hindu philosophy. Taken literally, their effect upon Mrs. Moore, Adela, and Fielding is, of course, completely negative. "Yet, the caves suggest, too, that a reality exists beyond time and space to which man's consciousness cannot fully reach."[1]

Now certainly these readings contribute much to the potentiality of meaning, but they are not entirely satisfactory because they approach the caves as rational elements. Actually, the caves are not only the setting for *irrational* experience, but they are themselves archetypal. We mean by this first that the caves function in a situation involving elements which derive, not from Forster's rational or conscious mind, or even from Adela's conscious mind, but from the dark ambiguous soil of the unconscious, which disguises its meanings in symbols, as in myths, fantasies, fairy tales; and second, that the cave, *as cave*, is itself a primordial image in mythology and psychology, hence as an archetype it is a constituent of the collective unconscious and not of the purely personal and conscious psyche.

Thus, it need not surprise us that, within the novel, we find no rational answer to Adela's question to Godbole and Dr. Aziz, "What are these caves?" Aziz frankly does not know; and Godbole the Brahmin replies only in enigmatic negatives which deny to the caves anything remarkable at all: they possess neither sculpture, holiness, nor ornamentation—not even stalactites. There is only "an entrance in the rock . . . and through the entrance is the cave."[2] Yet they also figure as "extraordinary" in both the opening sentence of the novel and the opening chapter of Part II, "Caves." And early in this section Forster does tell us that the Marabar Hills, in which are the caves, "are older than any-thing in the world" (p. 123). Thus they are primordial. What does this mean?

Recent archeological discoveries, as noted by G. R. Levy in *The Gate of Horn* (1948), suggest "the profound significance of the cave in the race-memory and traditions of more advanced peoples." The cave, it now appears, functioned in the most critical events in the life of early man—as far back, indeed, as Mousterian and Crô-magnon man. Bodies of Mousterian men were buried in trenches in the floors of their caves, with implements and offerings which, Miss Levy concludes, "indicates the existence, if not of the family, at least of the group or clan, whose unit-ing bonds were felt to extend through time . . . and suggest continuous relationship. . . . This is the earliest indication in Europe of belief in a non-physical existence."[3] Thus, at the beginning, we see the cave identi-fied with the concepts of unity and of a belief in an aspect of the spirit-ual. These suggestions are pertinent to *A Passage to India*.

A Passage to India presents, on the surface, a theme the opposite of unity and relationship. It is a novel of barriers—between matter and es-sence, between races, castes, religions, and sexes; and though some of the tensions are somewhat relieved in the resolution, we are left with a re-assertion of the barriers: "Why can't we be friends now?" Fielding asks Aziz, during what both know to be their last meeting. "It's what I want. It's what you want."

> But the horses didn't want it—they swerved apart; the earth didn't want it, sending up rocks through which riders must pass single file; the temples, the tank, the jail, the palace, the birds, the carrion, the Guest House . . . they didn't want it, they said in their hundred voices, "No, not yet," and the sky said, "No, not there." (p. 322)

Yet the underlying theme of *A Passage to India* is that which character-izes and charges all of Forster's novels: the implication of unity, to-getherness, "connection." So in *Howards End* Margaret Schlegel muses, "Only connect! . . . Only connect the prose and the passion, and both will be exalted, and human love will be seen at its height. Live in frag-ments no longer. Only connect, and the beast and the monk, robbed of the isolation that is life to either, will die."[4]

The cave, then, ambivalent in its combination of primal functions, both shelter and tomb, testifies to man's early sense of unity, both ma-terial and spiritual, and symbolizes here that unity of individuals, races, spirits which, Forster implies, is the only real solution to the problems, not only of an England and an India, but of all men. But as the place of burial the cave also means death or separation. Unity and separa-tion, as basic aspects of the human experience, are also basic themes of *A Passage to India*.

The separation or death-aspect is translated in the novel into Mrs. Moore's experience in the small black hole. Already in a strange depression when she enters the cave, she faces the darkness, is caught up in a momentary panic caused by the dark, the smell, and the strange pressures, she hits her head "and for an instant she went mad, hitting and gasping like a fanatic." There is also an echo, a sound which reduces everything to indistinction and futility: "Whatever is said, the same monotonous noise replies . . . 'Boum' is the sound . . . utterly dull. Hope, politeness, the blowing of a nose, the squeak of a boot, all produce 'boum'" (p. 147). The echo undermines Mrs. Moore's life; for, coming at a moment of fatigue, it murmurs to her, "Pathos, piety, courage—they exist, but are identical, and so is filth. Everything exists, nothing has value" (p. 149).

From this "double vision" Mrs. Moore never recovers her sense of the positive. As a Westerner, whose rational heritage discriminates between polarities, she is lost in a concept which sees good and evil, not as irreconcilable opposites, but as hyphenated; as essential, though contrasting, aspects of the same all-pervasive divinity. She could then have made no sense of Godbole's "explanation" to Fielding of Adela's experience in the cave: "Good and evil are different, as their names imply. But, in my own humble opinion, they are both of them aspects of my Lord. He is present in the one, absent in the other, and the difference between presence and absence is great. . . . Yet absence implies presence, absence is not non-existence, and we are therefore entitled to repeat, 'Come, come, come, come!'" (p. 178). As Mrs. Moore experiences it, however, this basic paradox can only paralyze her spirit, a blend of Western rationality and oriental intuition; for the intuitive part of her nature, though real, is not sufficiently developed to sustain and protect her. The moments in the cave simply reduce her to ill temper, cynicism, and an apprehension of spiritual decay and death which, only a little later, is paralleled by her physical death on the sea. Yet even this death is paradoxical; for even as her body is committed to the Indian Ocean, her spirit manifests itself to Adela during her testimony at the trial of Aziz; she is transmuted by the crowd in the street into an Indian goddess, Esmiss Esmoor; and still later she assumes identity as a cosmic aspect in the memory of Godbole.

The cave, then, is thematic in its implication of good-and-evil. But because this theme is so highly complex, it can be explored and dramatized only through a series of "variations." These variations, both negative and positive, are reflected in both Adela's experience in the cave and in its own implicit qualities.

Taken literally, Adela's experience adds up to hallucination, hysteria, and physical and psychic illness—to negation and evil; but this experience, though highly distressing to Adela and others, does not change the positive implications of the cave as symbol. Perhaps just here is an instance of the difference between plot and story in a Forster work. For we must differentiate between what Adela *thinks* happens—an attempt by Aziz to assault her—between, then, the *facts* of the *plot*, and the underlying truth, the *story*, which is carried by the cave-symbol. It is the old difference again (not confined to a Forster novel) between objective reality and a subjective interpretation of that reality. Here an ancient parable may help us.

Another cave has left its mark upon our imaginations, Plato's cave, in the seventh book of *The Republic*. This is the cave of Illusion, where "reality" is merely the shadow of a shadow, for the objects that cast the shadows are themselves artificial. And this cave too, like Forster's cave, has an echo. Because of Forster's long devotion to Greek thought and attitudes, we may logically assume that Plato's cave of Illusion underlies other symbolic implications of Forster's cave.

Yet *A Passage to India* is rooted in Forster's intimate knowledge of India, which he first visited in 1912–1913, and to which he returned in 1921, serving for nearly nine months as secretary of the Maharajah of Dewas State Senior, Sir Tukoji Rao III. *A Passage to India* was begun before the 1921 visit and completed after Forster's return to England. The story is given in detail in *The Hill of Devi* (1953). Here we need note only that Forster's immersion into Indian life—his contacts with the Maharajah, with the Maratha nobles and their women, even his dressing as a Hindu and participating in the eight-days' feast in honor of Krishna, the Gokul-Ashtami—all of this contributes significantly in theme, characters, events, and attitudes to the "rightness" of the novel. But even more important, this record of the Indian months suggests that the conceptual texture of *A Passage to India* is inevitably a blend: it is a combination of concepts both Greek and Indian. To the Platonic cave, with its concepts of earthly life as illusion and as the betrayal of the senses, we must now add a corresponding Indian concept—Māyā.

In *Philosophies of India* (1956) Heinrich Zimmer defines Māyā as "the illusion superimposed upon reality as an effect of ignorance." Māyā is the net of sense entanglement. In the Vedantic philosophy, to understand its secret, to know how it works, to transcend its cosmic spell, "breaking outward through the layers of tangible and visible appearance, and simultaneously inward through all the intellectual and emotional stratifications of the psyche"—this is conceived to be the primary human task. For this task the intellect alone is insufficient, for it sees life and experience as a dualism. But "it is a sign of nonknowing to suppose that because the dualistic argument is logical and accords with the facts of life, it is therefore consonant and with the final truth. Dualism belongs to the sphere of manifestation, the sphere of bewildering differentiation through the interaction of the gunas, and is but a part of the great cosmic play of Māyā."[5]

Adela's experience in the cave of Illusion is an instance of Māyā. This state is corrected during the tense moments of the trial in her clear if not temporary recognition that, whatever happened in the cave, it was not any act of Aziz, though it may well have been something entirely real, if entirely inward. Thus the critical question of what did happen in the cave includes both Adela's illusion, her misconception of the truth, and the reality; and obviously the reality includes all the value implications which the cave symbolically carries. Adela's hysterical flight from the cave is a rejection of these values. But since this rejection grows inevitably out of her total personality, we are also involved with the problem of what totality of psychic elements, what kind of personality, can apprehend truth or reality.

Adela is one of those persons to whom life must "explain" itself rationally. She wants to "know" India, to harmonize all of its paradoxical voices into one clear harmonious chord of being. Yet, unlike Mrs. Moore, Adela lacks the intuitive capacity which alone can grasp the disparities and resolve them into an image of cosmic wholeness. Only love, through intuition, Forster suggests, can do this; and with all the good will in the world, it is Adela's incapacity to love, her emotional and intuitive deficiency, which is her essential limitation.

When she enters the cave, Adela has just realized that she does not love Ronny, her fiancé. Her decision to marry him has never been based on strong physical or emotional need; it has been a restrained, rational decision, an on-again-off-again matter, revived, for instance, by an automobile accident which momentarily threw them into close contact. Preoccupied during these days with the question of love and marriage, she is also psychically involved (though on a below-rational level) with the physical contact implied. Her essentially virginal nature is obscurely troubled by this implication; yet she is also fundamentally honest, and now she sharply sees the incongruity: "Not to love the man one's going to marry! Not to find it out till this moment! Not even to have asked oneself the question until now! Something else to think out..." (p. 152).

In the first moments of this shocking recognition, she puts a blunt question to Aziz, which so embarrasses him that he darts into a cave to recover his poise. She enters still another cave. The emotional context of the moment is thus confused and negative. From her cave Adela emerges in deep psychic and emotional distress, half-falling down the hillside into cactus plants, hundreds of needles of which penetrate her body. This too is meaningful: it is as though nature itself enacts a violent impingement upon this woman who "hitherto had not much minded whether she was touched or not: her senses were abnormally inert and the only contact she anticipated was that of mind" (p. 193). It is not exaggerated perhaps to see some phallic symbolism in the penetration of the cactus-needles, a delicate irony. And it is significant that Adela's movement down the granite hillside is a wild descent, the physical plane correlating at the moment with the psychic plane.

Now from what "reality" has Adela fled? Her panic must have arisen out of what she felt to be a peril—primarily, the danger of contact or union. This brings us back to the cave in its implications of union with either the human or the divine.

The ancient cave consists of a shallow grotto which leads to a deeper recess. The Marabar Caves have a similar form: "A tunnel eight feet long, five feet high, three feet wide, leads to a circular chamber about twenty feet in diameter" (p. 124). Crô-magnon man used his grottoes, which were open to the daylight, as shelters and workshops. These represent the mundane activities of the group. But in the deeper recesses behind the entrance were enacted the essential ceremonies, what we may call the psychic life, of early man. Miss Levy tells us that these ceremonies were of a religious nature, "as yet inseparable from art, magic, and social and economic experiment," and that here "the signs of daily activities . . . are strikingly absent." This, then, is the place where early man enacted the rituals which celebrated critical moments in his life, moments during which he intuitively felt some aspects of cosmic truth. The cave was considered "the repository of mystic influence," in that both animal souls and divinity were felt to exist here. This aspect of the cave, as the site of divine power, underlies the other positive aspects. But these other aspects have each their special property and significance.

As the site of divine power, the cave is also the site of the masked religious or ceremonial dances, a deliberate means of approach to the animal nature and therefore to the divine nature. Again, it was a common belief that the primal emergence of the mythic ancestors was from caverns in or under the earth. To the cave the novice magicians repaired for their sleep of death and rebirth. The cave was the site of the sanctuary where were kept the churingas, the incised or painted objects of wood or stone which were believed to hold in union both animal and human divinity, and which were shown to every initiate at the moment of his passage from boyhood to clan membership. Since amulets and engraved blocks bearing female symbols have been found lying face down in contact with the earth, the cave is associated with female potency. "The cave was already a Mother." Both primitive and later civilized races, performing their ceremonies in caves or crypts, considered the cave the mother from whom they were born again. Such rites aimed at renewal through union with divinity, and were among the major ceremonies in the "rites of passage," celebrating the individual's birth, initiation, death, and rebirth. The initiation rites linked the religious and social aspects of group solidarity, and signified the spiritual rebirth of the individual (sometimes known as the moment when he "received his soul"). "The primary group-relationship known to us was not that of blood, but of a willed participation in a life both physical and non-physical, which stretched through time to include the dead and the unborn."[6]

Thus as a nature-symbol the cave is polyvalent: it appears as the site of the divine power; as the Mother, or female potency; as the link to mythic ancestors, thus to the past; as the place of initiation into adult and group privilege and responsibility, hence as a symbol of maturity and of the future, of rebirth and resurrection. Cumulatively, the cave appears as the site of the Divine Mystery, the creative life-force. Thus it implies the continuity between the past and the future.

Many of the archeological implications of the cave are supported by modern psychology, which sees the cave as an archetype, a psychic image of an inherited, unconscious tendency. Freud sees any object which has the property of enclosing a space or acting as a receptacle as a female symbol. Such objects as pits, hollows, caves, boxes, chests, and ships are, furthermore, "constant" symbols, occurring in dreams, mythology, folk-lore, religion, and art. And such activities as dancing, riding, climbing, being rhythmical in nature, may symbolically represent the sexual act. From this standpoint, it is pertinent to note that the physical aspects of Adela's experience—the climb up the hill (which would be seen as a male symbol), the violence in the cave (somehow the strap of her field-glasses is broken, a significant detail suggesting her loss of "sight"), and her frenzied descent down the hill—all constitute a kind of parody on the sex-act, really a symbolic rejection of it. This equates with Adela's rejection of the implication of union, which again is thematic.

According to Jung, the cave is an archetype for the Great Mother. "Phylogenetically as well as ontogenetically we have grown up out of the dark confines of the earth.... The protecting mother is ... associated with the ... protecting cave. The symbol of the mother refers to a place of origin such as nature, to that which passively creates, to matter, to the unconscious, natural and instinctive life."[7]

Neumann also conceives of the cave as a Great Mother symbol, linking it, through its "elemental containing character" with the womb. "The vessel lies at the core of the elementary character of the feminine. At all stages of the primordial mysteries, it is the central symbol of their realization. In the mysteries of preservation, this symbol is projected upon the cave as sacral precinct and temple."[8] But the cave is also a tomb, the "container" that "holds fast and takes back." So the elementary character of the Archetypal Feminine is also terrible. And the Terrible Female is one symbol for the unconscious. "The womb of the earth becomes the deadly devouring maw of the underworld, and beside the fecundated womb and the protecting cave of earth... gapes the abyss of Hell, the dark hole of the depths, the devouring womb of the grave and of death, of Darkness without light, of nothingness."[9] Forster notes of the caves, "Nothing, nothing attaches to them."

Finally, Neumann sees the cave as an archetype for the Way. "In a ritual still largely unconscious, the Way led prehistoric man into mountain caves, in whose recesses they established 'temples.' ... The 'hard and dangerous way' by which these caves could be reached formed a part of the ritual reality." Later, this archetype of the Way became a conscious ritual, until in Calvary, "the way of destiny becomes the way of redemption."[10]

Thus, as a psychological archetype, the cave is, again, the site of divinity; a symbol of the Good Mother; an aspect of the Terrible Mother, hence a symbol of the unconscious; and a symbol of the Way of spiritual rebirth. But because here it is also the cave of Illusion or Māyā, to Adela's vision these positive implications are distorted and obscured. Nonetheless, it is from these mythic potentials that she flees. Details of plot and character support this interpretation.

Neither very mature emotionally nor very profound, Adela's contemplations about love and marriage have occurred only at the top of her mind: in terms of herself as an Anglo-Indian, of the place where she and Ronny will live, of the kind of social and domestic life they will have. As she tells Fielding later, "I was bringing to Ronny nothing that ought to be brought. . . . I entered that cave thinking: 'Am I fond of him?' . . . Tenderness, respect . . ." (p. 263). These she has tried to make take the place of love. The cave forces violently upon her an experience involving her emotions, her unconscious psyche, her sense of herself as a woman. This, her undeveloped feminine psyche, is her basic limitation. Her disturbance in the cave is thus fundamental, for all of the cave's feminine implications—union, initiation, potency—are experienced as an attempt at rape, an ironic perversion.

Thus Adela must reject the cave as the spot of the mystic initiation, achieved through the individual's "willed participation" in some significant ritual. The cave *is* evil for her simply because in her flight she rejects all of its positive potentialities.

But Adela has other limitations. Frankly she admits to Fielding her lack of religious faith. Both, they confess to each other, are atheists; yet both sense a basic lack. "Were there worlds beyond which they could never touch, or did all that is possible enter their consciousness? They could not tell" (p. 263). Communicating at last on a rational level, they feel their friendliness is yet that of "dwarfs shaking hands," and they sense a wistfulness that marks the absence of something significant though indefinable.

So Adela can only fail to realize the religious implications of the cave. *The Secret of the Golden Flower* speaks of *"the cave of power, where all that is miraculous returns to its roots."*[11] But Adela must reject the cave of power, the finitely unknowable, for she is never able to define rationally what did happen to her there.

She does, however, confront something there. Since it is not rationally definable, let us call it the unconscious. Jung's system postulates for the woman, as for the man, a balancing element in the psyche. In the woman the masculine side is personified by the Animus, which thus represents the opposite of the dominant attitude in female consciousness. According to Jung's "function compass," Adela's dominant function is Thinking; thus her compensatory unconscious function is Feeling. Now, says Neumann, "the spiritual aspect of the unconscious confronts woman as an invisible stimulating, fructifying, and inspiring male spirit, whether it appears as totem or demon, ancestral spirit or god. In the woman, every psychic situation that leads to an animation of the unconscious . . . sets in motion the unconscious patriarchal structures of the animus."[12] I suggest that what Adela really encounters in the cave, what is symbolized there so violently that her unconscious (Feeling) function is activated, is the Animus, the male principle. Recognized and integrated into her consciousness, this principle would have initiated for her a greater psychic completeness, productive eventually of a real Self.

The Truth, then, was implicit in the situation; but only the Fact was experienced. Possibly evoked by her half-conscious ruminations as she entered the cave, some force which her intellect could make nothing of, spirit or flesh, denied god or demon, was objectified to her. But because she had never been really aware of her Feeling-self, she could only view this manifestation as evil, and reject it in panic and flight. In addition to the mythic implications of the cave itself, Adela has, then, also rejected the beginning of a meaningful Self-hood, or, in Jung's term, of the process of individuation.

Thus again we return to the cave as the place of Illusion, Māyā, of the false testimony of the senses. *What happened in the cave is a dramatization of the dualism in which cosmic truth states itself when seen only through the half-vision of the intellect alone.* The reality behind the illusion, the integration of the paradoxes, could appear only when not merely the intellect, the conscious psyche, is invoked, but also the intuitive powers of the unconscious.

Part of the significance of Adela's experience in the cave is that its implications transcend the limitations of an individual and/or fictional character. In her partial vision, Adela represents perhaps the major neurosis of modern man, the "split" between the conscious and the unconscious psyches. She cannot "connect," either within herself, or without.

In his psychological commentary on *The Secret of the Golden Flower*, Jung interprets this sort of experience, suggesting that such separation of consciousness from "the laws of life represented in the unconscious" is peculiarly characteristic of the Western Christian, and especially the Protestant "cult of consciousness." The more the intellect is developed, the greater is the gap between consciousness and the unconscious. Furthermore, "danger arises whenever the narrowly delimited, but intensely clear, individual consciousness meets the inner expansion of the collective unconscious, because the latter has a definitely disintegrating effect on consciousness." Although this danger may manifest itself as a "complex"—an autonomic psychic content—it may also appear as "more complex emotional states which cannot be described as pure and simple affects but are complicated partial-systems which have ... the character of persons. ... As we know, activated unconscious contents always appear first as projections upon the outside world." If, however, one denies the existence of the partial-systems, "they then become an inexplicable factor of disturbance which one assumes to exist somewhere or other outside. ... *The disturbing effects are now attributed to a bad will outside ourselves.*"[13]

So far as one may attribute psychological reality to a fictional character, the above comments seem remarkably pertinent to Adela's experience in the cave. Confronted in her low-toned state by the inexplicable "collectivity" of the cave, she can "know" her activated unconscious only as a projection upon the outside world—as, literally, an evil will directed against her, Dr. Aziz. Actually what she experiences suggests itself as a manifestation of her own state of psychic disunity.

What, then, did happen in the cave? Nothing. And everything. For negation and disunity are real too. Confronted by a deep and unprecedented experience of her unconscious, Adela is frightened, and rejects. Her engagement to Ronny is broken, and she can only return to England and to her orderly rational life there. True, she does develop under her ordeal. Fielding sees that she is no longer examining life but being examined by it, and that in this degree she has become a "real person." But India, the land of the intuitive and the mystical, can remain for her only an enigma, though not a Mystery.

Thus we may see Adela's experience in the cave as ambivalent: having both subjective and objective meanings. Subjectively, it reveals to her the painful knowledge of her own limitations. Objectively, it poses Western rationality against Eastern mysticism; time against eternity; the conscious against the unconscious. But for modern man, or at least for Western man, no integration of these polarities seems yet possible. Perhaps this is why, in the last lines of A *Passage to India*, Forster leaves us without any neat comforting resolutions of the basic tensions, knowing that, until our disparate psychic selves find some real integration, the voice of the cave, the mysterious echo, speaks still its "No, not yet."

Yet here, in the Cave, in the silence of the OM, the Mystery, is the site of the "transformation" that may produce the Self. For the cave is the Mother and the Tomb, the beginning and the end.

Notes

1. Sources cited in this paragraph are as follows: White, "A *Passage to India*: Analysis and Reevaluation," *PMLA*, LXVIII (Sept., 1953), 647; Tindall, *The Literary Symbol* (New York: Columbia University Press, 1955), p. 144; Warren, *Rage for Order* (Chicago: University of Chicago Press, 1948), p. 136; Allen, "Struc-

ture, Symbol, and Theme in E. M. Forster's *A Passage to India*," *PMLA*, LXX (Dec., 1955), 934–954; and McConkey, *The Novels of E. M. Forster* (Ithaca, New York: Cornell University Press, 1957), p. 140.

2. E. M. Forster, *A Passage to India* (New York: Harcourt, Brace and Company, 1924), p. 123. All references in the text are to this Harbrace Modern Classics edition.

3. G. R. Levy, *The Gate of Horn* (London: Faber and Faber, 1948), pp. 3–6.

4. E. M. Forster, *Howards End* (New York: Vintage Books, 1954), p. 187.

5. H. Zimmer, *Philosophies of India*, ed. Joseph Campbell (New York: Meridian Books, 1956), pp. 27, 394.

6. Levy, pp. 8–35 and *passim*. E. O. James (*Myth and Ritual in the Ancient Near East*. New York: Frederick A. Praeger, 1958, p. 22ff.) would agree with Miss Levy on the general significance of the cave, seeing it as a tribal sanctuary in which magico-religious fertility and hunting rites were performed, as well as rituals intended to "establish a beneficial relationship with the supernatural source of the food supply."

7. Quoted in Patrick Mullahy, *Oedipus: Myth and Complex* (New York: Grove Press, 1955), pp. 149–150.

8. Erich Neumann, *The Great Mother* (New York: Pantheon Books, 1955), p. 282.

9. Neumann, p. 149. It is further interesting to note that the experience of the Terrible Mother finds its most grandiose form as Kali. "In the very earliest Indian culture . . . in the temple sites of the Zhob River Valley, of northern Baluchistan, we find figures of the Terrible Mother" (Neumann, p. 150).

10. Neumann, pp. 8, 9, 177. Adela's approach to the caves is, of course, on foot; her descent, in its irrational violence takes on something of the exaggerated movement often characteristic of the primitive dance.

11. *The Secret of the Golden Flower*, trans. Richard Wilhelm, trans. into English by Cary F. Baynes (New York: Harcourt, Brace and Co., 1932), p. 62.

12. Neumann, p. 294.

13. C. G. Jung, "Commentary" to *The Secret of the Golden Flower*, pp. 96–111. (Italics mine.)

A Passage to India   Frederick C. Crews*

Is the novel, then a covert apology for Hinduism? Many readers have thought so, but at the expense of oversimplifying Forster's attitude. Hinduism is certainly the religion most able to cope with the bewildering contradictions one finds in India, but its method of doing this—accepting everything indiscriminately, obliterating all distinctions—has obvious disadvantages that are brought out in the course of the novel. The tripartite structure of *A Passage to India*, with its formal shifting

*Excerpted from chapter ten of *E. M. Forster: The Perils of Humanism*, pp. 151–63. © 1962 by Princeton University Press, and reprinted by permission of the author and Princeton University Press.

from "Mosque" to "Caves" to "Temple," suggests that various religious paths to truth are being problematically offered; and the inconclusive and frustrating ending of the book implies that each path, while having particular advantages that the others lack, ultimately ends in a maze.[1]

Those who favor a Hindu reading of *A Passage to India* rest their claims on the final section of the novel, where the setting has changed from Westernized Chandrapore to a Hindu Native State. In these surroundings there is, indeed, occasion for a meeting of East and West. But the meeting, which takes place at the peak of the Hindu festival of Gokul Ashtami, is effected through the capsizing of two boats in a furious rainstorm, and it is a moot question whether the momentarily reconciled parties have been drenched with Hindu love or simply drenched. It is a climax, Forster warns, only "as far as India admits of one" (p. 315), and in retrospect the festival amounts only to "ragged edges of religion ... unsatisfactory and undramatic tangles" (p. 316). If Hinduism succeeds, where Islam and Christianity fail, in taking the entire universe into its view, we still cannot silence the voice of Western humanism. What about man and his need for order? Are we to sacrifice our notion of selfhood to the ideal of inclusiveness? "The fact is," Forster has said elsewhere, "we can only love what we know personally" (*Two Cheers*, p. 45). And as Fielding thinks when he has quit India and recovered his sense of proportion at Venice, "Without form, how can there be beauty?" (p. 282)

These misgivings about reading *A Passage to India* in a spirit of orthodoxy are strengthened by an acquaintance with Forster's private statements of opinion about the religions involved. We know, of course, that such statements cannot take the place of internal evidence, but in this case the internal evidence is somewhat ambiguous; the temptation to ask Forster what he really thinks is irresistible. His attitude toward Christianity is hardly obscure, but Islam and Hinduism have aroused mixed feelings in him, and these, I think, find their way into *A Passage to India*. On his second trip to India, in 1921, Forster was Private Secretary to the Maharajah of Dewas State Senior, a Hindu Native State; his letters from there and elsewhere are sometimes revealing. "I do like Islam," he wrote to his mother from Chhatarpur, "though I have had to come through Hinduism to discover it. After all the mess and profusion and confusion of Gokul Ashtami, where nothing ever stopped or need ever have begun, it was like standing on a mountain."[2]

The nature of this attraction is evident in two essays reprinted in *Abinger Harvest*, "Salute to the Orient!" and "The Mosque." Islamic meditation, Forster explains, "though it has the intensity and aloofness of mysticism, never leads to abandonment of personality. The Self is precious, because God, who created it, is Himself a personality ..." (*Abinger Harvest*, p. 273). One thinks immediately of Forster's well-known individualism; the idea of selfhood is indispensable to his entire system of value. Again, Forster's liberalism and his contempt for superstition seem to govern the following contrasts between Islam and Christianity: "Equality before God—so doubtfully proclaimed by Christianity—lies at the very root of Islam . . ." and the Moslem God "was never incarnate and left no cradles, coats, handkerchiefs or nails on earth to stimulate and complicate devotion" (*Ibid.*, pp. 275, 276). Nowhere does Forster imply that he actually believes the dogmatic content of Islam; the point is that he is aesthetically gratified by a religion that is not grossly anthropomorphic. He is no more of a Moslem than he is a Christian, but Islam at least does not outrage his common sense and his love of modest form.

A Passage to India, of course, demands more of religion than this; the central question of the novel is that of man's relationship to God, and Moslems, Forster says, "do not seek to be God or even to see Him" (*Ibid.*, p. 273). Thus Islam can hardly lead Forster's characters to the assurance they need; as Fielding puts it, " 'There is no God but God' doesn't carry us far through the complexities of matter and spirit; it is only a game with words, really, a religious pun, not a religious truth" (*A Passage to India*, p. 276). And the refusal to abandon personality, which is the strongest bond between Aziz and the Westerners in the novel, turns out to be a severe limitation in their apparatus for grasping transcendent truth.

Forster's opinion of Hinduism is more clearly a dual one: he finds Hindu ritual absurd but Hindu theology relatively attractive. His letters about Gokul Ashtami are extremely condescending; he thought the spirit of the festival indistinguishable from "ordinary mundane intoxication," and he generalized: "What troubles me is that every detail, almost without exception, is fatuous and in bad taste."[3] Yet his admiration for the Maharajah for whom he was later to work led him to an early sympathy with Hindu doctrine. The following excerpt from a letter of March 6, 1913 explains part of the Maharajah's position and Forster's response to it:

"His attitude was very difficult for a Westerner. He believes that we—men, birds, everything—are part of God, and that men have developed more than birds because they have come nearer to realising this.

"That isn't so difficult; but when I asked why we had any of us ever been severed from God, he explained it by God becoming unconscious that we were parts of him, owing to his energy at some time being concentrated elsewhere. . . . Salvation, then, is the thrill we feel when God again becomes conscious of us, and all our life we must train our perceptions so that we may be capable of feeling when the time comes.

"I think I see what lies at the back of this—if you believe that the universe was God's *conscious* creation, you are faced with the fact that he has consciously created suffering and sin, and this the Indian refuses to believe. 'We were either put here intentionally or unintentionally,' said the Rajah, 'and it raises fewer difficulties if we suppose that it was unintentionally.' "[4]

Here again we may observe that Forster is not asserting a religious belief of his own, but is simply trying to be open-minded. Still, we can recognize the congeniality of Hinduism, in this interpretation, to Forster's opinions as we already know them. His disbelief in Providence, his sense of man's ignorance of divine truth, his rejection of the idea of a man-centered universe—all are reconcilable with his summary of the Maharajah's Hinduism. Yet the point at which the correspondence breaks down is even more striking. It is easy enough for Forster to entertain the theory that God is presently unconscious of man, but there is little provision in his philosophy for the moment of awakening; only the negative side of Hinduism accords with his temperament.

There is no escaping the impression that Hinduism is treated with considerable sympathy in *A Passage to India.* Its chief function, however, seems to be to discredit the Christian and Moslem emphasis on personality; the vastness and confusion of India are unsuitable for an orderly, benevolent deity whose attention to individuals is tireless. When the question of mystical union arises, however, Forster becomes evasive in the extreme. Gokul Ashtami, he remarks, presents "emblems of passage; a passage not easy, not now, not here, not to be apprehended except when it is unattainable..." (*A Passage to India*, pp. 314f.). Although Hinduism offers the most engaging fable to describe our isolation from meaning, it, too, like Islam and Christianity, seems powerless before the nihilistic message of the Marabar Caves.

The incidents in the Caves are of course the symbolic heart of the novel, where India exerts its force of illusion and disillusion upon the British visitors. These incidents are meaningful on all levels, making the hopeless misunderstanding between East and West vivid and complete, but their most important kind of meaning is clearly religious. The Christian Mrs. Moore and the Moslem Aziz, having befriended one another in a mosque, have previously been kept apart by social barriers, but now they are to meet, with Adela, on the ground of what Adela has called "the real India." The Marabar Caves will offer them an India more virginal than they bargain for, and will, through utter indifference to selfhood, challenge their very sense of reality.

The Marabar Hills, "older than all spirit," date back to an age long before Hinduism arrived and "scratched and plastered a few rocks" (p. 124). They are "flesh of the sun's flesh," and the sun "may still discern in their outline forms that were his before our globe was torn from his bosom" (p. 123). They are thus completely divorced from the works and history of man. Like the Hindu God, they seem to have no attributes: "Nothing, nothing attaches to them," says Forster (p. 124). And this analogy with Hinduism is highly suggestive, for Mrs. Moore's experience in the Hills is a kind of parody of the recognition of Brahma.

Hinduism claims that Self and Not-self, Atman and Brahman, are actually one, and that the highest experience is to perceive this annihilation of value. Value is indeed annihilated for Mrs. Moore; the echoing Caves convince her that "Everything exists, nothing has value" (p. 149).

Glen O. Allen has found several references in the *Upanishads* to the dwelling of Atman and Brahman in caves,[5] and one such passage seems especially pertinent here. "The wise who, by means of meditation on his Self, recognises the Ancient, who is difficult to be seen, who has entered into the dark, who is hidden in the cave, who dwells in the abyss, as God, he indeed leaves joy and sorrow far behind."[6] In the Marabar Caves Mrs. Moore discovers "the ancient," but it is not Brahma: "What had spoken to her in that scoured-out cavity of the granite? What dwelt in the first of the caves? Something very old and very small. Before time, it was before space also. Something snub-nosed, incapable of generosity—the undying worm itself" (p. 208). And though she does, indeed, leave joy and sorrow behind, the departure is utterly pedestrian. She has simply been thrust into the disillusion of old age: "She had come to that state where the horror of the universe and its smallness are both visible at the same time—the twilight of the double vision in which so many elderly people are involved. If this world is not to our taste, well, at all events there is Heaven, Hell, Annihilation—one or other of those large things, that huge scenic background of stars, fires, blue or black air. All heroic endeavor, and all that is known as art, assumes that there is such a background ... But in the twilight of the double vision, a spiritual muddledom is set up for which no high-sounding words can be found; we can neither act nor refrain from action, we can neither ignore nor respect Infinity" (pp. 207f.).

Readers who have claimed that Mrs. Moore has suddenly been transformed from a modest Christian to a mystical Brahmin have had to overlook the prosaic quality of her feelings here. She has had, in effect, an antivision, a realization that to see through the world of superficial appearances is to be left with nothing at all. "The abyss also may be petty, the serpent of eternity made of maggots ..." (p. 208).

Mrs. Moore's inversion of Hinduism is sharpened by the resemblance of the Caves' echoes—"boum" and "ou-boum"—to the mystic Hindu syllable "Om," which stands for the trinity of the godhead. He who ponders this syllable, says the *Prasna-Upanishad*, "learns to see the all-pervading, the Highest Person."[7] This is Mrs. Moore's ambition: "To be one with the universe! So dignified and simple" (p. 208). In an ironical sense she achieves this, for she does grasp a oneness underlying everything. Its monotony, however, is subversive of the moral and ceremonial distinctions that we require to reconcile ourselves to the Absolute. "... Religion appeared, poor little talkative Christianity, and she knew that all its divine words from 'Let there be Light' to 'It is finished' only amounted to 'boum'" (p. 150). The oneness Mrs. Moore has found has obliterated her belief in the categories of space and time, distinctions that are essential to a religion whose God has a sense of history. This is why she can be said to have perceived both the horror and the smallness of the universe; the Marabar Caves "robbed infinity and eternity of their vastness, the only quality that accommodates them to mankind" (p. 150). . . .

We may well ask at this point why Mrs. Moore, who seems to have a kind of second sight on occasion and who is certainly a morally sympathetic character, is visited with disillusionment. One answer may simply be that she *does* have second sight, that she perceives what truly subsists behind the veil of Maya; in this case her experience would constitute a thorough disavowal of Hinduism on Forster's part. Remembering Adela's hallucination, however, we may question whether Mrs. Moore has penetrated anything at all. Perhaps she has merely heard echoes of her own unvoiced misgivings about the significance of life.[8] It is impossible, in any case, to support the popular reading that she has experienced the merging of Atman and Brahman. Atman is the presence of the *universal* ego in the individual, the "God dwelling within," and the properly disciplined Hindu will find Brahman, the supreme soul, echoed in this "Self." Mrs. Moore, however, is unprepared to relinquish her selfhood in the narrow sense of personality. Instead of blending her identity with that of the world-soul, she reduces the world-soul to the scale of her own wearied ego; her dilettantish yearning for oneness with the universe has been echoed, not answered. Whether or not Forster considers the serpent of eternity to be made of maggots is a question we cannot answer on the basis of A *Passage to India*; in view of his skepticism it is doubtful that he would feel himself qualified to make any assertion at all on the subject. What does emerge clearly from the novel is that the Marabar Caves have not brought us into the presence of ultimate truth. The last words of India to Mrs. Moore, as she sails away to die, may serve also as a caveat to eager critics: "So you thought an echo was India; you took the Marabar caves as final? . . . What have we in common with them, or they with Asirgarh? Good-bye!" (p. 210)

Adela's experience in the Cave, though it has religious implications, lends itself more readily to analysis in psychological terms. This agrees with the Caves' function of echoing only what is brought to them, for Adela's yearnings are sexual, not mystical. As she climbs upward with Aziz her conscious thoughts are occupied with her approaching marriage to Ronny, but she is increasingly troubled by misgivings, until she realizes with vexation that she is not in love with her fiancé. Before entering the Cave, however, she commits the Forsterian heresy of deciding that love is not essential to a successful marriage; she will marry Ronny anyway. As in the case of Mrs. Moore, the Marabar Caves thrust to the surface a conflict between conventional and suppressed feelings.

The echo that is metaphorically sounded in Adela's hallucination (if it is a hallucination) of sexual attack is that of her unvoiced desire for physical love.

That this problematic assault should be attributed to Aziz is perhaps the central irony of plot in *A Passage to India*. Forster takes pains to let us know that Aziz's thoughts about sex are "hard and direct, though not brutal" (p. 102)—exactly the reverse of Adela's. Though he generally "upheld the proprieties ... he did not invest them with any moral halo, and it was here that he chiefly differed from an Englishman" (p. 103). As for Adela, he finds her sexually repellent ("She has practically no breasts," he tells Fielding; p. 120), whereas Adela, for her part, is attracted to him ("What a handsome little Oriental he was ...."; p. 152). Just before she enters the Cave, whose significance is apparently Freudian as well as metaphysical, Adela enviously ponders Aziz's physical advantages: "beauty, thick hair, a fine skin" (p. 153). She asks him, in what Forster calls "her honest, decent, inquisitive way: 'Have you one wife or more than one?'" (p. 153) And when the monogamous widower Aziz passes into a Cave to hide his embarrassment over her question, Adela enters a different Cave, "thinking with half her mind 'sight-seeing bores me,' and wondering with the other half about marriage" (p. 153). It is this other half, this wondering about physical gratification, that accosts her in the Cave; and, since Self and Not-self are confused there, she assigns her thoughts to Aziz.

An important difference between Adela's crisis and Mrs. Moore's is that Mrs. Moore adjusts her whole view of life to accord with the annihilation of value in the Cave, while Adela continues for a while to be torn between accepting and rejecting her experience. Mrs. Moore knows intuitively that Aziz is not a rapist, but she is weary of legalistic distinctions; the alleged crime "presented itself to her as love: in a cave, in a church—Boum, it amounts to the same" (p. 208). She does not stay to testify for Aziz, for the moral issue of the trial cannot interest her; if there is no value in the universe, there is surely none in distinctions between sanctioned and illicit love. Yet this very indifference makes it proper that Mrs. Moore, after she has withered out of bodily existence, should be resurrected as a Hindu goddess in the minds of the Indians at Aziz's trial. "When all the ties of the heart are severed here on earth," says the *Katha-Upanishad*, "then the mortal becomes immortal. ..."[9] The parallel is in one sense ironic, as we have seen: Mrs. Moore has been the victim of a travesty of Hindu enlightenment. On the other hand, the Mrs. Moore who originally befriended Aziz and who is remembered fondly by Professor Godbole has believed in loving everything that enters her consciousness, and such a love is the cornerstone of Hinduism.

Unlike Mrs. Moore, Adela lacks the imagination to be permanently shattered by her irrational experience. "In space things touch, in time things part" (p. 193), she repeats to herself, attempting to re-establish the categories that were imperiled by the Caves. Though she has been a freethinker, she turns to Jehovah for redress: "God who saves the King will surely support the police," goes her reasoning (p. 211). From the day of the hallucination until the climax of the trial she continually seeks to reconstruct the incident in direct logical terms. The dark savage has attacked her—but who has been the savage, Aziz or herself? Her virtue has been threatened—or has she simply rebelled against her starched prudery? Justice will be exacted upon the guilty one—but who is to cast the first stone in matters of sex? The psychological complexity of Adela's situation lends a kind of realistic support to Professor Godbole's doctrinal view: "All perform a good action, when one is performed, and when an evil action is performed, all perform it" (p. 177).

Forster would not assert this as a fixed principle, but we have often enough observed him recoiling from its opposite, the black-and-white attribution of guilt and innocence to separate parties. Before Adela can be freed from the echo of the Cave she must retreat a little from her simplistic Western notion of cause and effect. She is finally able to retract her charge because she has achieved a "double relation" to the controversial event: "Now she was of it and not of it at the same time..." (p. 227). In other words, she has begun to feel the limitations of a knowledge that is strictly bounded by her personality, her discrete selfhood. If she is never to know what occurred in the Cave, at least she will remember that there may be an order of truth beyond the field of her rational vision. Like Fielding, whose empiricism has brought him no closer to knowledge than her own resort to prayer, Adela has reached "the end of her spiritual tether... Were there worlds beyond which they could never touch, or did all that is possible enter their consciousness? They could not tell.... Perhaps life is a mystery, not a muddle; they could not tell. Perhaps the hundred Indias which fuss and squabble so tiresomely are one, and the universe they mirror is one. They had not the apparatus for judging" (p. 263).

A Passage to India, then, is a novel in which two levels of truth, the human and the divine, are simultaneously explored, never very successfully. Epistemological conclusions are reached, but they are all negative ones. Christian righteousness, we discover, helps us to misconstrue both God and man; Moslem love can scarcely reach beyond the individual personality; rational skepticism is wilfully arid; and the Hindu ideal of oneness, though it does take notice of the totality of things, abolishes the intellectual sanity that makes life endurable to the Western mind. The inescapable point of this demonstration is that God cannot be realized in any satisfactory way. It is a point that Forster dwelt upon at some length in his earlier novels, but always with a note of smugness; there was always the facile warning that we should restrict our interest to the world that we know. In A Passage to India, however, Forster's characters are given no choice; if they are to understand themselves and one another they must grapple with metaphysics. They do their best, but it is very little—not because they are exceptionally weak, but simply because they are human. Forster implies that we ourselves, his readers, are equally blocked off from meaning. We cannot fall back on reason and the visible world, for we see how these are falsely colored by personality. Even if we could, we ought not seek Mrs. Moore's "dignified and simple" identification with the universe, for this is nihilism in disguise. Nor can we assert with humanistic piety that our whole duty is to love one another; this, too, proves more difficult than we might have gathered from Forster's previous books. What finally confronts us is an irreparable breach between man's powers and his needs.

It is perhaps significant that Forster's career as a novelist comes to an apparent end at this moment of development, for the characters of a novel, as he has said elsewhere, "suggest a more comprehensible and thus a more manageable human race; they give us the illusion of perspicacity and power" (*Aspects of the Novel*, p. 99). *A Passage to India*, though it tells us more about its characters than they themselves know, tries to refute the very thought that our race is comprehensible and manageable; it casts doubt upon the claim of anyone, even of the artist, to supply the full context of human action. In writing one novel which pays full deference to the unknown and the unknowable, Forster thus seems to announce the end of the traditional novel as he found it; between pathetic futility and absolute mystery no middle ground remains for significant action.

Notes

1. The editions of Forster's works quoted from are as follows: *A Passage to India*, 1924; *Two Cheers for Democracy*, 1951; *Abinger Harvest*, 1936; *Aspects of the Novel*, 1927 (all published in New York by Harcourt, Brace and World, Inc.). Ed. note.

2. *The Hill of Devi* (New York, 1953), p. 123.

3. *The Hill of Devi*, pp. 160, 159.

4. Ibid., p. 45.

5. Glen O. Allen, "Structure, Symbol and Theme in E. M. Forster's *A Passage to India*," *PMLA*, LXX (December 1955), 934–954.

6. *The Sacred Books of the East*, ed. F. Max Müller (Oxford, 1884), Vol. XV: *The Upanishads*, p. 10.

7. Quoted by Allen, *PMLA*, LXX, 943.

8. The Caves not only deliver a dull echo in reply to every sound, they also offer reflections of light on their polished wall. The flame of a match and its reflection, we are told, "approach and strive to unite, but cannot, because one of them breathes air, the other stone" (p. 125). In symbolic terms this seems to support the idea that one will "see" his own thoughts imprisoned in Marabar stone, i.e. robbed of their context of human illusion.

9. *The Sacred Books of the East*, XV, 23.

A Passage to India:
Epitaph or Manifesto?

Benita Parry*

I

The symmetrical design and integrative symbolism of *A Passage to India*[1] confirm Forster's wish to make a coherent statement about human realities through art—for him the one internally harmonious, material entity in the universe, creating order from the chaos of a permanently disarranged planet[2]—while the deeper structure to the novel holds open-ended, paradoxical and multivalent meanings, discharging ideas and images which cannot be contained within the confines of the formal pattern. In a text consisting of a political fiction, an allegory, a philosophical novel, a social tragedy and a metaphysical drama, both centrifugal and centripetal forces are at work: the themes diverge from the axis and realign, the literary forms radiate and join, the ostensibly poised whole emitting ambiguity, dissonance and contradiction which are ultimately repossessed and transfigured in an affirmative if allusive coda. The novel's mythopoeic mode strains after models of universal and ahistorical order, composing an archetypal symbolism intimating that there exists a metaphysical wholeness of all the antinomies in physical reality, social formations and the psyche. Countermanding this vision of total connection is a pessimistic realism which perceives a universe apparently random and inhospitable to habitation, a disjunctive historical situation and the human mind divided against itself. The one orientation points towards an escape from the dislocations in the material world to the timeless womb of myth, the other confronts the present disarray in all its specificity and contingency. But finally, in the "not now, not here," "not yet, not there" (xxxvi, 304; xxxvii, 312), another direction is indicated, one which forecasts that the visionary and the secular will be reconciled. This anticipation of a future still to emerge, a tomorrow radically different from what exists, is rooted in the belief that institutions are not inviolable nor consciousness fixed; with this hope, the novel merges metaphor with realism, establishes that the flight into emblematic resolutions has been abandoned, and reaffirms history.

Forster's nonconformity was evident in his distance from both the orthodoxies and heresies of British society. Though he shared the ideology of the middle-class milieu to which he was born, he was at crucial points disengaged from it, was a part of Bloomsbury yet apart, a socialist without doctrine, a reverent humanist reassured by the sanity

*Reprinted from G. K. Das and John Beer, eds., *E. M. Forster: A Human Exploration* (London and Basingstoke: Macmillan Press; New York: New York Univ. Press, 1979), pp. 129–41, by permission of the author, New York University Press, and Macmillan, London and Basingstoke.

of rationalism and the sanctity of individual relationships, who came
to speculate on the satisfactions of sacred bewilderment and the dissolution of self in a transcendent other. With the accelerated disintegration of the old order after 1914, Forster's refuge in liberal-humanism,
never wholly proof against the elements, was drastically damaged. Confronted by the breakdown in established values, the ravages of European
competition, intensified class conflict within British society and growing
disaffection amongst the colonial peoples, he looked outside England
for a focus on this multiple disorder and, in choosing a route which
passed from fiction centred on the condition of England to the global
context created by imperialism, initiated a meeting with one of the
defining realities of his times.

Forster has written of his visits to India in 1912 and 1921 as trans-
forming experiences. For a small but significant number of English
writers, brought through circumstance or choice into contact with the
colonised world, the encounter exposed their consciousness to rival
conceptions of civilisation, culture and community, to cosmologies postu-
lating variant orderings to the universe, other definitions of the human
condition and alternative versions of personality structure. In negotiat-
ing the contrary modes of awareness, the divergent precepts and goals
devised by the west and by India, Forster produced a novel which
neither fully accepts nor entirely repudiates the standards and usages
of either. The text deliberately reveals the crisis of liberal-humanist
ideology—its impotence as a code in an embattled social situation where
moderation and compromise are not possible, its inadequacy as an explanation of a universe more extensive than the environment made by
human intervention, and the insufficiency of its insights into a psyche
whose experiential range exceeds ratiocination and sensory cognition.
Nevertheless, although the work ventures no affirmation of its creed,
it is the product of an intelligence and sensibility nurtured within the
cultural and intellectual context of liberal-humanism. It is because the
novel is mediated through this world-view and returns there for repose,
that the advance into new and profoundly astonishing perceptions is accompanied by retreats to the confines of known sterilities. The narrative
voice oscillates between faith and disbelief in the validity of humanist
mores, observing that within an India divided into cultural groups not
always sympathetic towards each other and ruled over by aliens hostile
to all, community is both a refuge and a laager, that if immersion in
mysticism wastes secular proficiency, then adherence to rationalism
atrophies other possible facets of personality, that whereas empiricism
can provide a rigorous arrangement of appearances, it misses essences,
and if exclusion and definition lead to functional and aesthetic excellence, it is the suspension of discrimination and the abolition of barriers
which makes for the unbroken circle.

To these polarities no resolution is suggested, yet because *A Passage to India* calls on resources outside the norms and priorities of western societies, summoning other social configurations, ethical codes and philosophical systems, evaluations which have been made of Forster's "medium mind" and his imprisonment within a superannuated system of ideas and values should be rephrased, for this novel both articulates in ontological and moral terms a radical dissent from the conventions and aspirations of the late bourgeois world, and omits to make the critical connection between these and the social and political structures they accompanied and sustained. Because of this, there is a vacuum at the core of the political fiction. Forster, always a cultural relativist, was amused at the rhetoric of a "high imperial vision" and came to applaud the colonial people kicking against imperialist hegemony,[3] but just as liberalism was unable to produce a fundamental critique of western colonialism, so is a consciousness of imperialism's historical dimensions absent from *A Passage to India*. Imperialism, the expression as well as the negation of modern Europe's values, inflicted a catastrophic dislocation on the worlds it conquered and colonised, generated new forms of tension within the metropolitan countries and brought the west into a condition of permanent conflict with other civilisations. Yet about this very epitome of the contemporary chaos, the novel is evasive; neither origins nor motives are rendered and the concept of exploitation is notably absent.

But if such elisions tend to disembody the critique, suggesting an evaluation of a superstructure uprooted from its base, the British-Indian connection is nevertheless composed as the paradigmatic situation of irreconcilable conflict, and the relationships brought into being by imperialism are perceived as grotesque parodies of human encounters. The chilly English circulate like an ice-stream through a land they feel to be poisonous and intending evil against them; British domination rests on force, fear and racism, generating enmity in articulate Indians sustained by memories of past opposition to conquest and mobilised by prospects of the independence to be regained. Here the novel asserts the confrontation of opposites as the essential reality of the social world. It is the politically innocent Mrs. Moore who challenges her son's brutal pragmatism with an appeal for love and kindness, a gesture towards humanising an inhuman situation, which is repudiated in the novel's recognition that hostilities will increase as Indian resistance grows (a process to which passing references are made) and British determination to retain power hardens. Aziz, the Moslem descended from Moghul warriors, and the Brahmin Godbole, whose ancestors were the militant Mahrattas, may have conflicting recollections of an independent Deccan resisting British conquest, but they are united by their distinctively expressed disinclination to participate in their own subjugation, a shared refusal which culminates in a Hindu-Moslem entente. On the other side, the British make up their differences and close ranks, with even Fielding throwing in his lot with Anglo-India and so betraying his ideals.

The effeteness of liberal codes in a situation such as that of imperialism is established in the novel by the catastrophic failure of British and Indian to sustain personal relations. The friendship between Fielding and Aziz disturbed throughout by differences in standards and tastes, is finally ruptured when each withdraws, as he inevitably must, within the boundaries of the embattled communities, and it is Forster's consciousness that social connections will fail which sends him in pursuit of spiritual communion between Mrs. Moore and both Aziz and Godbole. But perhaps the most eloquent demonstration of liberalism's impotence is its inability to offer any opposition to the enemies of its values. The obtuse, coarse, arrogant and bellicose deportment of Anglo-Indians, as realised in the novel, is the very negation of those decencies defined through Fielding: "The world, he believed, is a globe of men who are trying to reach one another and can best do so by the help of good will plus culture and intelligence" (vii, 56). When Fielding, after his courageous stand against his countrymen and women, aligns himself with the rulers of India, he is submitting to the fact of imperialism, deferring to a mode of behaviour and feeling made and needed by an aggressive political system and conceding that his liberal principles and hopes of doing good in India exist only by favour of a Ronny Heaslop. Forster's tone can be mild, but the integrity and toughness of his pessimistic acknowledgement that here there is no middle way to compromise and reconciliation marks a break with his previous, though increasingly hesitant, appeals to rapprochement between contending social forces.

II

In an essentially speculative novel, intimating a universe which is not human-centred and departing from the romantic humanism of his earlier works, Forster—without relinquishing reason—deviates from the dogmatic rationalist's scepticism about the numinous. The liberation to ecstasy and terror of the psychic energies subdued by modern industrialised societies, as invented in A Passage to India, is significantly different from Forster's former domesticated exhortations to connect the outer and inner life, the prose with the poetry, for the sublime now contemplated has heights and depths never discerned in dearest Grasmere or artistic Hampstead, and recognition of this augurs existential possibilities still to be assimilated by the west. "Inside its cocoon of work or social obligation, the human spirit slumbers for the most part, registering the distinction between pleasure and pain, but not nearly as alert as we pretend" (xiv, 125). The awakenings of two Englishwomen in India to what seems a surge from the deep and ancient centre in the universe takes cataclysmic form and results in derangement and delusion, the one mimicking in her feelings and behaviour the ascetic stance of isolation from the world but misunderstanding its meanings as meaningless, the other assailed by knowledge of sexuality and misinterpreting this as a sexual assault. When the urbane Fielding has intuitions of a universe he has missed or rejected, of that "something else" he is unable to know; when he and Adela Quested (a devotee of common sense) speculate on the possibility of worlds beyond those available to their consciousness, they are not yielding to concepts of heaven or hell, but admitting that some essential part to their beings is undeveloped.

What the novel creates in its transmutations of the numinous are dimensions to experience which are authenticated by their psychological truthfulness alone—expressing a hunger for perfection, a discontent with the limitations of the present and an aspiration to possess the future. The need for the unattainable Friend "who never comes yet is not entirely disproved" (ix, 97), the yearning after the "infinite goal beyond the stars" (xxix, 252), the longing for "the eternal promise, the never withdrawn suggestion that haunts our consciousness" (x, 106), these are signs of that permanent hope which will persist "despite fulfilment" (xxxvi, 294), just as the images, substitutions, imitations, scapegoats and husks used in religious ritual are figures of "a passage not easy, not now, not here, not to be apprehended except when it is unattainable" (xxxvi, 304). Significantly A Passage to India is a novel from which God, though addressed in multiple ways, is always absent—necessarily excluded from the Caves of the atheist Jains, and failing to come when invoked in the form of the Hindu Krishna or the Moslem's Friend—the Persian expression for God.[4] As invented in the novel, the numinous is not divinely inspired nor does it emanate from arcane sources; it needs no religion and meets with no God. Forster's disbelief in the power of the human spirit to "ravish the unknown" informs his transfigurations of the mystical aspiration:

> Did it succeed? Books written afterwards say "Yes." But how, if there is such an event, can it be remembered afterwards? How can it be expressed in anything but itself? Not only from the unbeliever are mysteries hid, but the adept himself cannot retain them. He may think, if he chooses, that he has been with God, but as soon as he thinks it, it becomes history, and falls under the rules of time.
>
> (xxxiii, 278)

What Forster does acknowledge is that faith confers grace on the believer during "the moment of its indwelling" (xxxiii, 275), and he affirms the gravity of religion's concerns, the fruitful discontent it speaks and the longings it makes known: "There is something in religion that may not be true, but has not yet been sung . . . Something that the Hindus have perhaps found" (xxxi, 265). This paradox signifies the meanings which Forster assigns the institutionalised routes to an understanding and changing of human nature and existence devised by India's religious traditions.

III

Theme and symbol in the novel's component texts converge on India. It is interesting that Forster's perceptions are in the tradition of Walt Whitman and Edward Carpenter, the one a passionate believer in popular democracy, the other a romantic socialist, both mystics and homosexuals disassociated by temperament and conviction from the conventions of their respective societies. Instead of the bizarre, exotic and perverse world made out of India by western writers in the late nineteenth and early twentieth centuries, a compilation serving to confirm the normality and excellence of their own systems, Whitman and in his wake Carpenter found in that distant and antique civilisation expressions of transcendent aspects to experience and access to gnosis, predicting that, when connected with the secular, these would open up new vistas to democratic emancipation, international fellowship and progress.[5] But if Forster's India does have affinities with these poetic evocations, the perspectives in A Passage to India are informed by enquiry into, rather than new-found belief in, alternative ways of seeing, and the altogether more complex configuration centres on the polarities of division and cohesion, separation and coalescence, the allegory pursuing the dialectical process from disjunction and fracture to a total, all-containing wholeness, while the realist mode composes a version of an internally splintered social formation moving towards solidarity against the outside source of conflict.

It is as if the defining concepts of the major Indian cosmologies are objectified in the landscape made by the novel, and this presents to the alien a new awareness that humanity's place is within a chain of being linking it with monkeys, jackals, squirrels, vultures, wasps and flies, and on a continuum of existence extending to oranges, cactuses, crystals, bacteria, mud and stones. Drawing on Indian traditions, the text constructs an ontological scale situating the species in a universe indifferent to human purpose and intent, contiguous to an unconcerned inarticulate world, planted on a neutral earth and beneath an impartial sky. It is a position which seems to reduce existence to a respite between two epochs of dust, inducing a view of people as moving mud and contesting the centrality of human aspiration and endeavour. The Marabars, as a figure of eternity, and the distance behind the stars, as the sign to infinity, create mythological time-space, challenging the myopia of empirical observation and measurement. In the environs of the Marabars, where hills move, fields jump, stones and boulders declare themselves alive and plants exercise choice, hylozoistic notions formulated by archaic philosophies and congenial to the traditional Indian mind are confirmed. To the rationalist this failure to delineate and define, this obliteration of distinctions, spells disorientation and chaos; to the metaphysician it speaks of a continuous series accommodating disparate modes of being within one coherent structure.

It is this organisation of reality that is produced through the multiplex metaphor of India: an India which with its various cultures, religions, sects and classes, is difficult, arbitrary, intricate and equivocal, a microcosm of the "echoing, contradictory world" (xi, 108), and an India which is the emblem of an intrinsic and deep harmony, an all-including unity accommodating paradox, anomaly and antinomy. For if "no one is India" (vii, 65) and "Nothing embraces the whole of India" (xiv, 136), it may all the same be the case that "the hundred Indias which fuss and squabble so tiresomely are one, and the universe they mirror is one" (xxix, 251). This possibility is translated in the gravitation of Aziz and Godbole towards a united front. Aziz attempts consciously to identify with India—"I am an Indian at last" (xxxiv, 284)—and unwittingly becomes absorbed, as had his ancestors, in India; Godbole, while continuing to live obediently within the sects and castes of Hinduism, assists Aziz in moving to a Hindu princely state and declares himself his true friend. But it is in the Hindus' ritual celebration of the entire universe of living beings, matter, objects and spirit taken into the divine embrace, that the conception of a dynamic blending of opposites is symbolically enacted, that enigmas and contradictions are ceremonially resolved and fusion is abstractly attained.

Although he was not a scholar of Indian metaphysics, Forster was familiar with the myths, epics and iconography of the country and found their innately dialectical style congenial. On rereading the *Bhagavad-Gita* in 1912 before his first visit to India, he noted that he now thought he had got hold of it: "Its division of states into Harmony Motion Inertia (Purity Passion Darkness)."[6] These three qualities, constituting in the classical Indian view the very substance of the universe,[7] are permuted in *A Passage to India* as Mosque Caves and Temple, a sequence with multiple meanings—one of which is the ontological and psychological significance pertaining to three major Indian philosophical-religious systems: they are figures, respectively, of consciousness and the present, the unconscious and the past, and the emergent metaconsciousness and the future. The novel offers this triad as the form of paradoxical differences contained within the unbroken whole: incorporated in the enclosing frame is the gracious culture of Islam in India, a society where personal relations amongst Moslems do flourish; the unpeopled Jain caves, place of the ascetic renunciation of the world; and the buoyant religious community of the Hindus, internally divided and internally cohesive. The approach to the component meanings of these systems is, however, profoundly ambiguous, moving between responsiveness and rejection, making the myth and subverting it.

Mystical Sufi tendencies are invented by the novel in the unmistakably Indian incarnation of Islam, a monotheistic and historically recent religion, dually committed to the mundane and the sacred. But having confronted the more ambitious theories of older India Forster now relegates Islam's consummation of the prose-poetry connection as too symmetrical, shallow and easy. With Caves, the novel passes back to the world-rejecting atheist tradition of the Jains,[8] a post-Vedic heterodoxy of the fifth century B.C. but, like Buddhism—with which it has historical and theoretical affinities—rooted in the ancient, aboriginal metaphysics of primal, Dravidian India. Here the novel produces a version of this uncompromisingly pessimistic outlook, one which disparages bondage to the phenomenal universe as the source of pain and suffering, and pursues liberation from all involvement with matter. The contemplation of negatives and Nothing within the text culminates in the transfiguration of the ascetic world-view, and if "Everything exists, nothing has value" (xiv, 140) is a statement of nihilism, it has an alternative meaning, one which acknowledges the material world as verifiable but assigns significance only to Nothing, to complete detachment: "Nothing is inside them, they were sealed up before the creation of pestilence or treasure; if mankind grew curious and excavated, nothing, nothing would be added to the sum of good and evil" (xii, 118).

There is a striking ambivalence to the imagery of the Caves; their "internal perfection" is evoked through crystalline figures of pure emptiness:

> There is little to see, and no eye to see it, until the visitor arrives for his five minutes, and strikes a match. Immediately another flame rises in the depths of the rock and moves towards the surface like an imprisoned spirit: the walls of the circular chamber have been most marvellously polished. The two flames approach and strive to unite, but cannot, because one of them breathes air, the other stone. A mirror inlaid with lovely colours divides the lovers, delicate stars of pink and grey interpose, exquisite nebulae, shadings fainter than the tail of a comet or the midday moon, all the evanescent life of the granite, only here visible. Fists and fingers thrust above the advancing soil— here at last is their skin, finer than any covering acquired by the animals, smoother than windless water, more voluptuous than love.
>
> (xii, 117–18)

But competing with and countermanding the delicate transparency of their interiors is the opaque menace of their external form:

> There is something unspeakable in these outposts. They are like nothing else in the world and a glimpse of them makes the breath catch. They rise abruptly, insanely, without the proportion that is kept by the wildest hills elsewhere, they bear no relation to anything dreamt or seen. To call them "uncanny" suggests ghosts, and they are older than all spirit.
>
> (xii, 116–17)

This speaks of the formless, primordial abyss before time and space, threatening to overwhelm consciousness; and the awesome possibility that the secret of the cosmos is not pristine order but ancient chaos is translated in the disasters which emanate from Caves.

Moving forward to the Hinduism of India's Aryan invaders, the novel creates that tradition's ecstatic affirmation of the entire world, the ceremonial celebration of all matter and spirit as originating from and sharing in the Lord of the Universe. But if the text participates in the ambition of Hinduism—itself compounded over aeons through the assimilation and reworking of many other existing beliefs—to tie, weld, fuse and join all the disparate elements of being and existence in a complete union, it withdraws from the incalculable and unassimilable enormity of the enterprise. While *A Passage to India* applauds the refusal of the present as it is, the wish to supersede all obstacles in the way of wholeness, it rejects emblematic resolutions. The impulse to the ceremonies is shown as magnificent:

Infinite Love took upon itself the form of SHRI KRISHNA, and saved the world. All sorrow was annihilated, not only for Indians, but for foreigners, birds, caves, railways, and the stars; all became joy, all laughter; there had never been disease nor doubt, misunderstanding, cruelty, fear.   (xxxiii, 278)

But when the celebrations end, the divisions and confusions of daily life return. Just as consciousness of political conflict and social divergence transgresses against the will to union, so is there here a humanist's repudiation of symbolic concord. The allegory is over before the novel ends, the aesthetic wholeness dismembered by the fissures and tensions of the disjoint, prosaic world that the novel invents; the permanent is dissolved in the acid of contingency. In the last pages emblems of reconciliation and synthesis compete with their opposites: "the scenery, though it smiled, fell like a gravestone on any human hope" (xxxvii, 311). The illimitable aspiration is not consummated: "a compromise had been made between destiny and desire, and even the heart of man acquiesced" (xxxvi, 297).

In retrospect it is apparent that the authority of the allegory is throughout seriously undermined by other modes within the text; as each positing of universal abstractions is countermanded by perceptions of the specifics in the human condition, so the cosmic is cut down to size by the comic—the squeals of a squirrel, though "in tune with the infinite, no doubt" (x, 105), are not attractive except to other squirrels; trees of poor quality in an inferior landscape call in vain on the absolute for there is not enough God to go round; there are Gods so universal in their attributes that they "owned numerous cows, and all the betel-leaf industry, besides having shares in the Asirgarh motor omnibus" (xxxv, 289), and a God whose love of the world had impelled him to take monkey flesh upon himself. From the infinite the novel returns to the ordinary, from eternity there is a bridge back to the mundane. The worth of human effort, ingenuity and creativity is restored in the view Mrs. Moore has on her last journey across India:

> She watched the indestructible life of man and his changing faces, and the houses he had built for himself and God . . . She would never visit Asirgarh or the other untouched places; neither Delhi nor Agra nor the Rajputana cities nor Kashmir, nor the obscurer marvels that had sometimes shone through men's speech: the bilingual rock of Girnar, the statue of Shri Belgola, the ruins of Manu and Hampi, temples of Khajraha, gardens of Shalimar.   (xxiii, 199)

The balance is redressed, and in the retreat to the Mediterranean it is overturned in favour of the secular and the "normal." The relief and pleasure known by both Adela Quested and Fielding on their return voyages from India is shared by Forster, whose paean to Venice is eloquent of a deep ambivalence towards the alternatives he had so courageously posed:

> the harmony between the works of man and the earth that upholds them, the civilisation that has escaped muddle, the spirit in a reasonable form . . . The Mediterrannean is the human norm. When men leave that exquisite lake, whether through the Bosphorus or the Pillars of Hercules, they approach the monstrous and the extraordinary; and the southern exit leads to the strangest experience of all.
>   (xxxii, 270–1)

Forster's knowledge, feelings and experiences outside this putative standard cannot stem the flood of his response nor discompose the peace it offers.

But neither this tenuous repose nor the symbolic solutions, neither the inevitability of compromise nor the permanence of conflict is the final word, for these are superseded by the generation of hope in a future when the obstacles the novel has confronted will have been overcome in history. On their last ride together, Aziz and Fielding, after misunderstanding, bitterness and separation, are friends again "yet aware that they could meet no more" (xxxvii, 307), that "socially they had no meeting place" (xxxvii, 309). But Aziz, anticipating the time of freedom from imperialist rule, promises "and then . . . you and I shall be friends" (xxxvii, 312); and when Fielding asks why this cannot be now, earth, creatures and artefacts intercede to reject the possibility: "they didn't want it, they said in their hundred voices, 'No, not yet,' and the sky said, 'No, not there.'"

A Passage to India is Forster's epitaph to liberal-humanism; in search of alternatives he had turned to other traditions only to withdraw, and had looked beyond the bleak present towards a transfigured tomorrow. He was at the height of his powers and he wrote no more novels; as fascism, war, the death-camps and the repression of the colonial struggles brought force, violence and chaos near and made the "not yet" seem more distant, Forster retired to essays, criticism, biography and broadcasts, forms through which it was still possible to state belief in liberal values, in full knowledge that the ideology sustaining these had been drained of vitality and was without relevance to the changing historical situation. Conscious of new threats, he had the independence and courage in 1935 to attend the International Association of Writers for the Defence of Culture in Paris, and before a largely communist audience reiterated his creed of individuality, personal decency, tolerance, justice, culture and liberty;[9] with Aldous Huxley, he was the only British writer to sign the Manifesto of that Congress. Forster needed no critics to tell him of the ambiguities and contradictions in his vision of life; he saw his faith crumbling and could find no other.[10]

Notes

1. *A Passage to India* (1924), Abinger Edition, 1977. Page references to this edition appear in brackets in the text. Ed. note.

2. "Art for Art's Sake" (1949) in *Two Cheers for Democracy* (1951), Abinger Edition, 1972, pp. 87–93.

3. "Our Diversions: 2, The Birth of an Empire" (1924), *Abinger Harvest* (1936) 44–7; "The Challenge of Our Time" (1946), *Two Cheers for Democracy*, 54–8.

4. A call echoed in Forster's need for a perfect Friend.

5. "Passage to India" (1871) in *Leaves of Grass*; "India, The Wisdom-Land" (1890) in *Toward Democracy* (Swan Sonnenschein, London, 1911). In his essay, "Edward Carpenter" (1944), Forster wrote: "As he had looked outside his own class for companionship, so he was obliged to look outside his own race for wisdom" (*Two Cheers for Democracy*, 207). It is open to conjecture that the predominantly "feminine" nature of India's civilizations, their cultivation of the imagination and intuitions, the pursuit of the unseen, and an eroticism in the visual arts, myths and epics which is conceptually androgynous—the absolute as the two-in-one, the male-female principles as coexistent—may have had an especial appeal to male members of what Carpenter called the intermediate sex.

6. Quoted P. N. Furbank, *E. M. Forster: A Life*, I, 1977, p. 216.

7 Heinrich Zimmer, *Philosophies of India* (1967) p. 231 (first published 1952).

8. The significance of Jain cosmology to the ideas and images in "Caves" is discussed in my *Delusions and Discoveries: Studies on India in the British Imagination 1880–1930* (1972).

9. "Liberty in England" (1935), *Abinger Harvest* (1936) 62–8.

10. In addition to the works referred to in these notes I wish to acknowledge a more general debt to the following books: John Beer: *The Achievement of E. M. Forster*; Malcolm Bradbury, Editor: *E. M. Forster: A Passage to India: A Selection of Critical Essays* (Casebook Series) 1970; Frederick C. Crews: *E. M. Forster: The Perils of Humanism*, 1962; Furbank I; June Perry Levine: *Creation and Criticism: A Passage to India*, 1971; Wilfred Stone: *The Cave and the Mountain: A Study of E. M. Forster*, Stanford, California, 1966; Lionel Trilling: *E. M. Forster*, 1944; Peter Widdowson: *E. M. Forster's Howards End: Fiction as History* (Text and Context Series), 1977.

INDEX